D0422766

DISCARDED

Enemies of Democracy

PAUL McCORMICK

Enemies of Democracy

HX
249
.M16

Temple Smith · London

139587

Acknowledgements are due to the Estate of Robert Frost and Jonathan Cape Ltd for permission to include the poem 'Fire and Ice' from *The Poetry of Robert Frost*, edited by Edward Connery Lathem (and to Holt, Rinehart and Winston, Inc for publication in the USA). I found Jacka, Cox and Marks: *Rape of Reason* (Churchill Press, 1975) of assistance when writing the Chapter on Marxist Methods.

First published in Great Britain in 1979
by Maurice Temple Smith Ltd
37 Great Russell Street, London WC1

© Paul McCormick 1979
ISBN 0 85117 168 0 Cased
      0 85117 169 9 Paper

Typeset by Mason & Weldon Ltd
in Journal Roman Medium

Printed in Great Britain by
Billing & Sons Ltd
London, Guildford & Worcester

This book attacks certain left-wing groups as enemies of democracy. It is therefore very important for me to state that I also unequivocally condemn fascist groups. Being opposed to left-wing extremism does not mean (except in Marxist smears) that you are an extreme right-winger. It is my view that in attacking left-wing extremism one is thereby helping to weaken right-wing extremism too.

Furthermore, I wish to make it absolutely clear that nothing in this book should be taken to mean that I advocate or condone any persecution or denial of civil rights to individuals belonging to extremist groups, however bad their views may be. This book shows a way to oppose them vigorously and effectively without stooping to their level.

Contents

Dedication

THIS BOOK IS DEDICATED TO THE ORDINARY
WORKING MEN AND WORKING WOMEN AND
THE RETIRED WORKERS OF NEWHAM WHO
WITHOUT THE BENEFITS OF WEALTH OR
YOUTH OR HIGHER EDUCATION OR
PROFESSIONAL TRAINING CAME FORWARD
WHEN ALL THE REST HAD FLED THE FIELD
TO FIGHT THE BATTLE FOR DEMOCRACY;

and in particular

FREDDIE BAMENT
(a retired worker who, after a road accident when he
was knocked from his motorcycle which damaged
his legs and back, still had the fortitude to attend
countless acrimonious meetings and launch a
lawsuit)

DORA LOVEJOY
(a working wife and mother with a serious heart
condition who has never flinched from hostile
meetings or legal action)

PATRICK MILSOM
(a bus driver who has kept on fighting and fighting
against the enemies of democracy, and who even
now struggles on alone in his Party branch, single-
handedly holding the Marxists at bay when even the
loyal Moderates have given up)

ALF DEACON
(a life-long trade unionist who, even when family tragedy struck, went out of his way to continue to assist the democrats)

JOHN PAGETT
(a bus driver who remained loyal throughout, despite threats and pressures, to the cause of democracy)

DAISY TURNER
(a retired lady with a lifetime of service to the Labour Party as a member, officer, and organiser who took up the cudgels for democracy)

WALLY HURFORD
(a prominent trade unionist, councillor, and local Labour Party President who, in his eighties, waged an unceasing fight against the enemies of democracy)

AND TO THOSE OF EVERY CLASS AND COUNTRY WHOSE FIGHT IN HUMBLE CAPACITIES OR OBSCURE ARENAS AGAINST THE ENEMIES OF DEMOCRACY HAS PASSED UNNOTICED AND UNRECORDED BY HISTORIANS AND POETS — FOR THEY ARE THE UNKNOWN SOLDIERS OF DEMOCRACY.

Preface

This book will annoy a lot of people. Many of them are vociferous people whose unrepresentative political views have been heard too often and too loudly. I should be more concerned if it did not annoy them. I aim to lend my voice to those whose views are rarely sought, and still more rarely heeded — the ordinary people. Too many books on Politics are written by politicians or academics for an exclusive audience as if democracy were a private affair. This book is from an unknown to many unknowns. It champions the cause of the Forgotten People — the people who are supposedly supreme in a democracy, yet so often are overlooked.

I should like to thank Anthony Morton for making certain papers and correspondence available to me.

I should like to thank Daisy Turner and Dora Lovejoy for their help, and the many others who must remain nameless. Anyone reading the text will see that Julian Lewis deserves great praise for his brave and unstinting efforts often in unpleasant circumstances.

I should also like to commend most warmly those, such as Alec Kellaway, Eddie Lee, Fred Jones and others, who, though they were more professional than the Newham workers to whom this book is dedicated (Alec is an Oxford graduate with roots in Newham, Eddie is a trade union official, and Fred Jones has been trained on Labour Party courses), also played their part in the battle for democracy.

Paul McCormick
May 1979

Introduction

The enemies of democracy are the political extremists of left and right, such as Communists and Fascists. This book is about left-wing extremists usually referred to as Marxists on account of their claim to be followers of Karl Marx. Some call themselves International Marxists; some, Workers' Revolutionaries; some, Communists (members of the Communists Party); others, Trotskyists or Trotskyites (followers of Trotsky). Like detergents with different brand-names but all made of similar substances, there is little to choose between them.

They all share allegiance to a form of Marxism which was adapted by Lenin and which puts the emphasis on a small, highly organised, dedicated and ruthless group seizing power, either directly or through infiltration of existing parties and institutions, and, by using illegal, violent or unconstitutional methods, to harness the full power of the State to transform the whole of society into a communist society.

There are other, more orthodox, forms of Marxism which are less vicious (but still dangerous). Those who subscribe to them I term 'Marxians'. It is likely that Marx himself, who once said 'All I know is that I am not a Marxist', would disown the Marxists described above. He would have recognised that their political proposals and methods were a recipe for political dictatorship.

Whilst the Fascist makes no secret of his dislike for democracy and openly opposes it in principle, the Marxist is less straightforward. He not only conceals his contempt for democracy but he uses the facilities provided by democracy in order to undermine it, and he characteristically claims to be acting in the name of, and on behalf of the people.

Democracy is not easy to define in a few words. Nor can

democrats easily agree upon a form of words. But it is easy for all to see the difference between regimes such as those of Communist Russia or Nazi Germany and other types of dictatorships, and those such as in Britain, America, France, Australia, Canada, Holland, which despite their many differences, are unquestionably democracies. Marxists, in particular, have done their best to sow confusion and blur the distinction between true democracy and the bogus forms. The phrase 'liberal democracy' is often used to distinguish democracy proper from the false sorts. Democracy is *not* simply 'one man: one vote', nor is it the doctrine that a majority of the people can rule and do as they like. You cannot have a democracy without the Rule of Law. The best account of democracy is to be found in the writings of John Stuart Mill.

Briefly, democracy is a system of government in which ultimate authority resides in the whole people to whom the government is accountable and by whom it is removable, in which state officials and powerful groups in society are subject to the same law that applies to everyone else, in which all resident adults are citizens with the right of access to the political process, in which power is exercised according to stipulated rules and procedures laid down by the government, and in which there are protections for the citizen against abuse of power by the government. Democracy does not mean that public opinion is king, but government policy should be broadly in line with the wishes of the bulk of the people.

It is generally considered necessary for democracy that there should be a free press; free speech, freedom of association and other civil liberties; a multi-party system; no excessive concentration of political, social or economic power; an independent judiciary; and either some division of political power through federalism, bi-cameral legislatures, division of executive and legislature, divisions within executive bodies, or some check on political power such as a written Constitution with judicial review; a plurality of pressure groups; an Assembly of Representatives; an adequate level of social welfare; independent universities; free trade unions; and periodic general elections with universal suffrage, a secret ballot and safeguards against electoral corruption (i.e., independent returning officers, careful regulations over ballot boxes, laws against bribery, etc.).

A system of this kind (which is true democracy or liberal democracy) may be called a constituional and representative democracy — constituional because it requires that all citizens' rights be protected, representative because it requires responsiveness and accountability to the popular will and insists that ultimate authority resides in the whole people. In such a system politicians hold their power on trust from the people, not by Divine Right.

Just as the extremists seek to invade our political institutions, they have laid claims upon our political vocabulary and call all sorts of funny things 'democracy'. There are certain so-called 'people's democracies' in Eastern Europe where the people are subjugated by a political elite, denied the most basic civil rights, and exercise little influence, let alone control, over government policy.

In this book, I refer to 'representative democracy' in order to lay particular emphasis on the representative aspect of true democracy. The Campaign I set up was called the Campaign for Representative Democracy (CRD). The name was apposite because we were fighting against attempts to turn MP's from representatives of all the people in their constituencies into mandated delegates taking their orders from a clique. We were campaigning against minorities of extremists who were seeking to impose unrepresentative views on the whole community, and we were fighting to ensure that all institutions, bodies and organizations in society where power is exercised should be run by people who are representative of the mass membership of those institutions and not of some self-appointed elite within them.

Politics exists on three levels. We can imagine them as being under the ground, on the ground, and above the ground. On the ground we can see the familiar battle *between* the Labour Party, the Conservative Party, and the other parties. It is partly over policy, partly over posts and partly over personalities. It is what the average man probably thinks of as being the whole of politics; at any rate it is the most familiar and obvious part.

If we look up into the air we may be able to see the less obvious jockeying for position and in-fighting over programmes and policies that occur between factions *within* each of the political parties. This forms the day-to-day political life of those who are active in politics. But as elections loom up this internal politicking is temporarily put aside as each party frantically pulls itself together to present a united front for the battle between the parties.

Very occasionally an earthquake parts the ground and reveals, what is normally invisible under our feet and forgotten, the third and most basic level where subsist the values and principles that underlie the party struggle and which concern the existence of the very political system and social framework in which this struggle takes place. It is at these times, when something is seriously amiss, that we all need to get back to the fundamental principle (of democracy) on which our society is based. This is not easy to do. It is much easier for the party politician to forget his own party's internal wranglings for a while and concentrate on the factors that unite it than it is for him to forget his own party and consider the principles that unite him with his fellow-members of society. Yet this is what, from time to time, he has to do.

Everyone in politics really has a pyramid of values. At the apex is the particular position we take up. One person may be a Social Democrat, another a Tribunite; one person may be a left-wing Tory, another, right-wing. At the apex level we divide according to such views. At the middle level lie our more basic allegiances as Labour men or Tories or whatever. Now and again the action shifts to the bottom level, the base on which the whole pyramid rests. At this level we regroup into democrats and anti-democrats, because here we are fighting the war for democracy itself. There will still be a lot of people far more concerned about their apex position as Social Democrats or left-wing Tories, or their party position as members of the Conservative, Liberal or Labour parties, than they are about their position as democrats. The most charitable interpretation is that they are ignorant of what is at stake.

If the world were to be under threat of invasion from bloodthirsty Martians we would surely sink our differences with the political extremists in our own country and the Russian Communists to form a united front on behalf of the human race against the alien invaders. If this happened we would have reached a still more basic level, the level of humanity, of the human species. It would be a fool indeed who refused to cooperate because of political differences.

All such differences would be overridden by the common underlying purpose. So it should be when it comes to dealing with questions affecting the fundamental principles of our own society. We must be democrats first, party supporters second, and faction supporters third.

I have already said a certain amount about the enemies of democracy, but not a word has been said so far about its friends. Maybe there are not too many of them. Certainly they form no organised group. It is very difficult to get people to unite round the banner of democracy, even though there are many who will take her name in vain. There is no party of democracy or league of democrats. The enemies of democracy are highly organised, the friends are scattered, isolated, and too often timorous and silent. Is it possible for a democracy to survive in the long run without institutions and groups prepared to defend it and put it before all else?

John Stuart Mill, the philosopher, was one of the very mildest of men as well as one of the most enlightened. He hated the thought of violence, such as the suppression of the revolt in Jamaica by Governor Eyre. Yet it was John Stuart Mill who wrote: 'Representative institutions necessarily depend for permanence upon the readiness of the people to fight for them in case of their being endangered.' The word is not 'whisper', 'persuade', 'speak', 'complain' or even 'shout'. It is 'fight'. In the weakest sense a 'fight' is a struggle involving organisation, meetings, legal action and so on; in its strongest sense, it involves the use of force.

I have defined democracy both in terms of its general principle and its characteristic institutions. Though there is room for debate and disagreement over details, there is a great gulf between the political extremists who reject the principle and the institutions, and those of us, the vast majority, who, whatever our other differences of opinion, firmly support the democratic way of life. Most of us have little difficulty in recognising that the political extremists hold views which, if we allow them to foist them on us, will bring about a dictatorship. But we do not always do very much to resist them.

This book is about a fight against enemies of democracy. It is the very fight that John Stuart Mill urged all citizens to wage if their democracy were to be preserved.

1

British Marxist Groups

Lenin, the founder of the Soviet State, created a special kind of Marxism, often called Marxism-Leninism, to assist him in his scheme to seize power in Russia. This is the form of Marxism I am chiefly concerned with in this book.

When Lenin died there was a power struggle between two of his lieutenants, Stalin and Trotsky. Stalin was the bureaucratic hatchetman, Trotsky the ruthless General. Stalin won and later had Trotsky murdered, having taken over many of his policies. The rivalry between them was personal rather than over policy where the disagreement was less. There was only room for one dictator and Stalin seized the position. But there was little to choose between them in their degree of ruthlessness. The forcible collectivisation of agriculture that murdered millions of Russian peasants was advocated by Trotsky and implemented by Stalin. Stalin became as notorious a dictator as Hitler (who admired Stalin for his ruthlessness). Stalin organized many purges of his political opponents, but Trotsky was no kindly and humanitarian intellectual. In 1921 he suppressed a sailors' revolt for democracy with the utmost brutality. If you ever meet a Trotskyite ask him to justify 'Kronstadt 1921'. The fact that Trotsky was outmanoeuvred by Stalin does not mean that he was a nice person or that things would have been the opposite of what they were had he won. There would have been little difference — except that now our left-wingers would be saying 'If only Stalin had won everything would have been all right'.

It is a feeble excuse to say Stalin was an accident. What guarantee is there that there will not be countless other 'accidents'? The truth of the matter is that Stalinism was, and is, a natural offshoot of Marxism-Leninism. If you have a system which concentrates enormous power in a party machine and a dogma that glorifies the exercise of untrammelled power, then it is always on the cards that someone like Stalin will rise to the top. You do not get men like Stalin rising to power and holding on to it for over thirty years in a Western liberal democracy. If the system produces Stalinism, then there must be something wrong with the system. This simple point is apparently beyond the comprehension of most left-wingers.

Stalin has become the universal scapegoat for Marxists. Every failing is offloaded onto him. He has been awarded, posthumously, the burden of the Cross — he has to bear on his shoulders the sins of the whole Marxist world. The process began as soon as he died. Accomplices, lieutenants and stooges immediately started to put all the blame on him for their own wrongdoings. The 'Blame Stalin' gambit is now the most popular Marxist defence. The fact of the matter is that Leninism, Trotskyism and Stalinism were three branches of the same upas tree of Marxism-Leninism. If the tree yields poisoned fruit then there is something wrong, not just with the lowest branch, but with the whole tree. The Marxist must justify — if he can — Lenin *and* Trotsky *and* Stalin.

Lenin had little time for democracy: 'Democracy is by no means a boundary that must not be overstepped'. In practice Lenin presided over a terror (a mini-terror by Stalin's standards, but a terror nevertheless), dissolved Parliament (the Constituent Assembly) at gunpoint, and banned all other parties. He did not believe in 'bourgeois' morality; lying, cheating, using violence, causing disruption and chaos, even making the lot of the worker worse, are all justified by the formula that whatever aids the Party in its attainment of power is permissible. Lenin said: 'Our morality is entirely subordinated to the interests of the class struggle of the proletariat'. When the going was rough people had to be shot. Lenin turned on the Mensheviks (orthodox Marxians) and said: 'For the public advocacy of Menshevism our revolutionary courts must pass sentence of death'. If the Mensheviks claimed that the revolution had gone too far and requested to repeat this assertion, Lenin's counter-request was: 'Permit us to put you before a firing squad for saying that'. So much for freedom of speech!

Trotsky was no democrat either. He said that terror was

necessary to subjugate class enemies: 'The problem of revolution consists in breaking the will of the foe, forcing him to capitulate and to accept the conditions of the conqueror'. As for terror, 'Terror can be very efficient against a revolutionary class which does not want to leave the scene of operations. Intimidation is a powerful weapon of policy, both internationally and internally'. With regard to democracy, Trotsky said: 'As Marxists we have never been idol-worshippers of formal democracy'. This is very similar to Stalin's remark 'For us, the interests of the Party are above formal democratism.'

What have these three Russian gentlemen got to do with contemporary Britain? I am not suggesting that Stalin is alive and well and living in Newham North-East. But they are of great relevance today, just as Marx is. And it is worth remembering Trotsky's views and conduct when we look at those who call themselves 'Trotskyites'.

Our present-day Marxists are working for Marxism-Leninism, and they are within its tradition in not being prepared as a matter of principle to respect democracy, individual liberty, the rule of law, freedom of the press, and free speech.

Some Marxists may not *realise* that Marxism is fundamentally undemocratic because they have only a nodding acquaintance with their own doctrine. Some Marxists may fervently *wish* to be democratic without appreciating that the necessary consequences of the measures they advocate will be to destroy democracy. All types of Marxism are fundamentally anti-democratic. There is, and can be, no such thing as democratic Marxism: one might just as well talk of Christian devils.

Many Marxists, however, are well aware of the position even as they speak with sirens' voices: 'Trust in us, we will work within a democratic framework'. What they mean is that they will use democracy to destroy democracy. In Lenin's striking phrase, they will support it 'as the rope supports the hanged man'. There are many nursery tales about the nefarious activities of wolves and foxes. They usually manage to con their victims and make a good dinner out of them. They never learn even when warned by the survivors of the previous generation.

What can one say to people who think that the Marxists

they deal with are somehow different? 'Go back to the
nursery and learn your political ABC'. One can at least urge
them to use a simple test of the reality behind political
protestations. The questions to ask are these: 1) What are
the personalities and attitudes of the persons concerned?
2) What are their politics and what implications flow from
them? 3) How is their party or faction organised? 4) What
methods do they employ in political disputes?

What is particularly galling is that often this test is unnecessary, because the Marxist, bold as brass, will announce
himself openly as a Marxist. Thus the wolf carries a placard
saying 'I'm a wolf'. But people still will not believe him.
They will say he is exaggerating. The same sort of people
read Hitler's *Mein Kampf* and called it poetic licence.

Let us look at the Marxist camp in Britain today. It consists of Marxists, Quasi-Marxists who are Marxists in all the
essentials, and Camp Followers who may disagree with parts
of the Marxist doctrine but who support many of the crucial
doctrines and align themselves with the Marxists at the
crucial times. Those who generally support the Marxists,
whatever their reasons, must be regarded as part of the
Marxist camp. What counts is which side they are on when
the chips are down.

This Marxist camp, spread over several political parties,
represents the numerical strength of Marxism-Leninism as a
political force. It is a substantial body of people. Of course,
they are a small proportion of the population — between one
and four percent. But that is still a lot of people, between
half a million and two million people; and one must never
forget that forty active people can dominate a thousand
people quite easily, even though it is only four percent. A
small band of resourceful, disciplined men can easily prevail
against an inchoate multitude. When Lenin took over Russia
in 1917 the Bolsheviks were less than one percent of the
population. This strange phenomenon of the few prevailing
over the many recurs again and again in our story. But it is
not so odd. We can think of the samurai, whose skill as
warriors made each one equivalent in fighting terms to perhaps thirty ordinary men. We can think, in a more homely
analogy, of the single sheepdog rounding up a whole flock of
sheep. I shall call this phenomenon the *samurai effect* — the

ability of a tiny, organized minority to impose its will on a large group of people.

The differences between the Marxist groups are ostensibly (and to some extent actually) over tactics, but undoubtedly personality clashes, pride, the desire to be a big fish in a small pond, the need to justify your own organisation's separate existence, and the desire to win power and not to have to share it, have all played their part in creating and perpetuating splits between the Marxist groups.

Sometimes a rough division is made between those Marxists who seek to 'smash the system' — the system including the established institutions and bodies like Parliament, the Labour Party, and the trade unions, and those who seek to 'work within the system' to change it into a Marxist system. The truth of the matter is that the distinctions between groups are largely ones of nomenclature. They give themselves particular names and set up separate organisations — and that is the main difference between them. Groups drift in and out of different tactical positions. One day a group may be working within the system genuinely, believing that it can achieve success within it. The next day the same group may be working within the system insincerely, using the system to sabotage it from within. Later on the same group will be operating outside the system. The Marxist groups are like strange planets that can move in and out of different orbits through different strategies, at one time working within the system, then outside it, then back within it once again. Some of these planets have their own 'moon' or 'moons' — smaller groups that each orbit round a planet. Such a moon may have once split off from the planet, or it may have split from a different planet, or formed itself; but its tactics and approach are such that it can be seen as operating within the wider orbit of a particular planet. It may not be formally or even informally attached to it but there is a kind of gravitational pull holding it in position.

The Marxist universe is exhibited in the diagram overleaf.

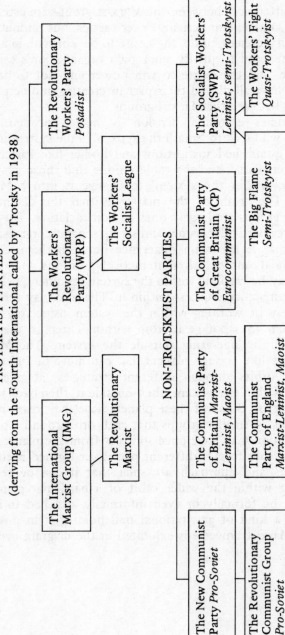

MARXIST GROUPS IN BRITAIN TODAY

TROTSKYIST PARTIES
(deriving from the Fourth International called by Trotsky in 1938)

The International Marxist Group (IMG)

The Revolutionary Marxist

The Workers' Revolutionary Party (WRP)

The Workers' Socialist League

The Revolutionary Workers' Party *Posadist*

NON-TROTSKYIST PARTIES

The New Communist Party *Pro-Soviet*

The Revolutionary Communist Group *Pro-Soviet*

The Communist Party of Britain *Marxist-Leninist, Maoist*

The Communist Party of England *Marxist-Leninist, Maoist*

The Communist Party of Great Britain (CP) *Eurocommunist*

The Big Flame *Semi-Trotskyist*

The Socialist Workers' Party (SWP) *Leninist, semi-Trotskyist*

The Workers' Fight *Quasi-Trotskyist*

MARXIST GROUPS IN BRITAIN TODAY (continued)

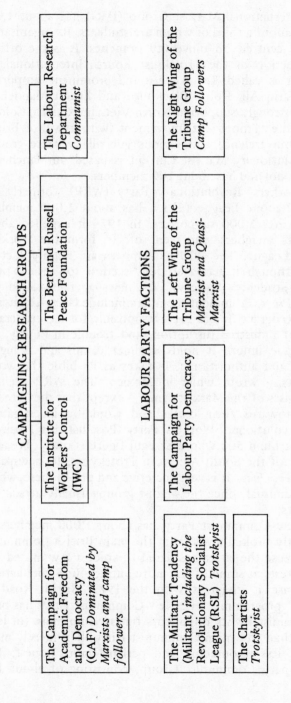

CAMPAIGNING RESEARCH GROUPS

| The Campaign for Academic Freedom and Democracy (CAF) *Dominated by Marxists and camp followers* | The Institute for Workers' Control (IWC) | The Bertrand Russell Peace Foundation | The Labour Research Department *Communist* |

LABOUR PARTY FACTIONS

| The Militant Tendency (Militant) *including the* Revolutionary Socialist League (RSL) *Trotskyist* | The Campaign for Labour Party Democracy | The Left Wing of the Tribune Group *Marxist and Quasi-Marxist* | The Right Wing of the Tribune Group *Camp Followers* |

| The Chartists *Trotskyist* |

The International Marxist Group (IMG) has about 1,000 members about a third of whom are students. Its organisation is mainly centred on university branches. It is the official British Section of the Trotskyist Fourth International. Its newspaper is called *Red Weekly* and prominent supporters include Tariq Ali, Robin Blackburn and Ernest Mandel. Its members strongly supported North Vietnam, Castro, Colonel Gaddafi, the 'Troops out' movement (withdrawal of British troops from Ireland) and various guerrilla warfare groups. The Revolutionary Marxist Current is based on Manchester and Liverpool and has about 100 members.

The Workers' Revolutionary Party (WRP), formerly the Socialist Labour League (SLL), has about 1,000 members and a further 5,000 supporters. In 1974 it expelled about 200 of its members who went off to form the Workers' Socialist League. The WRP's members are mainly factory workers, though it has a student section too (the Young Socialist Students' Society). Its newspaper is called the *Workers' Press*. Prominent members include Gerry Healy and Vanessa Redgrave. It has been responsible for a considerable amount of industrial disruption, and trouble in Equity, the actors' trade union. It holds summer camps and is highly organised and authoritarian. It takes as its bible the works that Trotsky wrote while in Mexico. The WRP are the scientologists of the Marxist camp — except that they are less friendly towards their critics and would-be investigators.

The Revolutionary Workers' Party (Posadist) is a Troskyist group of around 500 whose St Paul figure is one J. Posadas, the leader of the South American Trotskyists. Its newspaper is called *Red Flag*. It is very secretive and pro-Chinese, which is rather unusual, since the Maoist groups usually attack the Trotskyists.

The New Communist Party has about 1,000 members. It has recently broken away from the main British Communist Party because the latter has dared to voice a few muted and weak protests at some of the more outrageous Soviet actions and because it disagrees with the 1977 'British Road to Socialism' programme. The New Communist Party has been called Stalinist by its opponents but it is no more (or less) Stalinist than the main Communist Party; it is merely more rigid and less resourceful, and perhaps more honest. The Revolutionary Communist Group, consisting of about 100 members centred on Bristol and producing a magazine *Revolutionary Communist*, seems to have originated from the International Socialists but nevertheless holds views virtually identical to those of the New Communist Party.

The Communist Party of Britain (Marxist-Leninist) is a Maoist Party of about 500 members which has some official recognition from the Chinese authorities. It is the largest Maoist party in Britain. Its founder was Reg Birch, a leading figure in the engineers' union. Its newspaper is *The Worker*. This party has expressed support for armed guerilla struggle for the working class. The Communist Party of England is smaller but it seems to be very affluent and it publishes the *Workers' Daily*. Industrial disruption brought about by Maoist groups is increasing in importance. There are a number of other Maoist groups in operation.

The Communist Party of Great Britain (CP) has about 25,000 members. A number of its members had become exhausted by the end of the 1960s by what had been several decades without any real advance and membership fell from a peak of around 35,000. If the CP started to make real discernible progress towards power it is probable that some 10,000–15,000 lapsed members would rejoin. The CP also has a number of sympathisers who would probably join the Party under these circumstances. The potential strength of the CP is probably therefore nearer 50,000. The CP is by far the best organised Marxist Party in Britain today, as well as being the best funded. It has a very powerful hold in the trade unions, especially in the National Union of Miners, the shop workers' union, ASLEF (the train-drivers' union), the civil service union, ASTMS (the white collar union run by Clive Jenkins), the National Union of Railwaymen, the Engineers' Union (AUEW), the Transport and General Workers' Union (the biggest trade union in the country) and many others. It has an efficient students' section (there are about 1,000 students in the CP) which runs the Student Broad Left and has had Communists elected as Presidents of the National Union of Students. Prominent members include Bert Ramelson, Sue Slipman, Digby Jacks, and Mick McGahey. Every summer the CP organises the 'Communist University of London', a week-long summer school of Marxism at which 400 to 750 people turn up. CP publications include the newspaper *Morning Star* (circulation about forty thousand, the magazines *Comment*, *Marxism Today*, *Labour Monthly* and *Labour Research*. They have their own publishers, Lawrence and Wishart, who turn out reasonably cheap and well-produced versions of Marxist-Leninist writings. The Communist Party has recently moved a little away from Soviet Communism towards Eurocommunism, though there is not a tremendous difference between them. In terms of organisation, discipline, patience, long-term motivation, funds, size, and political know-how the Communist Party outclasses all other Marxist groups. Though apparently tame it is like the pet tiger.

The Socialist Workers' Party (SWP) has about 4,000 members. It used to be called the 'International Socialists' (IS) and its present magazine is called *International Socialism*. The International Socialists used to be called the 'Socialist Review Group' or the 'Cliff Group' after its leader Tony Cliff. The change of name to Socialist Workers' Party came when they decided that the International Socialists were largely academic and they needed to win support from manual workers. This was called 'the turn to the class'. Its newspaper *Socialist Worker* has a circulation between 25,000 and 30,000. Leading members include Paul Foot, nephew of Michael Foot the former Deputy Prime Minister, and (like Tariq Ali as well as his uncle) a former President of the Oxford Union. Other leading members are Duncan Hallas, David Widgery, Mike Kidron, and Chris Harman. The SWP has been associated with the 'Right to Work' campaign, various anti-racist organisations, and the Rank-and-File movement within the National Union of Teachers, and other unions too. They have their own publishers, the Pluto Press. Paul Foot's recuriting book *Why You Should be a Socialist* urges people to join the SWP with the words 'We socialists are not fanatics . . . We want the commitment of workers who laugh and love . . .' However, there has not been much love or laughter when SWP members have put the boot in against the police at anti-National Front demonstrations, and they have been described quite accurately as 'Red Fascists'. They have also been responsible for a considerable amount of industrial disruption, and have become particularly strong in the Midlands. Their views are close to those of the Trotskyists though they prefer to call themselves Leninists.

The Workers' Fight, a breakaway group from the International Socialists, has about 100 members and is centred on Manchester.

The rather quaintly-named Big Flame is an exotic group with about 100 members based mainly in Liverpool, though it seems to be growing rapidly. It has caused a certain amount of industrial disruption through shop stewards in the Liverpool docks and also it has managed to set up another disruptive branch in Fords at Dagenham.

There are a number of other Marxist groups not shown on the map. The most worthy of these, and the one which I feel is the most genuine, is the Socialist Party of Great Britain which publishes the *Socialist Standard*. It has been running since 1904 and is refreshingly open; indeed its internal organisation is much more 'democratic' than that of the Labour Party. It has no leaders at all and never has had, and its Executive Committee meetings are open to everybody (even non-members). There are very elaborate safeguards, including a referendum, before anyone can be expelled. This contrasts powerfully with the frequency of expulsions, often in bitter and unfair circumstances and nearly always on the narrowest points of tactics, which exposes the intolerance of other Marxist groups. If this is how they treat each other, how on earth would they treat us if we gave them the chance?

I have left out the various anarchist groups because although some of them are borderline Marxist groups, such as the Libertarian Communists (formerly the Anarchist Workers' Association), a number of them such as 'Freedom' and 'Black Cross' are not Marxist at all. It is significant that although many anarchist groups have been influenced by Marx, every single one has rejected Marxism-Leninism and criticised it as illibertarian. Even the one closest to Marxism-Leninism has this to say about it: 'However, we are not un-critical of the more mainstream, Leninist revolutionary tradition in Britain. Most of the groups in this tradition have a rigid and elitist view of the nature and role of revolutionary organisation. They also seem to have at best only a paper commitment to democracy in the revolutionary process and to the control of the means of production by the working class as a whole' (*Libertarian Communist*, January/February 1978).

It is gratifying to see, on reading through socialist

literature, how much support can be found in the criticisms
the groups make of each other for my strictures on the whole
lot of them. Group A says Groups B and C are undemocratic,
Group B says Groups A and C are undemocratic, Group C
says Groups A and B are undemocratic. And I say they are
all absolutely right. The Socialist Party of Great Britain has
seen both the Trotskyist Parties and the non-Trotskyist
Parties in my map for what they are — Enemies of
Democracy. In the *Socialist Standard* for February 1978 it
spelt out its official view:

> The Eurocommunist position on Russia is in fact very
> similar to that the Trotskyites have been peddling for
> years: that it is basically a 'workers' or 'Socialist' country
> but that it suffers from 'bureaucratic deformations'. This
> is nonsense; how can the oppressed and exploited workers
> of Russia, who are unable even to organise genuine trade
> unions, be in any way regarded as the rulers there? It is
> nevertheless a convenient argument that allows those who
> hold it to have their cake and eat it: they can support and
> criticise Russia at the same time! This ambiguous attitude
> of the Eurocommunists to Russia inevitably calls into
> question their sincerity when they proclaim a commitment
> to democracy as an inseparable part of Socialism. For how
> can they hold this opinion, yet at the same time regard the
> obviously undemocratic system in Russia as somehow
> Socialist? Only by practising 'newspeak', defining demo-
> cracy in a different way from normal, just as they did in
> their bad old Stalinist past.

This comes, one should remember, from a Socialist group
that was right about the Russian Revolution — not in 1968,
nor in 1956, nor in 1939, nor even in 1929 — but in 1917.
They condemned it as soon as it had occurred.

We now turn to the Campaigning Research Groups. The
Campaign for Academic Freedom and Democracy (CAFD)
should not be appearing on the map at all. It is a disgraceful
state of affairs that a body set up by the National Council of
Civil Liberties (of which I am a member, and which, for all
its faults and left-wing biases, does make some effort to be
non-partisan) should be a vehicle for promoting Marxism —
because this is what it amounts to in practice. CAFD has not

been even-handed — it has put its main emphasis on defending Marxists, yet it has shown no indication of appreciating that they are the very people who pose the greatest threat to academic freedom in the universities and polytechnics in Britain today. The NCCL should break all links with this organisation and set up a proper one to replace it.

The Bertrand Russell Peace Foundation was set up by Bertrand Russell to campaign against imperialism. It was linked with the Vietnam War Crimes Tribunal. Bertrand Russell was never a Marxist, nor even a camp follower. He was a radical — half-socialist and half-anarchist. To his credit he was one of the few foreign observers to criticise Lenin and see the dangers of Marxism-Leninism. However, after his death his organisation has been run by others belonging to the Marxist camp. The leading light is Ken Coates and he is a Marxist. He is effectively in charge not only of the foundation and its funds, but also of its publishing house 'Spokesman'. Furthermore he has set up a body called the Institute for Workers' Control (IWC). This has been operating for over a decade now as a Marxist powerhouse of tactical stratagems, of pamphlets and publications, of seminars and research groups. They have organised large conferences of trade unionists and academics numbering between 1,000 and 2,000. Ken Coates is a particularly clever tactician and persuasive polemicist, which makes him an important figure in Marxist circles. He has very close links with Tony Benn, and the IWC provided such intellectual ballast as might be discovered behind Benn's industrial strategies. Ken Coates has not only been working on establishing workers' control over industry, but also on campaigning for the Labour Party leader to be elected by the Annual Conference, which would give Benn a tremendous advantage over the other contestants. He has written a little book arguing that it is only rationality, common sense, decency, and democracy for the leader to be chosen in this way and 'Spokesman' published it for him. Coates also seems to be closely linked with Frank Allaun, the left-wing Labour MP who is always calling for disarmament, and attacking our defence capabilities. Allaun was the editor of the left-wing Labour newspaper *Voice of the Unions* which was closely associated with the IWC. Ken Coates is one of the foremost exponents of the view that Marxists can and should seek power through the Labour

Party.

The Labour Research Department has misled many people into thinking it is an official Labour Party body. It is in fact a Marxist research group run by the Communist Party. Trust the Communists to call it Labour. They knew full well it would cause people to have the wrong ideas about it.

We now come to Labour Party factions, and the first of them, the Militant Tendency, is the centre-piece of our story. It is a shadowy and secretive body of dedicated Trotskyist revolutionaries who are working secretly deep inside the Labour Party. They are shrouded in mystery. Nevertheless I have pieced together the following facts about them. The Militant Tendency is the name given to the supporters of the newspaper called *Militant* and sub-titled 'The Marxist Paper for Labour and Youth'. They call themselves 'a tendency' because the Labour Party Constitution forbids Labour Party members from belonging to any unconnected 'political organisations' (a) 'having their own Programme, Principles and Policy for distinctive and separate propaganda' (b) 'possessing Branches in the Constituencies', (c) 'engaged in the promotion of Parliamentary or Local Government candidatures,' (d) 'owing allegiance to any political organisation situated abroad' (Labour Party Constitution As Amended 1976, Clause II, my subdivisions). Militant offends against (a) and (b) certainly, and probably against (d) as well. It does have its own separate programme, policies and principles. It has a large number of branches in constituencies up and down the country. (Incidentally, members of all the Trotskyist and Non-Trotskyist parties we have looked at would be offending against most of these clauses – all would offend against (a), many would offend against (b), a number would offend against (c), all the Trotskyite parties owing allegiance to the Fourth International would offend against (d), so would the Maoists who owe allegiance to China, and so would the CP and the New CP because of their Russian sympathies. The Militant Tendency is directed by a kind of elite corps of dedicated revolutionaries. These constitute the Revolutionary Socialist League (RSL) which is an approved instrument but not a section of the Fourth International. This means that Militant is linked with the International Marxist Group and the Workers' Revolutionary Party and the Posadists which are members of the Fourth International.

The Militant Tendency pretends it is an unorganised tendency of like-minded persons who happen to read and support *Militant*. This is a lie. It is, in fact, a highly organised and tightly-knit body modelled on a guerilla army. It has a leadership, an elite corps (the RSL), and the ordinary Militant workers who form the main part of this secret army. The 1975 Report of the National Agent of the Labour Party (which is still being kept secret because its recognition of the extent of Marxist penetration into the Labour Party is political dynamite) has come into my possession. It states that *'Militant* has its own printing works and is associated with "Workers' International Review Publications" and *Militant Irish Monthly*. The scale of the tendency's activities is such that it requires direction by more than an editorial board. . . . Those who support the Militant Tendency openly declare that it is Marxist and claim that all but one of the eleven members of the LPYS (Labour Party Young Socialists) Committee are supporters of the Militant Tendency.' It reveals that the entire organisation at national, regional and local level of the Young Socialists (the youth movement of the Labour Party for those aged 16 to 25) has been captured by Militant. The National Agent drew attention to a proposal by Militant to use the Young Socialists (which ought to be an impartial body for all young Labour Party members) in order to raise further finance for the activities of the Militant Tendency! It is like using the Student Christian Movement to finance a heroin-smuggling ring.

Militant is growing by leaps and bounds. In 1974 it had about 500 agents in operation; by 1978 it had around 1,200. Its secret document *British Perspectives and Tasks 1974* (May 1979) discloses: 'Now that our horizon is extended, we should hold international schools involving members and contacts internationally, YS (Young Socialists) Schools also, but in addition, cadre schools under the banner of the Tendency.' This is how the secret army trains its agents. I have received reliable information from three sources that these secret training sessions have been held, lasting between three and seven days, and that they are increasing in frequency. Often they are held in Wales.

There is a rigid system of promotions and new members are carefully vetted before being permitted to enter; they then start to work their way up the promotion ladder by impressing one of the leaders. The document states: 'Workers willing to accept our programme and perspectives and willing to work actively for our aims once their level is raised sufficiently should be brought in.' That means once their level of political consciousness is raised, i.e. once they have impressed one of the leaders sufficiently by their pliability. Then: 'For the first 6, 12 or even 18 months new worker members should be treated as contact members.' Many people do not check out their wives-to-be as carefully as this! It continues: 'Individual discussion with leading comrades in the branch should continue regularly, comrades should be integrated socially as well as politically.' There is a touching concern for leadership for a group which preaches the religion of equality. Militant further divides its members into two categories — 'core members' and 'contact members'.

Militant is expanding rapidly in the trade unions; it has published Marxist pamphlets propounding 'Militant' or 'Socialist' or 'Fighting' programmes for the following unions: the postmen, the Civil Service union, the miners, the railwaymen, the engineers, the steelworkers, printworkers, the local government officers, the General & Municipal Worker's Union, the electricians, and the Transport and General Workers' Union. It has also brought out a pamphlet written by leading Leyland shop stewards (thus revealed as connected with Militant) entitled *Stop the Sabotage!* — though it might more appropriately be entitled 'Start the Sabotage!' The newspaper *Militant* is expanding its circulation, and so much money was coming in that it was doubled in size in 1978 from eight to sixteen pages. 'Our paper is the best in the World,' they declared in 1974. The expansion of *Militant* has been welcomed by Labour left-wingers: Frank Allaun MP sent a message in for the issue of 10 March 1978 saying '*Militant* will do a most valuable job if it helps to build a mass socialist youth movement.'

Vast sums of money are at the disposal of the leaders of the Militant Tendency. Some of this money is raised and announced openly but much of it is not. Confidential Militant documents in 1974 admit that in that year Militant had 20 full-time organisers. One Militant document already referred to (26 April 1974) comments that the summer schools and training facilities will cost a lot of money and adds: 'This amounts to an extra expenditure in addition to the expense of 20 full-timers. We urgently require a full-time industrial organiser; full-timers for the Southern, South West, Eastern, East Midlands and most regions; a full-time youth organiser. We need full-time workers on the press and for editorial work.' By 1978 the full-timers on political work had risen from twenty to forty (This is about half the number of full-time agents employed by the Labour Party). This was in addition to the staff on the paper. These people have to be paid; they do not live on air. Also they need expenses. At a rate of £3,000 per annum for salary plus expenses (a very modest estimate) a sum of £120,000 would be required merely to support the political agents in the field. In addition to this a further £10,000—£15,000 would be required for the central direction of these agents. In addition the summer schools and training camps cost a great deal of money — my information suggests perhaps a further £10,000 spent on these. Then there are all the costs of running the paper. The target openly set for 1978 in *Militant* (issue of 10 March 1978) was £70,000 for the year. I doubt if they will raise more than £30,000 of this through open appeals to supporters: in the first six weeks of 1978 they raised less than half the required amount for that period. The shortfall will be made up from secret sources. All in all the annual income for the Militant Tendency in 1978 will be in the order of £200,000 to £250,000. This group can look forward to an income of a quarter of a million pounds for 1979 and rising thereafter. With that money, 1500 agents, and 50 full-time paid organisers (estimates based on a modest 10 to 20 per cent growth which is less than they have achieved over the last four years), with a printing press, three newspapers, and branches up and down the country — Militant will be a formidable national political force inside the Labour Party in 1979 and 1980.

The sources of their funds are a great mystery. Some money is being raised by sale of the newspaper, but the appeals for money for the newspaper suggest that it is making a loss overall and is being subsidised to increase its circulation and thus its influence. *Militant*, like most Marxist news-papers, carries no paid advertisements, so it has no advertising revenue. Some money is raised directly by supporters, some is being creamed off from other socialist or Labour organis-ations. But there still remains a substantial sum unaccounted for. The evidence, though circumstantial, points to some foreign source or sources as providing these large sums. Presumably it would be a source or sources interested in fostering Marxism in Britain. Very little of the money is coming from trade unions — not surprising when one considers Militant's attitude towards them. It will work for power within them but 'We must never forget to train our cadres to the theoretical possibility of the Unions as organisations being thrust aside, in a period of revolution, or prior to an insurrection and that workers' committees or soviets could take their place' (Document, 26 April 1974).

The leaders of the Militant Tendency include Ted Grant, a South African, who belonged to the Revolutionary Communist Party, Peter Taafe the Editor of *Militant*, Andy Bevan, of whom we shall hear more than enough later, and Nick Bradley, formerly head of the Young Socialists.

The Chartists are a Trotskyist group centred round the newspaper the *Chartist*, sub-titled 'Labour's Revolutionary Voice'. They also published a quarterly journal the *Chartist International*. They appear to be close to both IMG and Militant (most of the members originally came from IMG). They work exclusively within the Labour Party. They take up slightly more extreme positions than Militant (for instance they openly attack Tony Benn whereas Militant for tactical reasons is prepared to work with him), but they also work in cooperation with Militant. The Chartists are sometimes known as the 'Revolutionary Communist League' which is their official title. They have several hundred members, are growing in strength, and seek to impose a 'revolutionary programme' on the Labour Party. They are active within the Labour Party Young Socialists. The Chartists are best seen as an annexe of Militant connecting them ideologically with IMG, the WRP, and the Posadists.

The 'Campaign for Labour Party Democracy' has got a cheek. It is not campaigning for democracy at all. What it seeks is a change in the system so that MPs can be kicked out by their local party activists. In practice this will work strongly in favour of the Marxists. This they know very well. It is really a 'Campaign for Labour Party Marxism'. The Secretary of this body is called Vladimir Derer. This campaign is very active in the following areas: London, Cleveland, East Kent, Essex, Medway Towns, Nottingham, Oxford,

Bradford, Huddersfield, Sheffield, York and Bristol. The campaign publishes a bi-monthly newsletter, and it is growing steadily in size and influence. Needless to say everyone in the Marxist camp is fully in favour of this campaign. Our friend Frank Allaun, MP, has been elected President of the Campaign. Its Vice President is Joan Maynard, MP. This campaign is also determined to make 'Annual Conference decisions binding on the Parliamentary Labour Party'.

The Tribune Group is a group of left-wing Labour MPs. It has grown steadily from about 20 MPs at its inception in 1964 to about 80 in 1978. All the people who belong to it are left-wingers; additionally there are other left-wingers, like Tony Benn and Judith Hart, who do not belong but are closely associated with it. Some people who know nothing much about politics will raise their eyes at my classification of the left wing of the Tribune Group as being composed of Marxists and quasi-Marxists, and the right wing as being composed of camp followers. A few members of the Tribune Group are mavericks who fit into neither category, but it is true of the bulk of them. I say the left-wing Tribunites are Marxists having carefully studied their voting records, their public speeches and comments, their writings, their private talks in left-wing gatherings and their activities in internal Labour Party politics, and having discussed their views with other Labour politicians, political correspondents, and Party officials. These people, numbering some 20 MPs, are out-and-out Marxists. Some of them have views which are indistinguishable from those held by leaders of the Communist Party of Great Britain (Eurocommunist) and some have views that are indistinguishable from those of the pro-Soviet New Communist Party. When people say 'There aren't any Communists in Parliament' it is necessary to correct them: 'There may not be any Communist Party members in Parliament, but there are at least 20 Communists who sit as Labour MPs.' It is a sobering thought that while there is not one single Fascist in Parliament, there should be 20 Communists. In addition to these there are about 40 camp followers belonging to the right-wing of the Tribune Group, leaving about 20 Tribunites who do not really belong to the Marxist camp at all. Some of the Tribunites may not realise just how close their socialism is to the Marxism-Leninism of the Marxists, but many of them do. The crucial test is not what they call themselves; it is the kind of society they are aiming for, the kind of methods they propose to use to achieve it, whom they vote for, and so forth. Some of them may indeed not realise what species they belong to: there may be foolish and ignorant wolves who think they are sheep, but that is not a good reason to open the door and invite them in to dinner.

Leading members of the Tribune Group include Eric Heffer, Frank Allaun, Norman Atkinson, Joan Lestor, Ian Mikardo, Sydney Bidwell, and Arthur Latham. Eric Heffer is an able and underestimated man. He is a lynch-pin for the extreme left, and over the past twenty years he has been at the forefront of moves to unify it. He himself travelled from the Communist Party to the International Socialists and then got himself elected as a Labour MP. At the Socialist Wortley Hall Conference over twenty years ago Eric Heffer said: 'Let us get down to the real task of rebuilding the movement, particularly in Britain, so that we can create a genuine Marxist movement." That is precisely what he has been doing ever since. His most recent efforts in the autumn of 1977 were to argue that Eurocommunism should not have been condemned by Harold Wilson and David Owen. Heffer's book *The Class Struggle in Parliament* (1973) takes a Marxist approach. Heffer could fairly be described as the father of Labour's left wing. He is one of the few politicians who have got principles: it is a pity they are the wrong principles.

Frank Allaun is also a former member of the Communist Party and he holds very left-wing views. His great hobby-horse is British disarmament; he supported CND and the Labour Peace Fellowship. His views must be very popular in Moscow and he is not exactly noted for his anti-Soviet criticisms. Indeed he criticised a Soviet (Socialist) dissident, Dr Lubarsky, at a Tribune meeting saying that support for Soviet dissidents might be misinterpreted as support for capitalist enemies of Soviet Socialism (the *Guardian*, 22 November 1977).

Ian Mikardo, too, is doubtless popular in Moscow. He fosters good relations with the Soviet bloc as a businessman running an East-West trading concern.

Norman Atkinson is renowned as an extreme left-winger. His views and voting patterns in the House of Commons over the last ten years put him squarely within the Marxist camp.

It is not generally realised what an extreme left-winger Joan Lestor is. In my assessment her position is close to Ian Mikardo's. Both she and Mikardo effectively by their actions defended Alex Kitson, a prominent trade unionist, who made in the autumn of 1977 a series of nauseating speeches in Russia praising the 'achievements' of the Soviet government. Heffer, who is more keen on Eurocommunism than Soviet Communism, had a blazing row with them at a Labour Party meeting.

Sydney Bidwell attracted a great deal of attention to himself in 1977 when he announced that, unlike the Communist Party, he believed that violent revolution might be necessary to resolve the 'class struggle'. That gives a fair indication of his views; Lenin would have approved of his announcement. Bidwell is a former Chairman of the Tribune Group.

Arthur Latham is the very left-wing former Labour MP for Paddington.

The Tribune Group is a group of MPs. It does not formally exist outside Parliament. However, it has a large number of supporters. In this it is helped by its associated newspaper *Tribune* edited by Richard Clements which is the most widely-read Labour newspaper. In student politics there is an organised Tribunite group called 'Clause Four'. In the constituency Labour Parties there is no *organised group* of Tribunites though there are many individuals who call themselves Tribunites.

We have now done our trek round the Marxist camp. What has emerged? I could have dwelt at length on the very close links between certain sections of the Marxist camp and the Russian communists, and between certain sections and the IRA. But I do not want to direct attention to the spectacular and horrendous links of many Marxists. What I want to do is to emphasise how bad the whole Marxist camp is, not by looking at its worst members but by seeing what all the Marxists have in common.

Two things emerge. One is that the differences between the groups are slight and all are enemies of democracy. The other is that the Marxist camp has very considerable resources at its disposal, of personnel, of newspapers, and of money. When we consider that Militant alone will be spending some quarter of a million pounds on Marxist

activities in 1979, the total expenditure for the whole
Marxist camp in 1979 is unlikely to be less than a million. No
wonder they are making progress! They are *buying* the revolution. Purchasing power for them is not about the cost of
living but about buying their way into power. This excludes,
of course, the vast sums of money at the disposal of the trade
unions. AUEW-TASS is Marxist. Some others are already
virtually under the control of an alliance of Marxists and
camp followers. As we have seen Communist Party members
(to say nothing of other Marxists) are a strong force in many
of the trade unions. It remains to be seen whether the
Marxists will get their hands on the union money. Personally
I think that moderate trade unionists will probably just about
manage to keep them at bay in most of the big unions. But
they can still get a long way on a million pounds a year. A
million pounds and a million people can achieve a lot.

Now I can almost hear some people saying 'Don't worry.
They will fritter this million away squabbling among themselves. They are all at sixes and sevens with each other.' This
sort of thing is said so often. But imagine that you and I
tiptoed down the stairs to a dark basement where we ob-
served a gathering of feckless desperados in a violent
argument:'Let's strangle him,' said one. 'No, we say he
should burn.' 'Electrocute him!' cried others. 'Drop a brick
on his head,' a gruff voice interjected. 'Run a combine har-
vester over him.' They were talking about *you*. Now suppose
I said, airily, 'Don't worry. They're quarrelling among themselves.' And suppose I added 'Look, several of them have said
they only want to paralyse you,' (Marxism with a human
face). What would your reaction be? How complacent would
you be then?

The threat of Marxist unity (or, as the Marxists call it,
'Left Unity' or 'Socialist Unity') cannot easily be discounted.
In any case they only need to act in concert. They only need
to sink their differences for a while. They only need to agree
to polish off democracy first, and then afterwards fight it out
between themselves.

This book is about Marxists acquiring power through the
back-door by masquerading as democratic socialists or by
using democratic socialists. I am convinced that the best
hope the Marxists have of gaining a considerable amount of
real power is to work either through the Labour Party or in

conjunction with it. This will also involve working through the trade unions. A considerable number of Marxists, including many of the most able ones, evidently agree with me, because this is precisely what they are doing at this very moment. Increasing numbers of them are doing it with each year that passes. 1979 and 1980 will be worse than ever before.

2
The Infiltrators

Infiltration is a much-abused word. The story is about to unfold of how Reg Prentice was booted out as the Labour candidate for Newham North-East by Marxist infiltrators. But what precisely is an 'infiltrator'? It was never necessary to define such terms for the ordinary London East End worker; he knew exactly what a Marxist infiltrator was without any need for explanation. But this book is also addressed to educated people, who find problems with such terms. Being so much cleverer they get hopelessly muddled up with fine distinctions and intellectual red tape. So for their benefit ...

An infiltrator is a political tresspasser who gains entry into an organisation and works his way up within despite the fact that his views are inconsistent with the fundamental principle of that organisation. Democracy is the fundamental principle of the Labour Party — it comes before Socialism. (If it did not, Labour Party members would have to condone indefinite postponement of a General Election once a Socialist government were in power). As enemies of democracy, Marxists do not belong in the Labour Party. You do not have to be a doctrinaire Socialist ('Nationalisation and more Nationalisation') to belong in the Labour Party. This test would disqualify nearly all the Labour Party's leaders, many of its founders, and the vast bulk of its membership. The Labour Party has always aspired to be a democratic party of social concern and those who interpret socialism in terms of human emancipation and championing the lot of the poor and unfortunate belong in it. Those subscribing to 'revolutionary socialism' do not.

It is important to make a distinction here. Some people have called me, and my colleague, Julian Lewis, infiltrators because we moved from one constituency (Oxford) to another (Newham North-East), and they have equated this kind of 'infiltration' with the other. In fact they are two quite different things. The real infiltrators are those who move in to take over someone else's organisation for their own purposes. If another man tries to defend that organisation he is in no sense an infiltrator, even if he comes from a different geographical place. Suppose a ruthless speculator moves into a neighbourhood, buys up a block of flats and starts to evict the tenants illegally. And suppose that a lawyer whose office is in another borough tries to defend them. He and the speculator are both 'outsiders', certainly, but does that put them on a par? It is not where someone comes from that makes him an infiltrator; it is what he is trying to do.

Newham is the name given to three Parliamentary constituencies. They are all safe Labour seats. In 1974 the Labour majorities were 13,541 for Reg Prentice in Newham North-East, 13,381 for Arthur Lewis in Newham North-West, and 17,721 for Nigel Spearing in Newham South.

The geographical area covered includes East Ham, Forest Gate and Canning Town. You can get the flavour of the place by taking a long trip on the District Line out to East London and getting off at East Ham. You are struck at once by the grimy, desolate urban wasteland in which you find yourself. There are no parks, no trees, no theatres or cinemas or sparkling shop windows — only mean streets and cramped houses. Everything seems to be decaying and down-at-heel, without even the charm of being shabby genteel, for it never was genteel. It is a barren district with few social and cultural facilities and none of the zip of fast city life. The main industries are chemical manufacturing, the gas works at Beckton, and the docks. All are in decline.

There are severe social and economic problems in Newham. The Newham Rights Centre stated in its *1977 Annual Report* 'Poor housing plus dole queues equals Newham'. Also there are racial problems and the National Front is much in evidence. There are few professional people living in Newham. The professional and managerial element comprises only one twentieth of the Newham workforce, putting Newham in the lowest bracket of constituencies in this respect.

Newham is not unique. In most respects it is fairly typical

of many safe Labour seats. The bad conditions are not the
cause of the infiltration but they provide an invitation. Like
germs infecting an open wound the infiltrators home in on
this social disaster area determined to change things for the
better, perhaps, but also to exacerbate social tensions and
turn them to their own advantage. There are many legitimate
grievances to exploit.

The bad conditions do exist and the response to them has
been poor. However, it is unfortunate that the left so often
manages to corner the market in indignation and protest over
social problems. In Italy the Communist Party is adept at this
and has a proud municipal record: this reflects badly on the
other parties. The trouble is that there are so few far-sighted,
intelligent and compassionate centrists and right-wingers.

The most significant social and economic facts for our
story are that housing is cheap in Newham which means that
young middle class entrants into the area can afford to buy
houses on mortgages, and that the middle class element is
small. With such a small proportion of professional and
managerial people, new settlers with this background will be
like one-eyed men in the land of the blind. Being articulate,
educated and self-confident they will be in a good position
to brush aside the local working class people and lord it over
them.

But on the whole the social conditions are not relevant.
They only facilitate infiltration by providing social tension,
availability of cheap houses, and above all, little opposition.
The story is one of pure political tactics, in-fighting and
organization. It could happen (and indeed has happened)
elsewhere, where the social conditions were quite different.
The story is one of political power, not economic laws.
Ironically, the infiltrators themselves are a standing con-
tradiction to the Marxism they espouse. They are all
professional people doing very nicely out of the capitalist
system and being paid much better than the Newham locals.
Their activities have nothing to do with economic factors and
everything to do with political in-fighting. What happens
inside the Party depends not on external social factors, but
on the internal structure and organisation of the Party.

How do the infiltrators go about winning control of a
constituency Labour Party? The structure of constituency

Labour Parties is slightly complicated. Just like any other club it has members and officers. The Newham North-East Party has six officers: a Chairman (sometimes called President), two Vice-Chairmen, a Treasurer, a Secretary and an Assistant Secretary. In addition to individual members, other organisations can affiliate to it and become members too, so the members are the individual Party members plus the affiliated organisations. The Party is run by two important committees, a small Executive Committee (the EC) and a large General Management Committee (the GMC). These committees are composed of delegates elected by the individual members and other delegates elected by the affiliated organisations.

The individual members are divided into 'branches' corresponding to the geographical division into 'wards' made for Council elections. (Although technically incorrect, I will adopt popular usage and use the terms 'ward' and 'branch' interchangeably.) In Newham North-East there are nine wards: Manor Park, Wall End, Woodgrange, Castle, Central, Greatfield, Little Ilford, Kensington and St Stephen's. They are each entitled to send delegates to the GMC, the number depending on the number of members of the branch. If a branch wants to send an extra delegate it has to find another 50 members, and another 50 for each extra one after that. The delegates are elected at meetings of the branch. These meetings are very poorly attended; even at the Annual Meeting it is a surprising thing if more than 30 per cent of the members bother to turn up, and the number of members is itself fairly small.

In addition to the Party Branches, we have the affiliated organisations. Any organisation that is affiliated to the national Labour Party can affiliate to the Newham North-East Labour Party. This includes trade unions, and various socialist societies. They can each send delegates according to the number of their members up to a maximum of 6 delegates and they pay fees for this privilege which help to finance the Party.

In summary, then, the General Management Committee (GMC) consists of delegates from the nine Party branches (wards), the Party sections, the affiliated trade unions, the affiliated socialist societies, and the Co-op. The Executive Committee (EC) is elected by the GMC from its own membership.

The Party sections are special groups of members of the constituency Labour Party grouped together according to some common interest or characteristic. Thus young people (16 to 25) and women are very fortunate because not only can they exercise all the normal rights of branch members but in addition they have an extra set of rights by having their own section. The youth section is called the Young Socialists. There are also Women's sections. So women elect women's delegates as well as helping to elect their ordinary branch delegates, and the young members elect Young Socialist delegates as well as branch ones. These Party sections are also fortunate in that, whereas it takes 50 members to elect an extra branch delegate, these sections can have two delegates for only 11 members. A delegate here is 'worth' 5½ persons instead of 50 persons.

One other peculiarity is that for both trade unions and Party sections it is permissible for only 2 members to return one delegate. In this case a delegate is worth 2 persons. Thus, for example, a trade union with 90 members living in the constituency would be able to send 2 delegates to the GMC, whereas 10 different trade unions, each with 2 members living in the constituency, would be able to send 10 delegates.

The Rules of the Labour Party really are extraordinary. In many ways they are quite feudal. It is interesting to reflect upon the marked similarity between the Labour Party's Rules and British Parliamentary electoral systems before the reform of 1832. Prior to that there were rotten boroughs and pocket boroughs and so forth. Constituencies varied enormously in size: huge cities like Manchester were grossly under-represented and tiny villages were over-represented in Parliament. In some places a local landowner or noble had the borough in his pocket and he chose the MP. In Old Sarum, MPs were returned to represent a wall!

Under the Labour Party Rules two extraordinary conditions exist:

(1) Multiple voting: some people have many votes, others only have one.
(2) Vote-values differ enormously: some votes are worth 1/50 of a delegate others are worth ½.

The reason for this extraordinary state of affairs is that the

Labour Party treats organisations as well as individuals as members. Indeed, in its early days it did not have individual members at all.

The system can work perfectly well. Any old system will work provided you have co-operative people who stick to the Rules and agree on fundamentals, and in Newham the system, though bizarre, worked satisfactorily for many years. But it is a system wide open to abuse. We shall see in a moment how the infiltrators abused it.

In 1970 the Newham North-East Labour Party was a fairly torpid affair. Its Executive Committee consisted mainly of old men, and one or two women, in their sixties and seventies. For example, there was Daisy Turner, a delegate from Greatfield Ward. She is a delightful and cheery old lady full of fun and very kind. She had been a member of the Labour Party for about forty years, represented her locality on various regional conferences, organised a Newham Women's Section and won awards for her service to the Labour Party. There was Bert Simpson a tough, frank, no-nonsense man with a strong sense of right and wrong. There was Councillor Fred Bigland who had only got a few more years to live. The most powerful figures were the Chairman, Jo Taylor, the Secretary, Claude Callcott, the Vice-Chairman, Harold Lugg, and Councillor Wally Hurford. Jo Taylor was popular and pleasant and in such an easy-going set-up he made a good Chairman. But his health was poor, he had heart trouble and with his last heart attack he actually died on the operating table — though happily he recovered and is still alive today. Claude Callcott was one of the oldest EC members: he was getting on for eighty. All these people could be loosely classed as Moderates. Some were on the right wing of the Labour Party, others were in the centre. Harold Lugg was rather different. Like them he was a working man, in fact he had worked for many years as a milkman. But he had rather left-wing views and was a great schemer. He also had a rather sharp tongue and at meetings he sometimes seemed rather opinionated and bullying. His political style was rather different from that of the others. He was not a Marxist — he would not have understood what it was to be one. His views were, I suppose, somewhere within the Tribune Group. Councillor Wally Hurford, who was getting on for eighty, was the Grand Old Man of the Labour

right-wingers. He was by far the most subtle and intelligent
of them all and he had plenty of guts. He knew his way
around and was one of the strongest bastions of the Moderate
cause in Newham. But he was an old man and his wife's
health was poor. Wally was a delegate for the Transport and
General Workers Union (T&G).

The ordinary members of the Party were old too. Many
of them were retired.

The GMC tells the same story of domination by the
elderly. Newham North-East was run by a gerontocracy. The
'paper membership' (those who had been signed up to the
Party and had a Party card but took no active part) was
weighted towards the elderly, and the 'active membership'
(those who took an active part in the Party, regularly attending meetings, assisting at Party functions and so on) was
also predominantly elderly. For instance, Manor Park branch
in the early 1970s had a membership 80 per cent of whom
were elderly and there were no branch meetings so it was
almost entirely a paper membership. Bill Jones, a Labour
Party Regional Office official, commented in relation to
Newham North-East in the mid seventies: 'The care and
retention of OAP members in every Ward is commendable,
but the overall ratio is too high. One is fearful that a
bronchitis epidemic will decimate the membership.'

Imagine then how attractive it must have looked to those
roving ambassadors of goodwill, the Marxists. Surely it was a
prime target for infiltration? Infiltration is the official policy,
indeed the *raison d'être*, of the Militant Tendency. As early
as March 1959 the Revolutionary Socialist League brought
out a document called *Problems of Entrism* which is the
classic manual on entryism. Entryism is the name given to
the technique of entering the Labour Party and creeping and
burrowing up within it, capturing positions of power and
using them as fortresses. The technique was originally
developed by the Communist Parties, especially in relation to
the trade unions, but the RSL has perfected it. The fullest
account of the technique is to be found in a booklet
published in November 1973 called *Entrism*. Its Introduction
states: 'The stage at which we are in the YS will be repeated
in the adult LP and the Unions.' This means that since they
exclusively dominate the Young Socialists they seek to
achieve dominance in the Labour Party and trade unions. It

adds ominously, 'the real history of the tendency is only just beginning. We are only at the start of real entry work with the outline of those conditions laid down by Trotsky just beginning to take shape.'

Entryism has two underlying principles: the principle of securing power by entering a large and powerful organisation and the principle of entering secretively. Trotsky, Lenin and Stalin supported both. Trotsky wrote that 'every revolutionist who has not lost touch with reality must recognise that the creation of Communist fractions in the reformist trade unions is an extremely important task'. But it was Stalin who was the expert at this sort of technique. He had worked his way up into the dominant position by capturing control of the internal Party organs. Militant has no intellectuals or polemicists of any note, only bureaucratic hatchet-men. We have seen that there is no great difference between Stalinism and Trotskyism but it is ironical that those who claim to follow the banner of Trotsky should so strongly resemble his murderer in this respect.

Militant advocates entryism within the Labour Party and the trade unions. We know that Militant liked what it saw of the rather decrepit Newham North-East Party. The Militant document *British Perspectives and Tasks 1974* stated, 'We must dig roots in the wards and constituencies as we have in the YS [Young Socialists]. It then adds 'Many are still shells dominated by politically dead old men and women' — an unkind phrase. 'Politically dead' means that Militant disagrees with their views, but 'shells' of 'old' men and women is a fair description. It goes on: 'They are now ossified little cliques. they will begin to change with an influx of new members.' This, then, is the story of Newham North-East: a shell dominated by elderly men and women, and then an influx of Marxist infiltrators. The Militant leaders were acutely conscious of the need to proceed by stealth: 'we must be firmly against any adventurous courses ... The Chartists and the Workers' Fight are horrible examples of how not to work. We must proceed unsensationally and calmly ... building up in the Party and the Unions.'

We have seen what the Newham North-East Party was like in 1970. But in 1971/2 we can notice a change. The old faithfuls are still there but there is now a trace of a new element. Here are profiles of some of the new people in 1971.

Alan Howarth, age 23. Moved into Newham in 1971, joined Newham NE Party in 1971, immediately got on to GMC and EC; Profession — committee clerk to the Parliamentary Labour Party (since 1975); views — very left-wing.

Owen Ashworth, age 36. Joined Newham Party in 1970, got on to EC and GMC 1971. Profession — teacher; views — very left-wing; appearance — ginger beard.

Elaine Ashworth, age 31, wife of Owen Ashworth. Profession — teacher; Other details the same (except the ginger beard!).

Helen Abji, age 27, wife of Mr Abji. Moved into Newham 1971, joined Newham Labour Party late 1971, got on to GMC and EC 1972; Profession — teacher; Views — very left-wing.

Michael Brown, age 23; Son of local councillor; Profession — teacher; Views — very left-wing; Appearance — long hair.

Anita Pollack, age 25, unmarried. Joined Newham Labour Party 1972, got on to GMC and EC 1972; Profession — editor (book publishing); Views — very left-wing; Appearance — very pretty.

Philip Bradbury, age 26, Joined Newham Party 1972, got on to GMC 1972; Profession — lecturer in psychology at North-East London Polytechnic; Views — very left-wing; Appearance — long black hair and long moustache.

Kevin Mansell, age 24, married; Got on to Newham GMC 1972; Previously Vice-President of the Students' Union at Cambridge University 1967-8; spoke at the National Union of Students Annual Conference 1967; Profession — social worker; Views — very left-wing.

John Clark, age 23, married. Got on to the GMC 1972; Profession — administrator for the Paddington Churches Housing Association at a salary of about £6,000 p.a.; Views — very left-wing.

Michael Pemberton, age 24, married; Joined Labour Party 1972, got on to GMC and EC 1973; Profession — research chemist, trade union organiser, member of ASTMS Dagenham; Views — very left-wing.

This is a representative selection of the newcomers. They tended to come in couplets — Mr Pemberton brought Mrs Pemberton (a teacher) along, Mrs Abji took Mr Abji along, Philip Bradbury came with Anita Pollack. This was rather unusual for a local Labour Party (the old faithfuls did not generally bring their wives along) but it doubled the vote. The new arrivals came in husband-and-wife combinations, boyfriend-girlfriend combinations, and one or two other combinations. There was not exactly a community of women among some of the newcomers but there was a certain amount of cross-fertilisation. This bohemian touch for some reason upset a number of the locals much more than the extreme political views of the newcomers. However, it was the more staid and conventionally respectable couples who were often the more dangerous politically.

The prototype profile of the newcomer is: a middle-class professional, probably a teacher, social worker, lecturer or administrator, in his twenties, with very left-wing political views, with long hair and a Marx-like black beard or Che Guevara moustache, hitched up to the female version of this species.

The *annus mirabilis* for the newcomers was 1972, the year when most of them became seriously involved, often for the first time, in the Labour Party. The newcomers swung into action immediately. In no time at all they moved into key posts at all levels of the Party. In 1970 there was not a single Marxist on the Newham Party's Executive Committee or on the General Management Committee. The position soon changed. At a GMC meeting on 2 December 1971, 2 Marxists were present out of 29. The 2 Marxists, who came from different branches, signed their names in the attendance book in the same pen adjacent to each other, as they were to do at several subsequent meetings. This suggests they regularly came to meetings together, probably discussing tactics on the way. Of these two, one was fairly soon going to become Vice-Chairman, the other was going to just miss becoming the Newham Greater London Council candidate.

At a GMC meeting on 24 May 1972 there were 7 Marxists present out of 27. At a GMC meeting on 27 September 1972 there were 11 Marxists present out of 32. This was a pretty startling rise to power — from nothing to just over one-third of the active GMC in less than eighteen months.

No penetration of the Executive Committee took place in 1971; it continued to be composed exclusively of the old Party regulars. But in 1972, 3 Marxists had wormed their way in. In 1972 significant changes took place at the higher levels

of the Party. Alan Howarth became Youth Officer, and Helen
Abji became Assistant Secretary. According to an officer of
her branch (Little Ilford) at this early stage (1972) Helen
Abji was saying 'we will have to get rid of Reg.' Reg
Prentice's days in Newham were numbered.

Another significant change was that Harold Lugg, by some
deft organisation of his supporters, managed to beat Jo
Taylor for the Chairmanship in 1972. Lugg was Vice-Chairman and one of the old faithfuls in the Party, and his rise to
the Chairmanship was not the achievement of the Marxists,
though they backed him and may have encouraged him. But
it was a god-send for the Marxists because Lugg would never
take the lead in resisting them. Being fairly left-wing himself
and seeing which way the wind was blowing, he would
happily let Prentice be sacked.

How did the Marxists make such progress in such a short
time? They were very willing, for a start. Some of the old
faithfuls must have been rather pleased that a new generation
of eager helpers had arrived, keen, energetic young men and
women offering to do the Party chores. They would revital-
ise the Party and recruit new members. And indeed they did.
But the members they recruited were usually Marxists — a
doubtful blessing for the Party! The newcomers did not
usually advertise their views in the early days. Who, then, was
to suspect what they were up to? It is easy to see why the
old regulars were taken in; nothing like this had ever
happened before in Newham and they were caught by
surprise. Some of the branches of the Party were in a semi-
moribund state and had not held meetings for some time.
Many of them did not send the full complement of delegates
to which they were entitled. This meant that there were
vacancies and empty places and any newcomer could simply
walk into them. Any election would be a formality because
there were more places than there were candidates. Unless
there was some very good reason to exclude a person offering
his services there would be no problem for him in securing a
place on the GMC.

The newcomers were returned from the Party branches
based on the wards — the Ashworths from St Stephen's
branch, the Abjis from Little Ilford, Clark from Wall End,
Bradbury and Pollack from Manor Park, the Pembertons
from Woodgrange, Brown from Castle, Mansell from

Kensington. They were nicely spaced out across the constituency in twos and threes in the wards. The only two wards not to be penetrated at this stage (1971-2) were Greatfield and Central.

At the earliest stage the newcomers ran in harness with the old-timers: for example, a Party branch would return, say, a couple of newcomers and a couple of the old Moderates. The newcomers simply put themselves forward and became delegates to the GMC. But this was not enough. The next stage was to get control of the Party branches by becoming Chairman and Secretary (the two key posts) and after that the old-timers could be quietly dropped or 'knifed', or perhaps you could even wait for them to retire naturally if they only had a year or two to go.

By 1974 many of the Party branches had fallen to the newcomers. Philip Bradbury had become Chairman of Manor Park and Anita Pollack had become Secretary, Helen Abji had become Secretary of Little Ilford, John Clark had become Secretary of Wall End, Michael Pemberton had become Secretary of Woodgrange, Owen Ashworth had become Treasurer of St Stephen's and Elaine Ashworth had become Secretary.

Once they got control of a Party branch they could field their own men for the Council elections, because each branch selected which candidates the Labour Party would put forward for Newham Council from each ward. (Not all were safe Labour wards, because some returned Ratepayers.) What kind of people did they put up? Unsurprisingly they often felt their own services were likely to be superior to anybody else's. In time they could build up a big following on the Council, and eventually it could be taken over, for it was a Labour-dominated Council, though this would mean capturing Newham North-West and Newham South too, or at least one of them. When Coucillor Fred Bigland died in 1975 a by-election was called for Manor Park Ward, now firmly under the Bradbury-Pollack axis. The man who was put up as Council candidate was one Christopher Palme, 26 years old, a bearded social worker married to a teacher. Michael Pemberton became a Councillor too, and so did Michael Brown.

How did the Marxists win control of wards and secure the key positions in the Party branches? This can be explained in

two ways. First, they could go so far by consent. We have
seen how they easily slipped into various positions. They
were often welcomed. They were efficient and knowledge-
able, being educated professional people. They tended to
hide their real political views. There was a shortage of Party
helpers. The Rules of the Party are such that its structure is
expansive: there are no ceilings on Party branch delegates,
for example, so there is no lack of empty seats to create
competition. But this entry by consent can only take them so
far. After a while they will have to start elbowing the old
Party regulars out of the way. There may be plenty of space
at the bottom level of the Party but there is rather less room
at the top.

At the ward level much was achieved by a quiet entry.
Why stir up unnecessary fuss? The post of branch Secretary
can be an onerous one. In the old days the Secretary did not
have to do a tremendous amount because meetings were
often irregular and infrequent. However a new species of
'demanding member' had arrived. Our bearded friends
wanted to go on courses, debate international politics, re-
organise the pharmaceutical industry, change the organisation
of the constituency Party, hold branch meetings every few
weeks, have resolutions sent here, there, and everywhere.
Being educated people, they understood everything, and their
weighty deliberations on all sorts of obscure questions had to
be forwarded without delay to the appropriate authorities for
action. How could the old Secretaries cope with such busy-
bodies? Heavy demands were made on their time. The job
became more and more onerous. Why not retire and let the
keen young men do the work they had generated? This was
one important reason why, when there were perhaps only
two or three Marxists in a ward, one of them could end up
holding the all-important post of branch Secretary.

Another factor was geographical distribution. By spacing
itself out cleverly, concentrating on certain areas and ignoring others, a minority can become a majority. Suppose we
have 10 Party branches and an active membership of 10 in
each branch. Suppose that there are 64 Moderates and only
36 Left-Wingers. One would think that the left-wingers would
be in a minority. But suppose they concentrate on 6
branches, in each of which they provide 6 of the 10 active
members, leaving the other 4 branches wholly to the

Moderates. Then if each branch returns 4 delegates on a simple majority voting system, we end up with 24 left-wing delegates representing 36 left-wingers and 16 Moderate delegates representing 64 Moderates! Being young and mobile, with high incomes, and being newcomers to the area, the Marxists coming into Newham could easily position themselves for maximum tactical advantage. Let us take the case of one couple not mentioned so far; the wife was a lecturer and social worker who moved in to Newham in 1972 when she was 25 and immediately joined the Labour Party. They sold their house to another Marxist couple when they moved out of Newham (they were nomads, not settlers) and this other Marxist couple took over their branch offices. In other words they handed over control of the ward to them. Maybe it was advertised on the house sale prospectus: desirable residence and full amenities including control of local Labour Party ward! This case was not unique. There is extensive evidence of Marxists moving in and out of Newham North-East, picking a particular ward in the first place, and then moving from one ward to another, all in order to secure political control within the local Labour Party. It demonstrates how seriously they regarded their Labour Party infiltration and how well co-ordinated they were. Several wards were controlled by just one household — they were 'pocket wards'.

In 1972, then, the newcomers had established a formidable contingent on the GMC. In the final analysis it is the GMC that really counts because this is the committee that selects the Parliamentary candidate. By the end of 1972 they constituted about a third of regular GMC attenders and about a quarter of GMC members. They had had a phenomenal rise. But in 1973 they made virtually no advance at all on the GMC — one extra member to be precise. They constituted throughout 1973 only 12 out of 47 and at meetings through 1973 they never rose above one third. Only one significant event took place; the new man, Mike Mecham, a black-bearded administrator in his twenties, became the GMC delegate for Greatfield Ward. His wife was soon to become the Secretary of Greatfield branch, one of the two missing parts of the jigsaw. Of the nine branches, that left only Central branch. What rough beast, its hour come at last, was going to slouch into Central branch? Who was going to be the new Secretary of Central branch?

Until the tail-end of 1974 the story was the same; only one newcomer on the GMC. Why? Why, after a bold advance in 1972 from virtually nothing to one-third, should there be virtually no advance in 1973 and virtually no advance until the end of 1974? This points unmistakably, irrespective of any evidence, to a highly organised operation. If there had been a natural incoming tide of young professional people to the area and to the Party, why should there be no new people prior to 1970, then a great burst on to the GMC in 1972, then practically nothing in 1973, and nothing again until the end of 1974? This suggests there is nothing social and economic involved here. But why should the infiltrators take a rest in 1973 and 1974? My own view is that they saw they could not rid themselves of Prentice before the next election because their 1972 push had not taken them quite far enough. However, they did try to test out the water. Towards the end of 1973 they put a 'No confidence' motion in Prentice. It was defeated by a 2:1 majority. This fits exactly with my calculation that by the end of 1972 the Marxists constituted one third of regular GMC attenders and demonstrates that they made no further progress in 1973. The voting showed a very clear line of division: only the Marxist third voted against Prentice, the rest voted for him (they did not even abstain). The Marxists knew that the Labour Party's National Executive Committee would not let them drop him a year before the election and an election was widely expected in 1974.

The other factor is that the attention of many Marxists became turned to the work of two Marxist parties contesting the election against Prentice. One was the International Marxist Group (IMG). In February 1974 the IMG candidate polled a magnificent 202 votes (0.4 per cent of the poll) and lost his deposit. The actress, Vanessa Redgrave, did a little better for The Workers' Revolutionary Party (WRP) — 766 votes (1.7 per cent of the poll) — but she lost her deposit too. Mr Prentice with 24,000 votes (54.4 per cent) was not too worried by the electoral threat from the Marxist quarter: only 2 per cent of the voters, and much smaller than the Liberals, the two Marxist parties came bottom of the poll.

Now, you do not have to be particularly brilliant to think: 'If there are less than 1,000 members of the Newham Labour

Party and there are about 1,000 Marxist supporters in Newham why don't we go in and take over the Party, kick Prentice out, and put a Marxist in to replace him? Then our man will get the twenty to twenty-five thousand votes of the Labour candidate'. If they could not get in through the front door they would creep round the other side and get in through the back. If the electorate had been given an open, avowed Marxist candidacy and did not like it, never mind. Let them be given a secretive Marxist candidacy instead! And, if the Marxists could not succeed in getting one of themselves in, they could at least make sure they put Prentice out. So, soon after they lost the election, many of them started to think in these terms. Like the sneaky supporter of a boxer who has been fairly and squarely beaten in the ring, they crept up to stick a knife in the back of the victor as he climbed out.

In 1974 the Newham North-East GMC was blessed with a new arrival. His name was Tony Kelly. He was shrouded in mystery and his address at any particular time seemed uncertain. By a strange quirk of fate he was enrolled by a local councillor who was canvassing for Prentice at one of the General Elections in 1974. How he must have laughed to himself as he played the innocent and asked questions about the Labour Party. If he had wanted to join to help the Labour Party, he would surely have done so before the election, not after it.

This opportunity of being invited, instead of inviting himself, was too good to be missed. It provided him with a good cover: who would suspect a man who had been invited into the party by a well-known local councillor? While the election was proceeding Kelly's interest did not lie with Mr Prentice's candidacy. He is a semi-educated man — he cannot always write grammatically or spell correctly — but he was very clued up on the dry technicalities of Labour Party Rules and Standing · Orders. This is very rare among Party members, especially new members. The various reports he wrote later also bear traces of someone who has received special training in this field.

Tony Kelly's occupation was a great mystery. At one moment he appeared to be working for the railways, the next he did not seem to be working at all; then he would apparently work at something else for a week or two. Perhaps one reason for these sudden bursts of work was that he could thereby obtain trade union membership. It was normally necessary to be a trade union member in order to join the Labour Party. Furthermore, there was the possibility of becoming a trade union delegate. No one knew for sure how old Kelly was; he looked as though he was in his late thirties and usually wore jeans and looked pretty unkempt. The reader can guess which ward he resided in. It was indeed Central Ward.

1975 was the year when the tidal wave hit the Newham North-East Party. The new people came in fast and furious, one after the other. At the Annual General Meeting (AGM) on 26 February 1975 the two Mechams (who claimed to be Moderates) appeared as Greatfield Ward delegates, Tony Kelly appeared as a trade union delegate for the Transport Salaried Staff's Association (presumably in his capacity as a sometime ticket collector), and one of two Murphys appeared as a Little Ilford Ward delegate. A young lecturer by the name of Ade Brooks who worked at the North-East London Polytechnic appeared as a St Stephen's Ward delegate and a Ms Jan Tomlinson, a young woman aged twenty-two, appeared to represent Manor Park Ward, now safely under the collective thumbs of Philip Bradbury, another lecturer at the same Polytechnic, and Anita Pollack. Jan Tomlinson had a startling rise to fame. She had gained office in her own branch very quickly and then been elevated at this AGM to Assistant Secretary of the Party. This post of Assistant Secretary is well worth watching. It was first taken in 1972 by Helen Abji. She held on to it until 1975 when it was handed on to Jan Tomlinson. At the GMC meeting on March 26 the other Brooks appeared, as if from nowhere — Angela Brooks, a lecturer who had joined the Newham Party in 1972 at the age of twenty-two.

On 10 April 1975 Tony Kelly suddenly appeared at an Executive Committee meeting as the 'Minutes Secretary', an office which did not previously exist. It had been suggested out of the blue that the office should be created and before anyone knew what was happening he was in it. Less than two weeks later he had become Assistant Secretary. It was, of course, quite unconstitutional and illegal: officers of the Party can only be elected at the Annual Meeting (under clause XII (1) of the Party's Rules). But Jan Tomlinson and he had done a swop: she had become Minutes Secretary and he had become Assistant Secretary. The way this post of Assistant Secretary was passed, like a shuttle, from Abji to Tomlinson to Kelly is illuminating. It is further evidence of their acting in concert. This juggling of posts is pure manipulation. Why did not Kelly face the democratic verdict at the Annual Meeting by openly contesting the position? As for Jan Tomlinson, she was a nomad indeed. In 1975 she was at the centre of it all; in 1976 she disappeared and was never seen again.

At the April GMC meeting there were some new faces. They were not very nice faces. The worst was Tom Jenkins. Then there was Keith Baggs, in his early twenties. Tom Jenkins was a teacher. He had been at Swansea grammar school and Bristol University. I found him the least likeable of an unlikeable bunch of people. Then there was Carol Bevan. She was the wife of a person called Andy Bevan. He is usually described in the newspapers as a self-acclaimed Trotskyist, though I prefer the term 'self-confessed' Trotskyist. As a matter of fact it is a false confession: he is a Stalinist. The second Murphy had arrived, Marianne Murphy. She was the wife of Danny Murphy who was active at Fords at Dagenham. Later he was to go to Ruskin College, Oxford (the trade unionist college).

These new people got together with Tony Kelly in March 1975 to set up a Young Socialist (YS) section for Newham North-East. It had managed very well without one for many years — but now it was going to have one. Tony Kelly had been elected as Youth Officer for the Party at the Annual Meeting — another of those little elections that was sprung on everyone at the very end of the meeting. Consequently he was elected unopposed; no branches had had the chance to submit nominations or secure the permission of nominees. The advantage of a Young Socialist's section was that a handful of people could thereby elect 2 delegates to the GMC. I liked the phraseology of Tony Kelly's letter announcing the setting up of this new body: 'Further to my elections as Youth Officer for the constituency, I have succeeded in contacting a number of young people who would probably be interested in participating in a Youth Section.' A fine achievement — to 'succeed in contacting' the very people who had plotted with you to set the thing up! Everything proceeded at break-neck speed. Transport House fell over itself to facilitate things in the shortest possible time, so that from start to finish it took less than three weeks for the YS to be operational. The section had 9 members: Carol Bevan, Tom Jenkins, Hilary Jenkins (his wife), Maureen McDonald, Nirwala Mistry, Jan Tomlinson, Marji Patel, Valji Varsani, and Chindo Bhombra. They needed only 11 members to have two delegates! For a ward or trade union two delegates would require fifty-one extra members as the basic minimum. In fact they had 9 members, not even 11 at this stage, but who cared? They sent two delegates just the same, Carol Bevan and Tom Jenkins. These extra votes would be useful in getting rid of Prentice.

Nothing is more instructive than the speed with which Jenkins and Bevan moved, in cooperation with Kelly, in getting the YS launched. Tom Jenkins was a close ally of Andy Bevan — they had been at Swansea grammar school and Bristol University together — so Carol Bevan and Tom Jenkins were well known to each other before they came to Newham. It would be too much of a coincidence that Tom Jenkins and Carol Bevan should both suddenly appear in Newham North-East at the same time and find themselves working together on setting up the Young Socialists there. It is far more likely that Andy Bevan suggested that the YS should be set up there and that the three of them worked in collaboration. For a start, setting up the YS would require the permission and assistance of the National YS committee, of which Bevan, a former chairman of the Young Socialists, was the dominant figure.

So the spearhead of the attack on Prentice was to be the Newham North-East YS, specially set up a few months earlier for that very purpose. The Militant document 26 May 1974) stated: 'The control of the YS ... is an enormous weapon in our hands.' How right they were! And it added: 'The other work of the YS must be as a spearhead in ... the Labour Party wards and constituencies.' This was called 'carrying in Marxism'. Tom Jenkins and Carol Bevan were effective carriers. Tom Jenkins is a frequent speaker at Militant meetings. The fact that Tony Kelly permitted them to dominate the YS section which he set up is a sure indication that he was up to his neck in it with them: if he had distrusted them he would not have let them take the positions. He could easily have stopped them.

There is extensive evidence of other frantic work in early 1975 for building power bases. Daisy Turner told me that her women's section had a visitation from Margaret Kelly with Mrs Patel in tow. They had come presumably to 'case the joint' but decided there were no easy pickings. Margaret Kelly joined on 25 March 1975, attended the next two meetings on 11 March and 25 March (bringing Mrs Patel to the latter) and then never came again, nor did Mrs Patel.

In April, May and June of 1975 the ground was carefully laid for the coup to unseat Prentice. Then they struck. At a meeting of the Executive Committee on 12 June 1979 some of the infiltrators suggested that Prentice should be sacked. They demanded a special EC meeting. It was duly called for Monday 23 June. The motion was circulated that the EC should recommend to the GMC that Prentice should retire at the next election. Mr Prentice turned up at the meeting but his presence did not help him. It may even have done the opposite. The motion was carried.

All now depended on the GMC which had the final say. A special GMC meeting was called for 23 July. Mr Prentice described the meeting in the following words: 'It was a stifling hot night and the local HQ in a tumbledown condemned building was crowded and uncomfortable. The physical discomfort was matched by a mood of tense anxiety. The pavement outside was packed with people, including a noisy group yelling "Prentice Out" and other things not fit to print. A strong police contingent was necessary to get us all into the meeting and out again afterwards.' The meeting lasted for three hours and the motion calling for Prentice to retire was carried by 29 votes to 19. It was undesirable to deal with such a matter in the summer holiday season when some delegates could not attend.

It is obviously important to know who voted which way. I have engaged in a great deal of detective work to provide the reconstruction below, which has been checked and counter-checked and is extremely accurate. It tallies with the known overall voting figures although built up independently from them. The following key is used to indicate the degree of probability that a person voted in the way attributed to him: $\sqrt{}\sqrt{}$ = virtually certain, $\sqrt{}$ = very probable, ? = quite probable, ?? = more probable than not.

For the motion	Against the motion
Tony Kelly √√	Fox √√
Anita Pollack √√	Jo Taylor √√
Michelle Pigott √√	L. Mathews ??
York √	Curran √
Connie Clements √	E. Davies √
Denise Cohen ?	Bert Simpson √√
Elaine Ashworth √√	Jack Kemp ?
Mike Pemberton √√	Leeder √
John Clark √√	Wally Hurford √√
S. Brown ??	W. M. Brown √√
Danny Murphy √√	Grainger √√
Keith Baggs √√	Jack Hart √√
Hilary Jenkins √√	Alan Whincup √
Jan Tomlinson √√	Boyce √
Claude Callcott ??	Alder √
Philip Bradbury √√	Vi Willis ??
Ade Brooks √√	Daisy Turner √√
Alan Howarth √√	George Phillips √√
Kevin Mansell √√	Laundon √
Patel √√	
Owen Ashworth √√	
Mike Mecham ?	
Catherine Pemberton √√	
John Wilson √√	
D. Brown √	
Marianne Murphy √√	
Tom Jenkins √√	
Carol Bevan √√	
Harold Lugg ?	

This bare list spells out just what happened. All the weight of the establishment is concentrated against the motion. Those who voted against include several Aldermen and a number of councillors. More significantly, almost all the people who voted against were active in the Party before 1970. They are the old, long-standing members of the Party, people who have lived in Newham and been active Labour

Party members for decades. Contrast this with the people who voted for the motion. Only 3 out of the 29 were locally-based people; only 3 were members of the Newham Party prior to 1970; no more than 5 were members of any Labour Party prior to 1970. The only two figures of any substance were Lugg and Callcott who were influenced by the fact that the majority were against Prentice and they were themselves seeking re-election. If we deduct the 23 known newcomers that leaves only 6 'authentic' Party members for the motion. I do not know the details of 3 of these but I suspect they belong to the same category as the 23 rather than the other category comprising the 3 old timers. If it had not been for the two 'invasions' of the GMC in 1972 and 1975 the motion would have lost all but 6 of its supporters and been defeated by 19 votes to 6. In fact I doubt whether Lugg and Callcott would have voted for it then, and it would probably never even have been put.

What nonsense it is to suggest that Prentice 'lost' the support of his constituency party when he retained the support of the vast majority of local long-standing active Party members! What Prentice 'lost' was what he never had — the loyalty and support of extreme left-wingers, the vast majority of whom had entered Newham and Newham North-East Labour Party shortly before. Many, and perhaps most of them, joined for the specific purpose of getting rid of him.

The motion was proposed by a person I have not previously mentioned. He was John Wilson, an electrician, who had joined Newham Labour Party in 1970, aged 29. He was the very first man in out of the whole lot of them, arriving even before Helen Abji and the Ashworths. He profited very well out of the changed balance of power in the Party. In a very short time he became a Newham borough councillor, and in 1977 he defeated a prominent local man, the Chairman of Newham South Labour Party and the incumbent, to become the Newham North-East representative on the Greater London Council. He is still there now. Andy Bevan did not move in immediately. Before his personal appearance on the scene he exercised influence on events through his wife (who moved into Newham before him) and Tom Jenkins.

However, he was very quick to get in where the action was when he saw that the sharks had drawn blood from Prentice. He joined the Newham Labour Party in December 1975

(having moved in a few months earlier) transferring his
membership from Bristol South-East where he had got to
know its MP, Tony Benn, quite well. Tony Benn was hoping
to use young Marxists like Andy Bevan in his bid for the
leadership; Andy Bevan was hoping to use people like Benn
to make himself, and his cause, respectable. Is it not
fortunate for political extremists, including Communists and
Fascists, that there are always people ready to 'use' them?

What kind of person was Andy Bevan? Julian Lewis, who
is to appear at length later in this story, had gone to the same
school in Swansea as he and Jenkins. Julian knew him well,
since they were in the same form. Bevan was a revolutionary
even in his teens. Julian hated him and thought him a fraud.
He pointed out how Bevan always used to encourage other
pupils to neglect their work for revolutionary work; then
they would mess up their 'O' levels. He, of course, did all
right. He was always making grandiloquent gestures of
defiance but at the same time making sure he never got
punished for anything. He was fairly bright and articulate but
he had one terrible failing: he was absolutely hopeless at
logic. Julian said that he first learned what rationalisation
was, before he knew the term, by observing Andy Bevan's
mental processes at work. In his schooldays he was very
careless about expressing his opinions. He expressed support
for the Soviet invasion of Czechoslovakia (needed because
counter-revolutionary forces were at work) and regretted,
with crocodile tears, the need to liquidate counter-revolutionary elements in Britain when the revolution came. Bevan
championed the cause of unionising school pupils and was a
disruptive influence at the school.

Being an inverted snob he went out of his way to get
offered a place at Oxford University so that he could have
the pleasure of turning it down as 'elitist'. He went instead to
Bristol University and spent so much time on work with the
Young Socialists, the National Union of School Students, and
above all, Militant, that he obtained a poor degree. He is a
great worshipper of Lenin and of Trotsky and probably
thinks of himself as the British Lenin. But though his views
contain an element of fatuity he is a very capable tactician,
and a very hard-headed and hard-line Stalinist type of character. My own observations of Bevan, confirmed by those of
others who have had close contact with him, support Julian's

assessment of him as politically dangerous. He is undoubtedly the most able of all the Marxists I came across in Newham. He gives me the impression that he has a desire to exercise power over other people for its own sake and a desire to bend them to his will, combined with a certain vainglory at his own historical role. He seems to get a kick out of talking of the need for the working class to use violence and there are frequent references to violence, as well as violent imagery, in his speeches. The style of his speeches is very reminiscent of some of the 1920s speeches by Stalin.

Bevan was in a strong position, because the Young Socialist section had become the leading force in the constituency — the 'spearhead' for Marxist advance, just as it was supposed to be in Militant's scheme of things. By the Autumn of 1975 it had risen to 16 members. Just look at their influence. Of the 16 members no less than 10 (Baggs, Patel, Carol Bevan, Andy Bevan, Jan Tomlinson, Marianne Murphy, Danny Murphy, Tom Jenkins, Hilary Jenkins, Varsani) were on the GMC. Of these, 3 were on the EC and 3 held ward offices of Secretary or Assistant Secretary. No other unit of the Party had anything like that amount of influence. Not bad progress for a body which had not existed nine months earlier!

There was quite a change in 1975 in the way the Party was run. A Moderate Councillor on the GMC in 1975 said: 'In 1975 there developed an anti-Prentice group. For the first time there appeared to be the development of an organisation within the organisation. After the decision on Mr Prentice in July 1975 the General Committee fell into two wings. There was no longer mixed voting as in the past — members started 'group voting' even on trivial matters. This was a new phenomenon for Newham North-East.' Of course it was. It was an unprecedented infiltration. The Labour Party has few defences against it. There are supposed to be no parties within the Party. Consequently an organised secret group, operating like a guerilla force, can cut through the Party like a knife through butter. A wave of intolerance swept through the Newham Party. Councillor Wally Hurford, one of the oldest Party members and most respected figures in Newham, was hounded for his verbal opposition to the Marxist invaders. They voted to censure him for criticising them to the Press. This was to be a prelude to expelling him from the

Labour Party but they decided not to risk it in the end.

An extraordinary resolution was passed at the GMC meeting on 26 November 1975, calling for the expulsion of all Freemasons who were members of the Labour Party. The terms of the motion made it clear that the fact that the Freemasons were a secret organisation was objectionable. The motion came from Central branch and was Kelly's inspiration. It was very rich for him to object to secret organisations! Obviously, what he and his confederates feared was any organised group that might offer them any resistance: the tactical instinct was sound, however odd this persecution of the Freemasons might look. (Totalitarians always dislike the Freemasons; Hitler particularly hated them.) Other GMC resolutions called for the usual Marxist stuff — nationalisation of the '250 monopolies' and so on.

The YS section was a prolific manufacturer of motions. One called for Labour Party 'democracy', that is, for the Party leader and MPs to be chosen by unrepresentative extreme left-wing activists (i.e. themselves) and another proposed a motion of confidence in Tony Kelly which was carried. One interesting motion from an affiliated electricians' union branch called for condemnation of a police raid on the Workers' Revolutionary Party. Its new delegate was Comrade Rowse.

The year 1975 was a good one for the newcomers. Tony Kelly had good reason to feel pleased with himself for his year's work. He had referred several times to 'nineteen plums ripe for the picking', meaning nineteen Labour MPs that he and his comrades hoped to dispose of before the next election. It looked as if they had picked the biggest plumb of all — a Cabinet Minister. Of course, what they had done was quite unconstitutional and had it been challenged in the Courts it would almost certainly have been invalidated. There were many breaches of the rules. The Executive Committee was improperly constituted throughout 1975. The Executive Committee is elected at the Annual Meeting (clause XII [11]). The Annual Meeting took place in February 1975, and the Young Socialist section was not formed until March 1975. Consequently there should have been no YS delegate on the Executive Committee. Needless to say Tom Jenkins was at the EC meeting on 12 June, when the idea was mooted, and was there at the EC meeting on

23 June to cast his 'vote' against Prentice. Furthermore, the Newham rules provided for a maximum of 6 trade union delegates on the EC, yet no less than 9 trade union delegates purported to be members of the EC and attended and voted at either one or both of these meetings. In addition to this the Secretary was not eleigible to be a member of the Newham North-East Party because he lived outside it: he therefore was not eligible to vote or sit on the Executive Committee. Consequently, the EC resolution on 23 June 1975 was legally invalid and had the EC been a constitutional one without the extra invalid 'votes' the motion against Prentice would not have been carried. The GMC resolution on 23 July 1975 was invalid because Callcott should not have voted on the GMC either (indeed he was not eligible to be the Secretary of the Party at all). He had no authority to convene the meeting, and the motion put under the authority of an EC recommendation was invalid.

Perhaps the local Newham Moderates cannot be blamed for not spotting these irregularities. However, the infiltrators must have been quite conscious of them. Prentice, who was out of touch and not very sharp, did not notice them. Indeed I appear to have been the first person to spot them and publicise them. It does not speak well for the Transport House enquiry and the Labour Party's National Executive Committee that at the meeting of the NEC on 26 November 1975, when Prentice's appeal was heard, the NECs decision was: 'We are satisfied that the only breach of the Constitution related to the votes of the paid Secretary/Agent who is not qualified within the constituency, but this had no effect on the final decision of the General Committee,' and consequently 'it is recommended that the appeal of Mr R Prentice MP be dismissed.'

I suspect the irregularities I have noticed are only the tip of the iceberg: they are glaring and obvious enough for anyone to see. It casts a grave doubt on either the impartiality or the competence of Transport House and the NEC that these were overlooked. The NEC could easily have invalidated the resolution on the single ground of unconstitutionality which they noticed. Its decision used the usual Labour Establishment technique of blaming both sides for encouraging outside intervention, and put the usual sugar-coating on the pill in the form of a 'strong recommendation' that the Newham North-East Party and Mr Prentice should be reconciled. Ron Hayward (the General Secretary of the Labour Party, and a noted left-winger) was to be sent down to Newham to hold 'discussions' to promote reconciliation. This was empty verbiage, and they knew perfectly well it was worthless. It was a sop for the Press and the public. If the NEC had really wanted to stop Prentice being kicked out, it would have invalidated the resolution or at least suspended a decision and called for the party to think again.

The formal dismissal of Prentice's appeal gave the green light to the Marxist infiltrators in Newham. Why did the NEC not save him — or at least do its job properly and impartially? The answer is because there was a majority of extreme left-wingers on it! The NEC had itself been infiltrated. We shall hear more of this presently.

What a fine state the Newham Party was in, then, in 1975: no valid EC, no valid Secretary, and no valid Assistant Secretary (Kelly had swopped with Tomlinson). The newcomers had broken the rules, and what excuse has been offered for the blatant cheating? In the words of young Michael Brown, the teacher, 'Being a voluntary organisation, meetings will never be 100 per cent constitutional.' What a delightful way of putting it! They had barely been 10 per cent constitutional. On the same principle, a secretary who embezzled a Club's funds might as well say 'Being a voluntary organisation, officers will never be 100 per cent honest.'

For all this it must be said that 1975 was the year when the Marxists adopted a 'softly, softly' approach. They had crept in so surreptitiously and acted so suddenly that they had caught the old faithfuls by surprise. Only a suspicious-minded person like myself would have been wary of trusting the newcomers in positions of power in the Party. The long-standing Moderates like Daisy Turner, Jo Taylor or Bert Simpson took the new people at face value. Most people are pretty trusting and if they invite a guest into their house will not rush to check whether he has stolen the family heirlooms. The old members had similarly invited the newcomers in and made them welcome. They were disgusted when they realised they had been betrayed by people who had hidden their real political views to gain admittance and only came out in their true colours when they were on top.

In the Autumn of 1975 the Moderates started to fight

back. Although Prentice had lost his NEC appeal a new candidate had not been chosen. Indeed, the procedure for picking a new candidate had not yet been put underway. So it would not be too difficult to reverse the step already taken by simply building up a majority of Moderates on the GMC and EC and then rescinding the motion. Prentice started to organise the resistance, but he was a very poor organiser and the people who helped him lacked either resources or competence. A meeting or two was organised by Greatfield Ward with the assistance of one or two leaders of the Social Democratic Alliance (SDA) such as Dr Stephen Haseler; but this body is really a propaganda body, not an organising tactical force, and it had no resources for such a battle. There had also been a busload of people from the Oxford Democratic Labour Club who went down to canvass in Kensington Ward one weekend in November 1975. It was not a question of whipping up public support: Prentice had that already. It was a question of getting EC and GMC votes. The battle was a battle for delegates, not for ordinary Party members, still less for the public. Prentice did not properly understand this and he thought that because most people and most of the Press was on his side, he would win. But it was not what ordinary Party members thought that counted, it was what their 'delegates' thought. The two were quite different. A Marxist claimed to 'represent' his union or his ward and cast his vote in its name, but he voted the way *he* wanted to, not the way most members he represented wanted him to vote.

It was inevitable that even this half-baked counter-attack by the Moderates would roll back the Marxists, because the latter had very little public support. At no time did they have more than 20 per cent support from Labour Party members and 10 per cent support from Labour voters, and these are the most generous estimates. Yet with less than 20 per cent from Party members they had well over 60 per cent of the GMC and EC seats; conversely the Moderates with over 80 per cent support from Party members had less than 40 per cent of the seats. Obviously any organisational effort was bound to reduce the Marxist strength in the wards.

In two wards there was a Moderate breakthrough. Sylvia Jones, a fiery middle-aged blonde woman had walked up to Prentice at one of the meetings and announced her support. She was to be his most loyal follower. She was quite a wild woman: she had once worked in a jewellers and a thug had marched in to demand some jewels; she refused and put up a fight, ammonia was squirted in her eye, and she went round with a glass eye after that. She had a lot of guts but you never quite knew where you were with her. She used to bubble with fun and energy and woe betide anyone who annoyed her — one of her neighbours did, a great strapping man, and she clobbered him and damaged his nose! For a while she was bound over to keep the peace. But recently she has been made a Justice of the Peace! Who better to look after the Peace? She managed to get herself elected as Secretary of St Stephen's Ward. The other breakthrough was at Little Ilford Ward where Alec Kellaway, a young local man who had been to Oxford University, became active and was elected as Secretary. Alec had a much better grasp of the situation than the other Newham Moderates. His concern was more over the Marxist danger than a matter of personal support for Prentice, though he did support the move to have Prentice reinstated. These two semi-private initiatives were the only significant Moderate advances in 1975.

If the counter-attack had been properly organised, Prentice would have won the Annual Meeting in February 1976. As it was he was to go into the election with 4 wards largely on his side (Greatfield, St Stephens, Little Ilford, and Kensington) and the other 5 wards against him.

Prentice had been 10 votes down on the GMC in July 1975. The Moderate counter-attack started to erode this lead. It would have done so to the point where it was wiped out, but the Marxists did not stand still. We have seen how there was a first wave of infiltration on to the GMC in 1972 and a second wave in 1975. There was now a third wave. These waves of infiltration may be likened to an army moving one battalion on to the field, then another, then another. Each consisted of ten people. Out of the 40 Marxists on the GMC in 1976, more than 30 had move in in three batches of ten or more in these three years.

In 1976 a new organisation came on to the scene. A branch of the Socialist Educational Association was created. Owen Ashworth was very helpful here: he just happened to be on the National Executive of the Socialist Educational Association (SEA) just as Andy Bevan was on the National Executive of the Young Socialists to assist their new branch.

Shirley Williams MP is one of the SEA's patrons: why did she
not do something to stop this body being abused for partisan
political purposes? She had, after all, spoken at a public
political meeting on Prentice's behalf. Did she understand
what was happening, and if so did she lack the courage to
act? She could have raised objection to the frantic setting-up
of a new Newham branch weeks before the Annual Meeting
and at least delayed it past the Annual Meeting in February
1976. That would have been much more help to Prentice
than a speech which added no votes to his GMC total.

The SEA branch sent six delegates to the Annual Meeting
of the GMC. One was Owen Ashworth, another was the wife
of 'that nice young man' John Clark. People like the
Ashworths and Abji were like the vampire. You could kill
them off but each time they re-emerge in some other form.
Abji was driven out of Little Ilford but came back from the
Co-op. Elaine Ashworth was driven out from St. Stephen's
but came back from the SEA. What a farce the whole thing
was! The Marxists cannot stick to 'One Man: One Vote'.
Their principle is 'One Marxist: Ten Votes'. For a start the
more meetings they attended the more votes they cast. They
called more and more meetings. If they did not get their way
the first time they tried again and again so they got fifteen
bites at the cherry. This reduced the principle to 'one meeting: one vote'. The one-meeting man got one vote; the ten-
meeting man got ten votes. But in addition to this they also
took extra votes for acting in different capacities. Consider
people like Marianne Murphy, Helen Abji, the Ashworths,
and so on. They were like a property speculator who sold the
same house to ten different purchasers thereby acquiring ten
times its value. They were like actors playing six different
parts in six different theatres in the course of a week —
except that they played the same turgid, stale, political lines
to an empty auditorium. Here we have the archetypal
activist, someone like Marianne Murphy. On Mondays she
wears her Young Socialist hat and casts her vote; on Tuesdays
she wears her ward hat and casts her vote; on Wednesdays she
wears her trade union hat and casts her vote; on Thursdays
she wears her Women's Section hat and casts her vote; on
Fridays she wears her Co-op hat and casts her vote; on
Saturdays she wears her SEA hat and casts her vote. Does she
rest on the Sabbath, like the good Lord? Of course she

doesn't! She's off to the Newham North-East Anti-Racialism Campaign, set up in late 1975: Chairman, John Rowse; Vice-Chairman, Alan Howarth; Secretary, Andy Bevan; Treasurer, Philip Bradbury; speakers, Jim Lazyell (Chairman of the London Co-op Political Committee), Nick Bradley (remember him? Young Socialist representative on the Labour Party's National Executive Committee, leading Militant speaker, close ally of Andy Bevan), Carol Bevan, Tom Jenkins, etc. In other words, the usual lot. Will these people help the cause of good race relations? I very much doubt it. Are they not the hard-faced men who look as though they've done well out of the 'race war' — and the 'class war'? Each extra organisation is an extra amplifier for voices which are deafening already. Why should they have so many amplifiers to amplify a message with so little content? Is it not the supreme case of 'the loud mouth that spoke the vacant mind'?

The new left-wingers on the GMC in 1976 fit the now all-too-familiar profile. Prentice described them as Johnny-come-lately's. Only one of them, Mr Abe Woolfe, was a little bit different. He had been in the Labour Party for many, many years and was an old man, but prior to 1976 he was an isolated figure because of his very left-wing views. He was a great apologist of the need for greater understanding of the USSR. In 1955 he was one of a delegation of ten to the Soviet Union and he stayed there for some time. When a return Soviet delegation came in 1958 they stayed at his home. He arranged also an interchange of teachers. In 1977 he was to announce: 'We are attempting to form a branch of the British-Soviet Friendship Society in the Newham area.' The new turn of events meant that Abe Woolfe was an isolated figure no more. There were now a large number of comrades who would be only too happy to be friendly to the Soviets.

The other new GMC members fitted the standard profile much more closely: Adrian Hall was a young lecturer who moved in with Diane Hall (guess what? Yes, right first time — a teacher). They became SEA delegates. Margaret Kelly became a Central Ward delegate. The two Young Socialist delegates for 1976 were Andy Bevan and Mr Varsani. Tony Kelly had changed unions and transmogrified himself from a TSSA delegate to an ASTMS delegate. Keith Baggs and Tom

Jenkins appeared as Wall End delegates. No doubt 'that nice young man' John Clark, who was Secretary, was helpful to them, no doubt he had no misgivings about that well-known Militant, Tom Jenkins. The two Murphys reappeared as T & G delegates. Rachel Charles came in as an ASTMS delegate. A Mr Heinitz and a Mr Mann were the other two SEA delegates. Hilary Jenkins came as a Post Office union delegate.

The result of the battle for delegates shows a slight net gain for the Moderates at the Annual Meeting in February 1976. It is not altogether easy to interpret the voting because though there was a guaranteed straight 40 votes from the Marxists for each of the left-wing candidates there were a few voters who 'split the ticket' (voted for some Moderates and some left-wingers) or abstained. The results were:

Chairman: Lugg 47; Councillor Phillips 37
Vice-Chairmen (2): Owen Ashworth 45; Howarth 44;
Taylor 43; Beverley 37
Treasurer: Elaine Ashworth 44; Granger 38
Secretary: Tony Kelly 46; Alderman Jack Hart 40
Assistant Secretary: Baggs 43; Alder 39

The left-wingers swept the board. The voting margin between leftists and Moderates varied from 1 to 10. Most of the offices would have been taken by the Moderates with an extra 7 votes. This was an improvement on the situation in July 1975, when Prentice needed an extra 11 votes to win the motion.

In fact the Moderates were pulling ahead more than this suggests because a number of the left-wing votes turned out to be bogus votes, that is, people voted who were not entitled to. The SEA, remember, sent 6 delegates, although they were only entitled to send 2. When this was discovered after the AGM they replied to the effect, 'Sorry, it was an accident.' A very convenient accident it was too. They asked people to believe that they, of all people, who studied the Rules and took advantage of every loophole, did not realise that they had sent three times as many delegates as they were entitled to. Also, Tony Kelly turned out not to be a valid member of ASTMS (this issue went all the way to Clive Jenkins, the leader of ASTMS who ruled against him). So that was 5 votes they had which they were not entitled to have. There were further votes from the Co-op over the proper entitlement. Without the irregularities they would have lost control:

with the irregularities they won.

It would be tiresome to spell out all the other irregularities, but it is worth mentioning the extraordinary circumstances surrounding the election of the Executive Committee. The election was begun at the Annual Meeting in February and then a special meeting was called for 11 March which Kelly announced was to be the second half of the Annual Meeting. This was all unconstitutional. Never mind, it helped the left to sweep the EC. At the Annual Meeting in February there were 86 delegates present, at this special meeting there were 61. The missing 25 were, of course, mainly the Moderates. There was an unpleasant scene when a Mr Fox, one of the few Co-op Moderates remaining, pointed out that the Co-op (where the Moderates were still just in control trying to withstand a massive left-wing invasion) had made its election for 2 delegates to the EC. Kelly insisted that an 'election' be held on the spot among the 6 Co-op delegates and 2 left-wingers were 'elected' instead.

There had been a change in the Marxist approach. They were nice enough when asking to be invited inside in the early days. Once they were asked to leave, however, they turned nasty. No longer was there a 'softly-softly' approach. The fight was on and they started to resort to cruder methods. Cheating and intimidation became the order of the day. Some Moderates complained they were being followed about. A number of them started to receive phone calls from fictitious persons at two, three and four a.m. People were shouted down at meetings. One man got up to announce himself as a delegate and was told he was not. 'Sit down or I'll beat you up,' a Marxist shouted at him. All this was very frightening, especially for the elderly.

3

The Moderates Fight Back

It was reading a Sunday newspaper report in the Spring of 1976 that drove me to become involved in Newham. The paper recorded the votes at the Newham North-East Annual Meeting of February 1976 and, as I read, two things struck me forcibly. First, an important issue was at stake which could have consequences far beyond the boundaries of Newham. Second, although the battle had been lost so far, the margin was small and it could still be won.

At that time I was a student at Balliol College, Oxford. I had graduated in PPE (specialising in Philosophy and Politics) some eighteen months earlier and I had stayed on at Balliol to do a thesis on a rather abstruse topic in Political Philosophy. Although to some extent I conformed to the academic stereotype, I had always been interested in practical politics. Having arrived at some conclusion in political philosophy, many academics sit back in contentment, thinking that their work is done. I did not feel that this was enough. The academic has a wider obligation than scholarship alone. I had studied democracy at Balliol. I had also studied Marxism. After some six years' study at a theoretical level I had learned a great deal about them and reached the conclusion that they were incompatible.

Parallel to my studies I was actively engaged in various forms of student politics. I first decided to intervene when I noticed at Balliol that the Marxists, though a minority of students, completely dominated the Balliol students' association. Hardly anyone opposed them. At one time, for nearly a year, I was the only person to voice any opposition to them at the general meetings of Balliol students, and I incurred much hostility from them. My experience of their activities fortified my theoretical conclusions and led me to

step up my political activity, so that I started to oppose them
in Oxford University student politics as well as in my own
college. When the Marxists took control of the Oxford
University Labour Club, I helped to found a break-away club,
the Oxford University Democratic Labour Club. Roy Jenkins
became its President, and I was its first Treasurer. It was at a
dinner of this new club that I had met Reg Prentice, who was
made a Vice-President.

It was not, however, any personal feelings about Mr
Prentice that prompted me to become involved. It was a
sense of the importance of the Newham affair and the realis-
ation that if I did not do something, perhaps nobody would.
Millions of people must have read in the newspapers, or heard
on radio or television, that over in East London, in a constituency called Newham North-East, a Cabinet Minister was
being pushed out by Marxist infiltrators in the Labour Party.
Many sympathised with him in his plight. Still more were
very alarmed at the activities of his Marxist opponents. Yet,
outside Newham, not one person had done anything worth
recording to stop them. People watched, and muttered about
it, and expressed their concern — but they did not *do* anything.

I was confident that it would be possible to save Prentice.
From my Oxford experience I knew what it was like to fight
the Marxists. I guessed that the real situation in Newham
was rather different from what had come across in many
of the newspapers, that the fight on behalf of the moderates
was being run in a disorganised way, and that the people who
were trying to push Prentice out had little support among
ordinary Labour Party members. These predictions turned
out to be correct.

The attack on Prentice is the most famous case this
century of a leading politician being ousted by his local
Party. There is nothing remotely comparable to it except the
attempt to remove W E Forster in the nineteenth century.
What were the issues at stake? First, the time-honoured constitutional doctrine, first enunciated by Burke, that an MP is
a representative, not a delegate, that he owes his allegiance to
all his constituents, not to his party machine, and that it is
not for local party activists to order him to vote according to
their instructions on questions of policy.

Secondly, that Marxists, who are enemies of democracy,

should not be able to acquire power through the back-door by kicking out Moderates and replacing them by left-wing extremists.

Thirdly, that people who have given a lifetime of service to an area and a Party should not be callously dropped without very good reason and without the approval of the majority of Party members in that area. Mr Prentice had been a member of the Labour Party for thirty years and a local MP for nearly twenty years. Three opinion polls, two covering the whole Newham electorate and one covering Labour votes only, had shown overwhelming support for Prentice. In addition to the sacking of Prentice, the takeover meant that many respected, local Party figures and councillors would also be sacked. This was already happening.

Fourthly, there were major policy disagreements between the two sides. Prentice put the standard Moderate view (which the majority of MPs, as well as most members and supporters of the Labour, Conservative and Liberal Parties, would support): for example, the rule of law, the mixed economy, free speech, membership of NATO, adequate defence, and resolving issues through the ballot box rather than by revolutionary violence. Most of the people who were trying to get rid of him openly rejected these and advocated instead class war, political control of the judiciary, massive nationalisation until a hundred per cent of economic enterprise was in the hands of the state, withdrawal from NATO, massive cut-backs in defence, no free speech for 'racists' and 'fascists' (in practice, anyone with right-wing views) and the encouragement of revolution and violence to achieve social and political change.

Fifthly, it seemed wrong that someone should be punished for merely speaking his mind. How can we have free debate if our representatives are terrified to speak openly? As Mr Prentice himself said not long after the crucial vote against him: MPs will be 'always looking over their shoulder to make sure they have not committed any offence. They would have to toe the line, or get out. Cowardice would become a condition of survival' (speech in Newham, 11 September 1975).

Taking all these factors together there was a clear-cut choice between two diametrically-opposed positions. All sorts of other factors became superimposed upon these —

whether Prentice was a good constituency MP, whether he was a nice person, whether he saw eye-to-eye with his Cabinet colleagues, whether he had been a good Minister, whether he was right to support Britain's entry into the EEC, whether he was tactically inept and too outspoken and so forth — but in the face of such a basic conflict between democrats and anti-democrats all these other factors were merely the icing on the cake. In practical political terms the choices were very limited; you could not get rid of Prentice and replace him by another Moderate with slightly different views and a different personality. If Prentice were toppled, the practical political effect, as anyone with any sense realised, would be that the Marxists would gain control — because a number of his personal supporters would drop out, the Moderates would lose heart, they would have no standard-bearer to rally to, and they would be demoralised. The stark choice was between Prentice, warts and all, in the democratic corner, and the Marxists who had infiltrated the constituency in the other corner. Their front-runner for the MPs position at this time was Andy Bevan.

Having decided to intervene I wondered how I could, for I had accepted a Research Fellowship at Nuffield College starting in October 1976 which committed me to staying in Oxford. Then I had an idea. In a number of my political battles I had had an ally in a Balliol student who graduated the year after I did. His name was Julian Lewis. Why not suggest to Julian that he go down to Newham North-East? I knew he was going to spend a year in London anyway, because his research was based on records held in central London. Why should he not take a bed-sit in Newham, instead of somewhere else in London, and he and I could then keep in touch over the telephone? Julian would be a very good person to look after the Newham end of the operation and help to implement the strategy I had begun to devise.

I told him to write at once to Mr Prentice to offer our services. (We should have just sent a telegram: 'Don't worry Stop Cavalry on its way.') His response was friendly — he was interested in having our help — but he said that he did not need it just yet. If he were forced to go Independent in six months' time he would be very interested then and Julian could be a local campaign assistant. When he was pressed a little harder he said that his local supporters in Newham would not like an outsider coming into the constituency to organise his group. We pressed him to put the proposal to his followers and urge them to accept it. It seemed odd that, since the fight was to save him and it was being run by his own followers, he should not have the decisive say on whether or not expert help should be provided. Why should the local people veto assistance?

That was in the spring of 1976. The months trickled by. I was becoming anxious because I knew that the longer the delay the more difficult the task would be. On the other hand I did not want Prentice or the local people to be alienated by our moving in without their approval. But after nearly six months I said to Julian 'Never mind Prentice. You had better get in there immediately.' And off he went.

I came up to Newham for the first time in the Autumn of 1976 to meet Julian. He was looking for a bed-sit there, and found a place in Shrewsbury Road about five minutes' walk from East Ham tube station and the Labour Hall (the HQ of the Newham North-East Party) which were both on the High Street. He was bang in the middle of St Stephen's Ward — the ward that had been captured from the Ashworths by the fiery blonde, Sylvia Jones.

Julian had hardly been in the place a couple of weeks before he swung into action. He telephoned me every day and very soon after he had arrived he suggested a scheme for taking control of Kensington ward. It was a good scheme and I added a few refinements and worked out the steps required. It was all ready for action. I knew we had to prove ourselves to the local people. Our academic qualifications would not mean very much to them and our previous activity in Oxford was unknown to them. This move to take Kensington would show them we knew what we were doing. My part was to be kept secret at this stage so as not to alert the Marxists. If they knew the thing was being run by a politics specialist from Oxford University they would be really worried and draft in an extra contingent of their roaming infiltrators.

Julian had made contact with two Moderates in Kensington Ward. One was Ray Massey, a tall, slightly scruffy bloke with a thick accent. He had one of those 'I'm-a-very-forthright-straight-from-the-shoulder-sort-of-bloke' manners and prefaced his remarks with such phrases as 'To be quite

honest ... To be quite frank ....' When Julian went to see him
he was a little taken aback by Ray Massey's question: 'Not to
beat about the bush, what I want to know, quite frankly, is —
what's in it for you?' Julian explained that there was not
really very much in it for him at all, that he was worried
about the Marxists trying to undermine democracy, and that
he would work to put Prentice back and win control of the
local Party for the Moderates.

The other man was Eddie Lee. He was rather different. He
had a much smoother manner and though he was clearly
working-class he was articulate and polished and well dressed
and smoked long expensive cigarettes. Ray Massey was very
keen to go along with the scheme of voting the Marxists out
of Kensington at the next branch meeting and putting Ray
Massey in as Chairman and Eddie Lee as Secretary. Eddie Lee
was not so keen. He did not like the idea of our organising a
group of people to turn out and vote them out. His objection
as a professional trade unionist was that this sort of thing was
not regarded as good practice — it was a bit sly. Julian
argued with him on this, saying that there was nothing wrong
with it. I felt Eddie Lee was being too fussy, almost prissy,
over this, though we admired the fact that he was standing up
for a principle. However, he was standing up really only for a
principle of etiquette, conventional dealing, or gentlemanly
behaviour. This kind of principle was not the same as a moral
principle or a weighty political principle. As one well-known
person (who will have to remain anonymous) said to me
about this sort of attitude towards the Marxists: 'Do they
expect us to raise our hats before we kick their bottoms?'
Anyway, Eddie Lee was prevailed upon to cooperate after
Julian had poured a torrent of words at him to explain why
it was necessary and desirable.

Many of the ward meetings and those of the societies like
the Co-op, the Socialist Educational Association and so forth,
were held in various rooms of the large Labour Hall — a ram-
shackle, run down building. Julian had not yet joined the
Newham Labour Party: I was still at this stage arranging his
transfer from Oxford Labour Party — a delicate operation if
the Oxford end of the Marxist network was not to be alerted.
So technically he was a visitor. He had talked to many of the
long-standing members in Kensington ward. The vast
majority he found were disgusted at what had happened to

Prentice and even more disgusted by the antics of the Marxists. They were eager to cooperate. One of the most eager of them was Freddie Bament, an elderly man who hobbled about on a stick but was always full of fun. In no time at all a large number had promised to attend the meeting and kick the extreme leftists out of control. Julian told them to wait outside and he would call them in to the meeting.

Julian turned up to the Labour Hall on the evening of 4 November 1976, a little before the meeting was due to start. Who should he bump into but Andy Bevan? They had been at school together. 'Hullo Julian,' said Andy Bevan, absolutely astonished to see him there in Newham. 'What are you doing here?' Julian explained that he was now a member of Oxford Labour Party and left Bevan with the impression that he was visiting Newham. Though astonished Bevan was affable enough.

However, Julian went out and then marched in at the head of a huge throng of Labour stalwarts from Kensington ward. Normally a ward meeting had an average turnout of about 8 or 10. This time it was about 30. And 20 of them were led in by Julian. In they came, the old, the halt, the lame, many hobbling on sticks. There were other ward and socialist society meetings going on, so many of the standard Marxists were in the building. This was like a miracle of the loaves and fishes − no one had seen anything like it. The Marxists were aghast. They, who were always making ritual calls for 'more participation' had actually, for once, got this extra participation, and they did not like it one little bit. As this large contingent of Moderates poured in the Marxists must have felt like Macbeth when he saw the forest start to move towards his castle.

Andy Bevan re-appeared to size up the situation. His former bonhomie had vanished, now there was merely the keen-eyed and anxious look of the political activist; if you looked into his eyes you might have seen instead of the £ sign which is sometimes rung up in the eyes of the cat in a 'Tom and Gerry' cartoon − two numbers, in the left eye the number of Marxists at the meeting, in the right eye the number of Moderates. He blinked. It did not look right. The Moderates had the deadly 2:1 majority required to suspend the Standing Orders. But Moderates never had the wit to suspend the Standing Orders ... Too late! Standing Orders were suspended! But what's this? A motion that the Chairman leave the Chair? But the Chairman is one of *our* men! Too late! He's out! What's going on? These old codgers have just kicked two of our best people out of Kensington!

The door of the meeting bursts open. A wild unkempt figure with long hair and a desperate expression on his face bursts in. It's Tom Jenkins, the teacher! There is a hurried frantic consultation between Jenkins and Bevan who always work very closely together. But what can they do? Their own meeting has started in one of the other rooms. Grimly they march off to it.

The Kensington meeting went like clockwork. One of the extreme left-wingers who had been voted out sat at the front angrily muttering and biting his nails all the way through. From time to time the door would be flung open, a distempered Marxist face would peer angrily about for a few moments, and then the door would be fiercely banged shut again. Next door another meeting was proceeding. It was a smaller meeting of about 10 or 15 Marxists wearing their 'hat for the day' — I think it was an SEA meeting. From time to time, whenever there was a note of jollity at the Kensington meeting (and the old folk, to be sure, were rather enjoying the intoxicating spirit of freedom from the Marxist yoke) there would be a tremendous banging on the thin partition that separated the two meetings as the Marxists rained blows on it in their impotent fury.

Ray Massey had been put in the chair and Eddie elected as *pro tem* Secretary. Retribution was swift. This outburst of democracy had to be crushed at once. The Party's Executive Committee was called into emergency session, and voted to reinstate the extreme left-wingers who had been voted out by a 2:1 majority and to suspend from Labour Party membership Ray Massey and Eddie Lee. Both of them were furious. Eddie was absolutely livid. He had been a good trade unionist in the Post Office Workers' Union for many years, he always did everything by the book, and was a loyal member of the Labour Party — and here were a bunch of Marxists trying to kick him out of the Labour Party because he had been elected by a huge majority to replace the extreme left-wing Secretary! This act was one of the turning-points as far as Eddie was concerned. If the Marxists could act in this way he began to realise that any attempt to treat them with consideration and easy-going tolerance would just lead to their trampling on him.

There was another aspect to the question. At the Annual Meeting, Moderate officers had been elected for Kensington but had been hounded out of office. As the *Newham Recorder* quaintly put it (9 September 1976): 'Two pro-Prentice officers of Kensington Ward resign through pressure.' So the Marxists had no business to be in office in the first place!

The Labour bureaucrats were called in. A London Regional Office official, Bill Jones, came down to Newham to 'advise'. Like that of the Transport House officials the 'advice' has a compulsory character and dire threats are made to suspend or expel members or disband the local party if it is not taken. These officials are like Political Commissars from Moscow — or school inspectors (as they used to be). It was pointed out to Bill Jones that there is no power to suspend members from the Labour Party under the Rules and that no disciplinary action can be taken without going through the proper procedure. He rather grudgingly conceded this point and announced that Massey and Lee were to be reinstated. Of course, much of the damage had been done: the Moderates had been frightened by the suspensions and Massey and Lee had been out of action for a while. Bill Jones then announced that insufficient notice according to the Standing Orders had been given, so the extreme left-wingers were still in office. This was nonsense, as he must have known, because the point was that the Standing Orders had been suspended at the time the motion was put and carried and had been validly suspended with a two-thirds majority. If this was a specimen of the 'justice' we were going to get from the national Labour Party's officers we were clearly wasting our time with them. Jones took no action at all against the Marxist-dominated Executive Committee for its illegal suspensions of Massey and Lee.

The Kensington *coup*, though overturned by Bill Jones, had put some heart into the Moderates. In a couple of weeks we had scored the only major Moderate success since the battle had begun. The *Newham Recorder* pronounced it 'a moral victory' and commented: 'The key to the control of the party rests on the ability of one side to organise. The past

record of the Left Wing is excellent compared with the practically non-existent attempt at organisation by Prentice
supporters' (p. 1; 9 December 1976). As I said, I had expected the level of organisation on the Moderate side to be very
poor. It turned out to be absolutely abysmal. It is virtually a
law of political science that groups trying to exert influence
or exercise power are effective in direct proportion to the
degree and quality of their organisation.

The man in charge of the Moderate campaign until we
came in was Councillor Jack Hart. He was the leader of the
Newham Council. He was a short man with glasses and one of
those rather blank bureaucratic faces, as befits a town hall
'bat'. He was very popular in Newham among those who only
met him at civic receptions because he had cultivated a very
effective politicians' manner with people. He had two techniques he often used. One was to sidle up to people and
almost whisper in their ears as though he were telling them
something immensely confidential. This flattered their egos.
Then he addressed men in this sort of vein: 'How are you, old
boy?' When he was in difficulties, he managed to enlist
sympathy for himself by saying things such as 'I am hurt that
you could think such a thing of me.' When I met Jack Hart
later on this seemed pretty transparent to me, but most
people were very impressed by his self-proclaimed sincerity
and his little personal favours to them. Interestingly enough
some of the other old councillors who knew him very well
did not share the common view. One of them used to refer to
him disparagingly as 'the Rev. Jack Hart' and used to relate
with a certain black relish tales of how the Holy Man was not
quite so holy when it came to internal politicking in the
council chamber. What annoyed him was that he could not
openly criticise Hart because no one would believe that Hart
was not really a saint.

Well, saint or no, he was a lousy organiser. It is true, to be
fair to him, that he was a busy man as Council Leader, but
the efforts he made to organise Prentice's campaign were
pathetic. From August 1975 Hart had convened regular
meetings of a group of Moderates who became known as the
'Jack Hart group'. It was he who had been Chairman of a
public meeting on 11 September 1975 in the Town Hall, held
under the aegis of Greatfield Branch, at which Roy Jenkins,
Shirley Williams and Tom Jackson spoke up for Prentice. The

meeting was disrupted by both Trotskyist thugs and National Front thugs who threw flour and other things at the speakers.

There is no doubt whatever that if the Moderates had been properly organised from August 1975 onwards they would certainly have won in February 1976, and done so by such a large margin that, even with the massive amount of Marxist cheating that would have been sure to take place, they would have romped home. By the Autumn of 1976 the Jack Hart group was still flickering on but it was much weaker than it had been a year earlier. Mr Prentice explained this in terms of a gradual retreat for reasons of self-interest. In his article in 1977 in *Time and Tide* he wrote: 'In particular, there were certain Councillors, and would-be Councillors, who were anxious not to remain at odds with the local Party's left-wing bosses.' An equally important factor was the growing demoralisation of Moderates, especially ordinary people who wanted to help but who saw that the whole thing was a shambles and not getting anywhere. They became demoralised and gave up attending. Many of them became increasingly concerned at the behaviour of Prentice, whom they had ample opportunity to observe. Several of them said that they despaired when they realised that their standard bearer was tactically inept and liable to make political *faux pas*.

We had gone into Newham to fight for democracy. But we had set out to save Prentice whose fight was inseparable from the fight for democracy in this context. We started out with good opinions of him, and we were eager to help him. We were making a very considerable sacrifice of time and money, and we were interrupting (perhaps jeopardizing) our academic careers. He would be the main beneficiary of this sacrifice. It is true that he had not asked us to move into Newham, but he had assured us and the public and his Newham supporters that he was sincere and wholehearted in seeking to recover the Labour nomination for Newham North-East. We had taken the initiative in offering to help, but it had been in response to his private and public promises and assurances.

Disillusion with him set in very rapidly. We were very angry at the 'lost' six months. If he had not discouraged us from moving in in the spring of 1976 we would have sorted out the whole position easily by November 1976. As it was

we had only a little over three months before the Annual
Meeting in February 1977. It would be a daunting, and perhaps impossible task, to reverse the eighteen months' hard
organisational slog of the left combined with the five year
start they had on us. Normally one would expect to take a
couple of years to sort the situation out. The strategy I
devised, however, made use of some complicated short-cuts
and I could have swung it in favour of the Moderates had I
had those vital six months. Naturally we were absolutely
furious when we discovered after a few weeks in Newham
that the local Moderates had been crying out for a full-time
organiser to move into the borough for over a year. They told
us they would have been delighted to accept our offer of
assistance; but Mr Prentice had *not* told them of it, as he
had promised to do in Spring 1976.

What was Mr Prentice playing at? This question reared
its head again on 30 November 1976 when, out of the blue,
he resigned from the Transport and General Workers' Union
panel of MPs and made a speech attacking the whole system
of sponsored MPs. Some of his supporters had just about
organised the affiliation of two large bus garages of T & G
busmen, which would add about 800 members to the local
Party and yield up to 12 delegates. They had been working
on this for months. Just at the crucial moment this
resignation came like a bombshell. They had not been warned
of it in advance. It was read as an attack on the T & G and
all its loyal members were naturally very angry. What could
be more inept than sounding off to no purpose (for Prentice's
speech was not going to move reform of the Labour Party
one inch closer) at the worst possible time without warning
your supporters, thus ruining their work and leaving them in
an exposed position with a lot of egg on their faces? When
Julian went to have a chat with the Moderate busmen concerned the response was: 'Don't talk to us about that f - b -,
Prentice.'

Prentice had not warned the members of the Jack Hart
group either. They were more polite. They just raised their
eyebrows and shrugged their shoulders in despair. Julian was
invited to the Jack Hart group meetings. They agreed that he
should work on the campaign full-time and welcomed him.
He telephoned me after the first meeting. He was not impressed with them. He said that Eddie Lee was a first-class

speaker and that Jack Hart seemed a very nice man but that the group did not have any strategy and was just going round in circles.

In these early days conditions were very difficult for our campaign — especially for Julian, down at what he called 'the sharp end'. He had no phone in his bed-sit so he had to stand in a freezing call-box late at night when reporting to me the state of play, relaying the information I needed, making suggestions, and taking down long, detailed notes on what the next moves should be. We were paying for the expenses of phone calls, transport, stationery, photocopying etc. out of our own pockets. It was proving very expensive. I had a small amount of money from a twenty-first birthday present plus some money I had saved as an organist and choirmaster and from marking scripts, and this was being eaten into at a rapid rate. We were soon both running overdrafts. Julian had very thrifty views: he had never in his life run an overdraft before. He was very annoyed that Prentice would not pay for the installation of a telephone for him. Prentice had actually indicated that he might — but evidently his wife dissuaded him. So every phone call reminded him of the fact that Prentice would not, out of a Minister's salary which, with extras, came to well over £10,000 a year, pay for a phone — thus condemning him to stand in the cold at night in a poorly-lit call box trying to take down instructions for the following day. Prentice was soundly cursed every evening! Sometimes I was cursed too for giving too many instructions.

These were not the only troubles. We had no filing cabinets, no secretaries, neither of us could really type, and we had so little time. It was extremely difficult to get hold of the Rules. The Marxists guarded them carefully to make sure they did not fall into the wrong hands. It was difficult to get the lists of members for each ward — in fact it was virtually impossible. An approach was made to the Labour Party bureaucrats but they would not help at all. The Newham Labour Party was being run like a secret society. We could not get the lists of members, details of affiliation fees, or the constitutions of the Party sections or affiliated organisations either. In trying to devise a strategy for this situation I was like a geographer trying to map out the Dark Continent several centuries ago.

One of the most important things to do was to discover
what had been happening over the year since the last Annual
Meeting in February 1976. With difficulty I pieced together
the story. At the February meeting the Marxist camp had
swept the board. But there had been cheating. Mr Prentice
had put in an official complaint to the National Executive
Committee of the Labour Party. He should have known he
was going to get little change out of them. When the motion
against him had been put in July 1975 he had appealed to the
NEC, which turned down his appeal. They claimed in the
press that they did not have the power to reverse the local
party's decision unless procedural irregularities were proved.
As we have seen, it was in fact riddled with irregularities, but
in any case their claim was not true. Under the Rules for
Constituency Labour Parties the NEC has the power 'to confirm, vary or reverse the action taken by the General
Committee' (Clause XIV (7)). They said they had decided to
abide by a practice invented by Ian Mikardo MP when he was
NEC Chairman whereby they would only 'vary' or 'reverse'
decisions to drop sitting members if there had been procedural irregularities. In other words they would not look at
the merits of the case but only at the manner in which it was
done. It is quite obvious why Mikardo, a very hardline leftist,
invented this doctrine. He knew perfectly well that Marxists
were, and would be, trying to push out Moderate MPs, not
the other way round. He knew that it would not look good if
the NEC, which was dominated by Marxists, were to be *seen*
to be dominated by Marxists. What better than to give the
constituency Marxists a quiet wink and to say in public, in a
high-minded fashion, 'Of course, this is all very unfortunate,
but all the NEC can do is to see if the Rules were broken. If
not, there's nothing we can do. Sorry.' Mikardo knew this
nonsense would con the Press and most political pundits into
thinking that the NEC did not have the *power* to do otherwise. Thus the NEC pretended to have its hands tied, when in
fact it was making a political choice — a choice to act in a
partisan manner backing one side in the dispute, the Marxists,
against the other, the Moderates. Mikardo also knew that he
could smuggle this major, breathtaking, innovation through
without a squeal from the Labour Moderates, most of whom
did not even notice. If, by any mischance, the unthinkable
happened and a left-winger was booted out, some petty pro-

cedural irregularities could be invoked and the NEC would then save him.

So the NEC turned down Prentice's appeal but sent Ron Hayward down to promote reconciliation. This was as cynical a manoeuvre as it is possible to imagine because, once the appeal had been turned down, there was no incentive for the Newham left-wingers to compromise at all. It was known that they would not dream of backing down, and Ron Hayward, the chief left-wing Labour bureaucrat, was one of the last people who would want to fall over themselves to promote a left-wing climb-down. I am sure if he were asked he would say he tried very hard but unfortunately ....

Mr Prentice's complaint about the Annual Meeting in February 1976 *was* a complaint about procedural irregularities. They were blatant. Clearly the NEC, under the full glare of publicity, could not avoid doing something about it. In the case of the Socialist Educational Association which sent 6 delegates instead of 2, the national SEA had admitted that it was all wrong. It was so obviously wrong that something had to be done. Now, imagine for a moment that you are faced with the problem of how to *seem* to be acting to put right irregularities while in fact stretching over backwards to assist the Marxists. How would you do it? To assist you, here are one or two extra points to bear in mind. With the loss of 4 votes some of the left-wingers would lose their positions if the same people attended the re-run of the Annual Meeting and voted the same way. Furthermore, disgust at Marxist cheating might turn one or two votes the other way. An additional factor to bear in mind is that 3 people missed the February Annual Meeting because they had flu: they were known Moderates. All in all, a quick re-run within a couple of months could have put the Moderates into most of the offices. A Moderate victory stared them in the face, even though the left-wingers would still have been in a strong position with a majority on the Executive Committee.

I do not know what scheme, if any, you have devised, but here is what actually happened. The left-wing officers and Executive Committee which had been 'elected' (invalidly) in February 1976 were allowed to remain in office until the Annual Meeting was reconvened! In other words the Marxist camp derived all the benefits from cheating that it could possibly have hoped to have. If you were caught

cheating in an exam you would be disqualified, and rightly
so, but the left-wingers were allowed to remain in office.
That is like you cheating in an 'A' level, everyone having to
re-sit the exam because you cheated, but your being allowed
to hang on to your 'A' level certificate and use it to get a job
in the meantime. Naturally the left-wingers used this 'meantime' to good effect to strengthen and consolidate their
position. They set up new organisations to give themselves
extra delegates. One of these was a new women's section, the
Little Ilford women's section. The Transport House bureaucrats fell over themselves to cooperate to rush this new body
into existence. Of course, it was invalid because it was being
done by people who were not in office.

The 'meantime' lasted a very long time — from February
1976 to December 1976 to be precise. The only complaint
upheld by the NEC was the 4 extra SEA delegates, yet it
took the Labour bureaucrats, and in particular Reg Underhill,
no less than ten months to get a new Annual Meeting organised. The officers only had a couple of months to go before
the next Annual Meeting! They had the benefit of 80 per
cent of their term of office on the strength of an election
that was known within days of having taken place to be
invalid! No action whatever was taken against any of the six
delegates. When Reg Underhill was later challenged in a
court case as to why it took ten months for him to organise
a new Annual Meeting he swore on oath that it took such a
long time because of the need for a thorough investigation.
How thorough an investigation is needed when only one
complaint (of 6 instead of 2) has been upheld by the NEC?
It is noteworthy that on a later occasion it took Mr Underhill
less than three months to reconvene an Annual Meeting. On
the later occasion the Marxists were not anxious for it to be
postponed as long as possible. If it can be done in three
months in 1977, why should the same process take ten
months in 1976? Why should Marxists remain in office for
ten months when they are not entitled to hold those offices
for ten minutes? These are interesting questions. If you want
answers to them you should write to Transport House.
Perhaps they can think of a more satisfactory explanation
than the one Reg Underhill gave in court. We raised the
queries detailed above in a court case in January 1977, but
answer came there none. Reg Underhill swore in an affidavit

that he had no evidence sufficient to act upon that the SEA branch was set up to assist an organised left-wing takeover of Newham North-East. I make no comment on this.

There were other unsatisfactory aspects of the reconvening of the February 1976 Annual Meeting. A 'freeze' date was chosen so that only delegates elegible as on a certain day in May 1976 could vote at the reconvened Annual Meeting. It just so happened that the choice of this date just put Tony Kelly (who was in the middle of a 'hop' from one organisation to another) on the right side of the cut-off line and just put a couple of Moderates on the wrong side. In addition to this, the cut-off date was itself arbitrary and illegal. The legally-correct course of action would have been to remove the invalidly-elected officers, run the Annual Meeting again from scratch as a new Annual Meeting a couple of months after the abortive one, and impose a cut-off date just a few weeks before the election when the list of delegates is finalised. Any persons who had cheated should have been disqualified as delegates and for standing for office for at least a year. But if this had been done the Moderates would have won!

So what happened? The Marxists were given a ten months' clear run to consolidate their position, to 'put the frighteners' on Moderate delegates (leading to some Moderate resignations, the places being filled by Marxists), to set up new bodies to generate more delegates for themselves, to wield all the patronage at the disposal of the local Party, and to let some of the pro-Prenticites gradually drift away (because, as Mr Prentice indicated, councillors did not want to upset the local left-wing Party bosses, and even if those bosses were holding office illegally they were nevertheless the *de facto* bosses). The effect of these massive advantages was predictable. At the Reconvened Annual Meeting held on 8 December 1976 the Marxists won by a margin of 15 votes. If you remember, they should have lost 4 votes on the SEA and 3 votes from the return of the Moderates who had been away with flu. As they only had an average 6-vote lead, they would have been defeated by 1 vote. In fact they won by 15. That shows precisely what those ten months in office (invalidly), by the courtesy of the Labour bureaucrats and the National Executive Committee, were worth to them.

By the way, I cannot let the question of the new women's

section (an extra 2 invalid votes) go by without quoting from the letter sent when it was first set up. Elizabeth Mann had written in to say that a new women's section had been set up with such familiar names in it as Helen Abji (Treasurer) and Marianne Murphy ('Deputy Chairperson'). She wrote: 'I am pleased to inform you that a meeting of a group of Labour Party women took place at 195, Sixth Avenue. We decided to call outselves the North-East Newham Women's section of the Labour Party.' Savour that phrase — 'We decided to call ourselves ....' That just about sums it up. The whole Marxist farce begins and ends with these words — as in 'We decided to call ourselves ... the working class.'

Naturally, there were protests at this new women's section for 10 members with 2 delegate-votes, because there was already a women's section which covered the North-East. This time Transport House bureaucrats came down on them like a ton of bricks — they could have their two delegates all right, but by God, they were not going to call themselves the North-East Women's section, they were to call themselves the Little Ilford Women's section. Reeling from this blow, it took them at least two minutes to recover their composure. What a shock to suffer even-handed, impartial treatment from the Labour Party bureaucracy!

We have seen what happened over Prentice's appeal against the motion that he should retire (this is technically known as a 'de-selection motion'). The term 'retire' is used because when the Rules were drafted many years ago this word was chosen because it was envisaged that a constituency might want to retire an old MP who was 'past it' but refused to acknowledge the fact by voluntarily retiring. To complete the story, his appeal against the de-selection motion was rejected by an Enquiry Team of the NEC, the Organisation Committee (a sub-committee of the NEC) and the NEC itself. Both these two committees refused to let him speak to them on the matter. This was most unfair. In fact it was a denial of natural justice and he would have been entitled to a legal remedy. The lowliest worker is entitled to a hearing before being sacked — this denial of natural justice is amazing. In the *Time and Tide* article Prentice commented: 'I would be less than human if I did not feel sickened by the way in which the national leadership of the Party has handled this matter.' The Appeal on the de-selection motion went to the

Annual Conference in October 1976. There he was ruled out of order when he tried to raise the merits of the case, and he was told to stick to procedural questions.

Frank Chapple, the electricians' union leader and a veteran anti-communist, attacked the NEC decision, but he had very little support. When we talk of the Annual Conference what we really mean is the leaders of the six biggest trade unions, which carry the majority of the votes. In other words Jack Jones, Hugh Scanlon etc. found little to object to in Marxist infiltration of the Labour Party. They cast gigantic votes: out of his pocket Jack Jones pulls over one *million* votes. That is a lot of votes to be cast by one man! He is casting the vote of all his members for them. Has he asked them first how they want to vote? Of course not. He knows better than they do how their votes should be used. This system is called the 'block vote' system. It is indefensible — except that the Labour Party would be even more left-wing without it. The constituency activists also cast votes in the name of their local party. Once again they have not consulted the members either. In both cases we have the 'burglar's vote'; all these people have 'stolen' the votes of their members, are voting in their name, without their permission, and usually contrary to their known views.

Surely no democrat can possibly maintain that there is any justification for this? Surely each individual member of each organisation should cast his vote in *direct* elections for the posts that are being contested? If Jack Jones and his successor Moss Evans (both Presidents until retirement, like the Presidents-for-life in banana republics) will not cast their members' votes against Marxist infiltration, the same is unlikely to be true of the members themselves. No democratic trade unionist can possibly accept the blot on democratic trade unionism inherent in the indirect elections within trade unions for leadership positions and the power of trade union leaders to cast votes for their members like some feudal seigneur buying and selling land and valuing it at the number of 'souls' who live and work on it. The notion of anyone 'owning' over a million votes and treating them as his private possession is intolerable. The system must be given a radical overhaul.

Well, we have left Prentice 'de-selected', the local Party still stuck 'in the meantime' between the February 1976

Annual Meeting and the December 1976 Reconvened Annual Meeting. All appeals against de-selection have failed. But de-selection is one thing, selection of a new MP is another. It would not be possible to arrange a new selection before the next Annual Meeting in February 1977 so the matter would rest until after that meeting. Did anything else of any interest happen between February 1976 and December 1976?

Yes. One episode which interested me was a closely-typed seven sheet petition calling for structural changes within the local Party which would weaken the Moderates still further. It was very cleverly worked out and in my judgement was a collective effort by some of the best Marxist infiltrators in Newham. It had 76 signatures. This petition was handed to the National Agent on 7 May 1976. It was a considerable feat of organisation to get 76 signatures to such a document in such a short time. It shows how well organised the Marxists were, because only the real hard-liners who belonged to the Marxist camp would dream of signing such a petition. It provides further evidence to support my calculation of the number of Marxists who had infiltrated the Newham Party. We know that 40 of them had got on to the General Management Committee. The number of them who had become *members* of the Newham North-East Labour Party by 1976 was, in my assessment, between 70 and 100. The Newham North-East Party had about 1,000 members, all told. At the very least, 800 of them were Moderates: the other 100 I am not sure about. Some appear to have been undecided, some were mildly left-wing, some were left-wing sympathisers, others were Moderates. However, at no time were there ever more than 100 in the Marxist camp in the Newham North-East Labour Party. Of these around 60 were hard-line Marxists, and 40 of them were on the GMC.

Poor old Prentice! He was out of his depth when dealing with such a large number of skilled infiltrators. He also had to do his job as a Cabinet Minister and MP. It is not surprising he was out-gunned, out-manoeuvred, and outwitted. I do not really blame him or the 'Jack Hart group' for the fact that they were being beaten in 1976 by a large group of Marxists who had joined the Party (and in many cases moved into Newham) especially to get rid of Prentice and capture the local Labour Party. I *do* blame them for letting this lot in in the first place, and for sitting on their backsides oblivious to the fact that they were being taken over between 1972 and 1975. Granted the Marxists proceeded stealthily, but people who go into politics are expected to have a bit of wit.

I blame them even more for not fighting back earlier in 1975 and for not fighting back harder in late 1975. I blame Prentice for refusing our offer of help in the Spring of 1976. To his credit, in a rare moment of self-blame, he admitted that he should have organised resistance earlier. In *Time and Tide* he explained why the 'Jack Hart group' had not got going sooner: 'Why did the moderates ever allow the left to gain control? Why did we not see the danger approaching and organise to stop it? ... There is really no excuse, either for me personally, or for leading moderates in the local Party. But the plain fact is that moderates are not good conspirators.... They instinctively react against suggestions that they should organize in special groups. They do not want to be accused of splitting the Party.' The fact that the Newham Party was split already and that the left were organising hard took time to sink in.

Unfortunately, this perception was not reflected in the actions of Prentice and the Jack Hart group at the time. When I offered my specialist help in a memorandum setting out what needed to be done, it received a frosty reception from Prentice. Most of the locals were very keen on it and very willing to give it a try. People like Daisy Turner were enthusiastic. They were yearning for a lead and were frustrated at the slapdash way in which the resistance had been organised. Prentice and Jack Hart got together and tried to prevent my memorandum from being considered. They then spoke against it and tried to suppress it while pretending not to. Despite these efforts the local Moderates insisted that it should be given a try.

The memorandum recommended that Julian should be appointed as the local coordinator and organiser. A few days later he received a terse letter from Prentice saying that he was on no account to call himself or consider himself Prentice's assistant and that Prentice wished to make it clear that he was not associated with Julian.

We were both furious at this ingratitude. Some light was thrown on it when Julian talked to Mrs Prentice, and found out that she and her daughter did not want Prentice to fight through the Labour Party. She was sure that he would keep his seat at Newham North-East if he stood as an Independent. Indeed she felt it would be better for Prentice to win the seat as an Independent MP than to regain the Labour nomination. Julian explained that this was pure moonshine and that Prentice would not win as an Independent. Even if he did the act would be largely pointless. But she knew better.

It was also pointed out to Mrs Prentice that Prentice had gone on record time and time again, in speeches and writing, almost every week from July 1975 to December 1976, assuring everyone that he was going to fight all the way within the Labour Party. More importantly, he had promised his local supporters that he would fight within the Labour Party until it was absolutely hopeless and then he would warn them in good time. Many of them staked their local careers on his promises. He specifically promised that, whatever happened, he would do his best to assist the fight and nothing to jeopardise it before the next Annual Meeting in 1977. Having given such solemn public and private assurances it was unthinkable that he would renege on them. But his sudden decision to resign from the T & G panel shocked his local supporters. He was strongly criticised, and promised faithfully to consult with his local supporters before taking any other initiatives which might damage the local fight.

My memorandum laid down the basis on which the fight against the Marxists should be waged. It called for a formal administrative structure with a constitution and funds. This later became the CRD, the Campaign for Representative Democracy. The memorandum stated:

You are dealing here with no ordinary Labour Party situation but with what is known as 'entryism' — a collaborative infiltration by extremists who become Labour Party activists. In this situation the ordinary efforts of Labour Party stalwarts and old-timers are not enough and the Campaign cannot be successful if it is based on such efforts or on sporadic canvassing attempts and isolated initiatives. This has been proved by its lack of success in the past. What is needed is the application of specialist anti-infiltration techniques, backed up by advanced organisation and adequate financial resources ...

Reg Prentice has won the Press campaign hands down

but this has not been translated into GMC votes in Newham North-East. The battle cannot and will not be won in Fleet Street or at Transport House.... The campaign has been top heavy and aimed at the wrong audience. What the ordinary member of the public thinks will make no practical difference to the result. It is essential [to produce] a majority on the GMC.

I made a number of specific recommendations and concluded by saying:

A very tough and aggressive campaign is required in which the initiative is seized instead of merely responding to what the other side do. It will be a close fight because of the strength of the opponents, but it is a fight that can be won — though certainly not if fought in a half-hearted, part-time, soft-hearted, sporadic and disorganised manner, without adequate resources or proper utilisation of the resources available.

There was a lot of tut-tutting from Jack Hart at those last words. They may sound harsh, but I stand by them. I was not, of course, advocating anything illegal or immoral; simply vigour, firmness, organisation and persistence. I do not think there is anything to admire about a disorganised, feeble campaign. If there are people about who think it is worse to say boo to a goose than to let the Marxists take over then I think that they are harmful idiots (what Lenin called 'useful idiots').

Fortunately, there were a number of very good people in Newham. The further away from the power hierarchy one travelled, the higher the quality of the people one came across. Among the 800 Labour Party members with moderate views were some of the best people I have ever come across anywhere. When I say 'best people' I am referring to their moral qualities, their characters. These ordinary working or retired people were courageous, unselfish, kind, always ready to put themselves out, determined, but always humorous and never fanatical. They were serious without being tiresome and they had integrity without parading it. Even when they did not agree with us on tactics, they always gave us a fair hearing. They were open-minded and ready to listen to reason. None of them ever became stooges, though naturally as confidence gradually developed they were willing to take more on trust. They were very loyal to the Labour movement and to their own class and locality — but without that fierce hatred for other classes that the non-working-class Marxist displays.

I can particularly vouch for the quality of some of the local trade union secretaries and their members. It was also reassuring to find that all these people had a lot more mental and emotional toughness than many of their 'leaders' and were quite capable of learning from experience. They realised that a new strategy was required to beat the Marxists, and they provided the strongest support for the new strategy of my memorandum.

This book is not a hagiography, but it has its heroes none-theless. In a story filled with shoddy acts by shabby people it is as well to remember that there were a large number of good people with whom it was an honour to be associated. Julian and I both agreed that the main, and at times the only, comfort in the whole story was that we had struck this seam of quality after cutting through the rubbish. These people really were the 'Labour aristocracy' in the correct sense of the term — those who had lifted themselves above the ordinary level by their serious concern for their civic res-ponsibilities and their willingness to devote their time and energy to political activity without seeking for personal advancement of any kind. They were the first volunteers in the battle for democracy. It is to them that this book is dedicated.

I have now virtually finished relating the events of 1976, but two incidents have been left out. You will have heard about them a long time ago because they were both in all the papers, but for people in Newham at the time both came as a shock.

The first was the appointment of the Labour Party's National Youth Officer. This is a most important post, because the Youth Officer is the Labour bureaucrat in charge of the Labour Party's relations with the Young Socialist branches up and down the country and all the university Labour Clubs. In the Labour bureaucracy there is an assured and steady ascent. People appointed to the lower offices such as Youth Officer and Political Education Officer will one day have a good chance of holding the two highest offices, that of General Secretary (currently Ron Hayward) and National Agent (currently Reg Underhill).

And who did Transport House choose for this important post of National Youth Officer? They chose the probable architect of Prentice's fall, the best-known leader of the Militant Tendency, a man who openly called himself a 'Trotskyist'. They chose Andy Bevan. At one time he would have been expelled from the Party; now he was given one of its best jobs, with a healthy £4,000 a year salary — not bad for a young working-class champion of twenty-four. How had this come about?

Transport House staff are selected by a committee called the 'Staff Negotiations Committee', elected by and from the National Executive Committee. It had ten voting members in 1976 plus two non-voting assistants, one of whom was Mr Underhill. At a meeting in the late summer of 1976 a 'meeting' of the Staff Negotiations Committee was held. this is a euphemism for the fact that three members turned up. Yes, three members. The most important decision ever made by this Committee was reached with only three members present. Several reports (for example, the *Daily Telegraph*, p. 6, 22 November 1976 state that Nick Bradley, the Young Socialist's representative on the Labour National Executive Committee, was present. If the report is true, then he had no business to be there.

The Staff Negotiations Committee had had seven strong applications. Six were from Labour Party agents, the full-time bureaucrats who would normally be expected to fill this senior post. The short list had been whittled down to three people: two Labour agents and Bevan. Who were the three men who voted in this historic vote? Brian Stanley voted against Bevan; Bert Hickling and Ron Hayward voted for him. Ron Hayward, the General Secretary of the Labour Party, voted for a Trotskyist, the leader of the Militant entryists, to take up a senior and important post. What does this say about Ron Hayward's political position? Not only did Bevan have extreme views: he was a leader of a secret organisation devoted to a Marxist takeover of the Labour Party. Furthermore, completely contrary to all precedents, he was not a full-time agent and this, predictably, upset the Labour agents' trade union, NULO (National Union of

Labour Organisers). There was supposed to be a 'closed shop'. Such is the hypocrisy of Bevan and his supporters that though they approve the closed shop — for everyone else — they make an exception for themselves.

So far the 'Bevan affair' has shown up Hayward and Hickling, and perhaps shown just how active Nick Bradley has been on behalf of his political associate, Bevan. Nick Bradley and Andy Bevan, the two Militant leaders who work very closely together, stood to form a powerful combination. With Bradley on the NEC and Bevan in Transport House, Militant would have a very powerful hold within the Labour Party. This Bevan-Bradley axis became of increasing importance in 1977. But the 'Bevan affair' went much further: it gave us a glimpse into just how far the Labour Party had fallen to the Marxists. In the Autumn of 1976 it boiled up into a major row within the Party. Even people like Callaghan and Shirley Williams could not ignore it. For once they tried to do something about it. They actually made an effort to stop the appointment of Andy Bevan, but the final decision lay with the NEC.

The line-up on this issue was revealing. It was not a left v. right, but a right, centre and left v. Marxist issue. Tony Benn, who has been cultivating a proletarian image by changing his name from Lord Stansgate to Anthony Wedgwood Benn to Tony Benn (even Anthony Benn doesn't quite sound working-class) reducing his entry in *Who's Who* until he only wanted 'Tony Benn — Member of Parliament' in it and the editors very sensibly cut him out altogether. Tony Benn who in the 1960s was preaching hare-brained stuff about white-hot technological revolutions and similar nonsense, had decided to support the growing Marxism within the Labour Party. It appears to me as if he would rather the Labour Party go Marxist with him as leader than not go Marxist under someone else. In fairness to him it must be recorded that he claims he is not a Marxist and I accept this.

Tony Benn wrote a huge letter published in full in *The Guardian* (p. 11, 13 December 1976) arguing that Marxism had a place within the Labour Party and that Andy Bevan would make a good National Youth Officer. He wrote 'I therefore hope ... the National Executive will not allow the fact that Andy Bevan declares himself to be a Marxist to provide grounds for declaring him to be unsuitable.' Benn knew

Andy Bevan: as I mentioned earlier, Bevan was a member of his local Labour Party, Bristol South-East before he moved into Newham. But just listen to these nauseating words with which Benn rounds off the letter:

> In my judgement, Andy Bevan has much to offer the Labour Party.... Andy Bevan's speeches about socialism have also, in my presence, drawn a response from older members of the party, who recognise in what he said the authentic voice of a political faith they had not heard advocated with such moral force since their own youth, many years ago at Socialist Sunday schools and street corner meetings.

That really is enough to make the cat sick! I suppose people used to say the same sort of things about Stalin and Trotsky in their younger days. Benn ought to think very carefully about playing with fire. There has been no comparable flirting with enemies of democracy on the right wing by Conservatives. It is a dangerous game and an evil one too.

On the other side of the fence the Prime Minister argued very strongly that Andy Bevan should not be appointed. So did the Labour Moderates. They pointed to such comments of Andy Bevan's as the one he made on BBC Television (19 October 1976): 'We proudly describe ourselves as Marxists, and what we mean by that is that we stand on the traditions of Marx and Engels, Lenin and Trotsky.' In dubbing him a Marxist-Leninist I have said only what he himself is happy to admit to. Perhaps he knew that by October 1976 the Marxists in the Labour Party were powerful enough for him to be as brazen as he pleased.

So extreme were Andy Bevan's views that even Michael Foot, a left-winger, found him too extreme and said he was worried about his views. He actually voted against his appointment. Surely with the Prime Minister, the Deputy Leader of the Party, and all (except Benn) of the Cabinet members on the NEC against Bevan he would lose?

Not a bit of it. On 15 December 1976, by 15 votes to 12, the NEC ratified Bevan's appointment. This was a humiliating snub for Callaghan and Foot. *The majority of the National Executive Committee of the Labour Party was prepared in 1976 to take the unpopular course, against the unanimous opposition of the Labour agents' trade union, and against the public appeals of the Labour Prime Minister and the Deputy Party Leader, of appointing a Marxist of especially extreme views to a senior administrative post at the Labour Party HQ.* This illustrates how bad the position had become. A few of the 15 might not openly call themselves Marxists or think of themselves as such. But in politics you are as you do. If you vote for Marxists and 95 per cent of the time do precisely what they want, in what sense are you not a Marxist? It is the action not the talk that counts. People sometimes take comfort from the divisions within the Marxist camp, but they all voted the same way this time. When it comes to acquiring power, Marxists back Marxists. Trotskyists on the NEC (like Nick Bradley), sympathisers with Soviet-type societies (like Alex Kitson) and sympathisers with Euro-communism (like Eric Heffer) all came together to vote for Bevan. When it comes to the crunch, as far as democrats are concerned, it is democracy to be done in first, and then they will settle scores between themselves later.

In the light of the 'Bevan affair' it became crystal clear why the NEC and the Labour bureaucracy had acted as they did over the motion to de-select Prentice and the Annual Meeting of February 1976. In particular, it explains why they did nothing to stop the Marxist infiltration of Newham North-East, whatever they thought of Prentice. They *wanted* the Marxists to take over.

On 21 December 1976, Prentice resigned from the Cabinet. This was a bombshell to his local supporters. Not one of them had been informed beforehand, let alone consulted. He announced that, although he was resigning from the Cabinet, he would continue the fight within the Labour Party to hold on to his seat. This was absurd. The only useful contribution he could make to the fight to save the local party was to stay in the Cabinet, to avoid making speeches that harmed his own cause, to intensify his constituency work, and to generate some cash to pay for the expenses involved in organising the fight. Obviously he was in a much weaker position as a back-bencher because he had, by resigning, distanced himself from the Labour government. Above all he had broken his solemn promise to his local supporters.

A common explanation for Prentice's fall is that he was a bad constituency MP. But though he was not one of the best constituency MPs (he hardly could be as a Cabinet Minister) he was at least average. He fulfilled his duties towards his constituents fairly satisfactorily and his relations with active Party members were surprisingly good. He was on first name terms with most GMC delegates and he even attended ward meetings. Mr. Callcott, the old Secretary, in his January 1975 report spoke glowingly of Prentice's constituency and West-minster record. This was a matter of months before the move to drop Prentice.

It is clear that Prentice's resignation from the T & G panel of sponsored MPs, followed a month later by his resignation from the Cabinet, was part of a steady process of disengage-ment from the Labour Party. This disengagement owed little to the general logic of the political situation or to the timing of leftward moves by the Labour Party. Indeed, in December 1976, it looked to many political pundits who hang on politicians' words that the Moderates in the Labour Establishment were starting to fight back. On 4 December 1976 Harold Wilson made a speech in Batley, Yorkshire, in which he attacked as 'political asset-strippers' infiltrators who sought to take over local parties and unseat respected Labour MPs. He referred to the people whom 'we in York-shire call comers-in' and he also called the infiltrators 'the predatory-minded, the take-over bidders' — phrases as blood-curdling as any I have used!

On 5 December 1976, the *Sunday Times* (front page article by Michael Jones) reported that Callaghan had made a 'fierce denunciation' in Leeds on 3 December of those who had infiltrated local Labour Parties. The article states: 'He told party workers that the most hateful slogans he had heard recently were: "What do we want? Everything! When do we want it? Now!" "That's not socialism, that's fascism," Callaghan said. "There are too many of these people who have infiltrated this party already. Get them out!" ' Needless to say, not one single infiltrator has been got out between that day and this. The article went on to suggest that the issue was moving towards a crisis, that a historic debate would begin, etc. It all fizzled out. Interestingly, the article quotes a motion tabled for the following NEC meeting which deplored 'unsubstantiated and hysterical allegations' which were part of a campaign to stir up 'a frenzied witch hunt'. Guess who tabled it? Eric Heffer and Joan Lestor. The extreme left-wingers keep bobbing up time and time again whining about witch-hunts, when they are the ones who are doing the hunting!

Christmas passed. It was a poor and short Christmas for Julian and me. We had work to do. The priority in January 1977 was to capture a couple of wards. All the ward (branch) meetings were held in January. My calculation was that we needed to take two wards. I told Julian that we should go for Kensington and Central. Kensington could be recaptured. It had had Moderate delegates in February 1976. They resigned in unpleasant circumstances, and left-wingers took over. We kicked them out in November 1976: Transport House reinstated them. Sure enough we beat them handsomely in January 1977. I emphasised to Julian the vital necessity of choosing for our new delegates people who would not resign under pressure, who would stay the course, turn up to the meetings, would not be people who could be either bought off or frightened off, and who were sound Moderates who appreciated the need for action. We discussed over the telephone the merits of the various possible candidates. I liked the sound of Massey: he sounded tough and straightforward and very cooperative. I was a little more wary of Eddie Lee. He sounded a rather prickly character who might pursue an independent line, but on the other hand he was a very good speaker, a good administrator, and he had loyally supported us over the arguments within the Jack Hart group. Julian liked him.

Ray Massey was elected as Chairman; Eddie Lee as Secretary. Best of all I liked the sound of Freddie Bament, an old man with a lot of pluck and a real fighter. He was installed as one of the delegates. Kensington went very satisfactorily from our point of view. The other ward annual meetings largely left no change. Julian was by now a ward delegate from St Stephen's and we both found ourselves in regular contact with the fiery Sylvia Jones, its Secretary. Indeed, I had met her for dinner a month or two earlier and found her very lively. We discussed her libel action against Tony Kelly and the *Guardian*.

But Central Ward went up the spout. Central was Tony and Margaret Kelly's ward, but Tony Kelly had left Newham at the end of 1976. (He thought his work was done and Prentice was finished, so off he went to Leeds, where he applied to join the local Labour Party. The MP, Cohen, would have been in trouble within a short time, but they would not let Kelly in. Very wise. *Tribune* and *Militant* have been complaining bitterly about it ever since. They still are.) A Moderate councillor in Central Ward, Mr Elson, was confident he had got the ward 'sown up' for the Moderates. 'Don't worry,' he said 'I've got it all in hand.' I was uneasy about this and told Julian that I thought we should take over Central ourselves. But there were two problems. One was getting a list of the existing members: the official list was in the hands of left-wing officers who refused to allow us to have access to it. Elson refused to cooperate, and there was no time to sign up new ones, which would have been best of all. The other was that Elson was Jack Hart's brother-in-law and if we stepped too hard on his toes, Hart would become difficult. Since Hart had shown himself to be opposed to the tough strategy anyway I felt inclined to risk his displeasure, but we had lost time and there was still the problem of the secreted lists. In the end, reluctantly, we had to leave Elson to it. He botched it completely. He produced a derisory number of votes (about 5) and the other side produced about 15. We could have easily captured it had he not got in the way. The blame for this rested with Hart as well, since he vetoed our overriding Elson. He said that if Elson said he had it all in hand then we need not worry, Elson could be relied on to come up trumps. Later on we learned that Elson was the Councillor who had recruited Tony Kelly, having stumbled across him on an election canvassing drive, and who had proudly announced that he had found a very keen new recruit for the Party!

We managed to squeeze in some extra trade unionists. Julian beavered about on his motorcycle contacting people and persuading them to get their unions affiliated and come back as delegates. Quite a few delegates were added in this way in the space of about five weeks. But time was so short. How easy it would all have been with the extra six months, or with Prentice's and Hart's cooperation.

In January 1977 we showed that we meant business. The Marxists were already very worried from their experience with us over the previous couple of months. At Julian's first GMC meeting he showed his mettle. Harold Lugg was in the Chair. There was some departure from the Rules. Lugg would not let Julian speak or vote because he had arrived 'late' (he had been to a union meeting). Julian tried to raise the issue on a Point of Order. 'Point of Order, Mr Chairman ...' 'Shut up!' said Lugg. Julian: 'On a Point of Order ...' (Shouts of 'Shut up,' 'Fling him out,' 'Christ!' and other expletives not fit to print.) Julian: 'Mr Chairman, on a Point of Order ...' Lugg: 'Shut up. Now as for Item 4 on the Agenda....' Julian: 'Order, Mr Chairman.' Lugg: 'We will have a speech of 2 minutes....' Julian: 'Point of Order, Mr Chairman, Mr Chairman, on a Point of Order, I have a Point of Order, Mr Chairman, Points of Order take precedence, Mr Chairman, Mr Chairman on a Point of Order, on a Point of Order, Mr Chairman I shall persist my Point of Order until it is taken, on a Point of Order, Mr Chairman....' At this point the meeting was abandoned. The Marxists had not determined how to deal with such a situation, they had never faced it before. They went off to work out 'the line' on Points of Order. But they had been served notice that the standard tricks of ignoring Points of Order, shouting people down and excluding them from speaking or voting were now to be challenged. From now on things were going to be very different.

On 26 January 1977 a new Labour Council candidate for the Greater London Council was chosen. The sitting councillor was Tom Jenkinson, a perfectly capable and well-respected local man who was Chairman of Newham South constituency. No one suggested his work had been unsatisfactory. Yet he was not even put on the short-list. This was humiliating and outrageous and it provoked a local outcry. But the Marxists were unmoved. The choice was narrowed down to two very left-wing candidates: Michael Brown, the young teacher, and John Wilson, the man who had proposed the de-selection motion against Prentice. John Wilson got it.

The ruthless treatment of the old stalwarts by the Marxist infiltrators was a great source of ill-feeling. People who had given their whole lives to a particular part of the local Labour movement found themselves summarily booted out. The ingratitude and callousness shocked and angered them. There was a pretty systematic purge which was starting to get under way. There was to be no room whatever in any significant Party position for local Labour Moderates, whatever their abilities or past services. The Newham Co-op had been taken over, and people who had nursed it and done all the work for it for years were all purged virtually overnight. This lack of ordinary humanitarian feeling is typically Marxist.

We now came into February 1977, the month in which the Annual Meeting was normally held. For a long time, indeed since I had first thought of starting the Newham campaign, I had been thinking about the problem of what to do over Marxist cheating. The reports in the Press had stressed the role of cheating in the Marxist success in February 1976. I put the question to you: what would you do if you knew that you could win if the Marxists did not cheat, but that you might lose if they did? Perhaps you would say, 'Let's take a chance on it and hope they don't cheat.' *But what if you thought that they would very probably cheat, and cheat to a sufficient extent to achieve a victory however hard you campaigned, and the harder you campaigned the more they would cheat?* Many people will say that the answer is to appeal to the National Executive Committee and Transport House to stop them cheating. But what if those bodies simply refused to act, or acted in such a way that the Marxists got the full benefit of the cheating? If the NEC were partisan, what then? What would you do?

But the NEC is *not* partisan, people say. Is it not? Look at how they acted over the de-selection motion, over the February 1976 meeting, over the reconvening of that meeting. Is it possible to imagine for a moment they were not being partisan? Was it not the NEC which by 15 votes to 12 in December 1976 appointed Andy Bevan as National Youth Officer? Andy Bevan was now in Transport House as one of the Labour bureaucrats! Andy Bevan was now leader of the Marxists in Newham. Who is on the NEC? Who are its leading figures? Why, they are Joan Lestor (Chairman), Norman Atkinson (Treasurer), Ron Hayward (General Secretary), Eric Heffer, Ian Mikardo, Alex Kitson (the man who likes Russia), Tony Benn, Frank Allaun (the Man-of-Peace-Committees), Joan Maynard (more extreme than any of them) and Nick Bradley (Andy Bevan's friend and a leader of Militant). Anyone who knew anything about politics would know that the NEC favoured extreme left-wing proposals between 1973 and 1976 and was dominated by extreme left-wingers. Such a person would know in advance, as we told the Appeal Court in January 1978, that there was not a cat's chance in hell that these people would take effective action against left-wing constituency activists of their own political persuasion on behalf of the Moderates they so despise. If you have followed the events described in this book as well, then you would be absolutely certain that it would be a waste of time appealing to them. Having seen what they had done in 1976 I had no confidence whatever in them.

So I return to the question: what would you do? Would you give up and let the Marxists cheat you out of a democratic victory? Would you let them walk all over you? Would you say 'You cheat: you win?' A lot of people would. They do not like it put so starkly, but they would rather that the cheats got away with it than do anything effective to stop them, however blatant and excessive the cheating. This is understandable. But is it *right*? Of course, it is not. In a civilised society there are institutions which exist to provide fair, completely impartial judgement, to be used as a last resort when methods of persuasion and agreement fail. They are called courts. This is the purpose of law, to provide the ultimate device for solving disputes in a civilised manner without resorting to force. In extreme and unpleasant circumstances such as existed in the Newham North-East Party there were only two alternatives: abject surrender to Marxists who cheated, manipulated, falsified, and intimidated (further details are provided in a later chapter on 'Marxist Methods') – or to take legal action. I am confident that anyone who thinks really carefully about this issue will be forced, however reluctantly, to agree that legal action was the only way. It is nothing to be ashamed of. It was the right thing to do. I do not regret for one moment the decision that legal action should be taken.

I told Julian at the outset that legal action might be required. He knew nothing about the law but he had no reservations about the need to use it after I had explained to him what situations might arise. Having assessed the position in Newham North-East I decided in December 1976 that legal action would probably be required. I therefore set about improving my knowledge of all the relevant parts of the law. It is a small and specialised and, to some extent, obscure branch of the law and I went very deeply into it. Julian made himself responsible for finding people prepared to act as plaintiffs, for securing the financial backing (we would need about £1000) and for indemnifying the plaintiffs and explaining the case to them. I concentrated on the legal aspect of the problem. We were now ready to take the Marxists on if they cheated.

Sure enough a hideous irregularity emerged. Julian had finally obtained a copy of the local Party's Rules and he had come up to visit me in Oxford. I was sitting in my room in Nuffield College idly swinging on my chair glancing at these rules when my eyes alighted on the notice required for the Annual Meeting. I questioned Julian on the matter. It was quite clear that the required notice had not been given. My hours of study had not been wasted! This was it ... legal action!

After Kelly had disappeared John Clark became Secretary. He had a nicer manner than Kelly though politically he was just as hard-line. His wife had been one of the illegal 1976 delegates. He had given only two days' notice of the Annual Meeting due on Wednesday 23 February 1977 at 8.00 pm at the Labour Hall.

I had to act really quickly on this and went without sleep for forty-eight hours over this period. I dictated affidavits, worked out the form of the writ, and worked on the legal points, cases, authorities and so on. Doing it all from scratch for the first time was interesting but not easy. We had found four plaintiffs (litigants), who had to be members of the local party to have *locus standi* in the action. They were Gerard Falvey, Alec Kellaway, Julian Lewis and Ray Massey. The defendants were Harold Lugg, the Party Chairman, and John Clark, the Secretary. I told Julian to phone them to warn them, that if they persisted in going ahead with the meeting legal action would be taken. They ignored his warning and refused to call it off, perhaps thinking it was a bluff. It was not.

We were so close to the meeting now that only legal action could save the day. Even if the NEC were impartial it could not possibly act quickly enough. It meets monthly, and its next meeting was not due for a week or two. This was a twenty-four-hour job. The courts have special emergency procedures. We applied for an emergency Injunction and this was granted by Mr Justice Stocker. He was very hesitant about granting it (I think he knew there would be a rumpus over it) but he had no choice: the case was so clear and overwhelming.

The Injunction was given to Julian who took it down to a local firm of 'process servers' (the people who serve Injunctions as a profession, though any citizen can do so with the permission of the plaintiff) and told them to 'serve' it on Lugg and Clark. To serve an Injunction you have to inform the person what it is and hand it to him, preferably reading it to him first. If he refuses to take it, he should be tapped lightly on the shoulder with it and it should be put to rest as close to him as possible. It has then been 'served'. People do all sorts of things to avoid being served and you have to be a bit of an Artful Dodger to keep up with them.

I had decided to travel to Newham on Wednesday to survey the ground again and meet some of the Moderates. I arranged to meet Julian in his room in the evening and travelled down on the Tube. I was debating with myself whether or not I should stop for a Kentucky fried chicken, but decided not to. This was just as well because when I got there I found everyone in a state of consternation. What should they do? The Injunction had not been served! Julian was very concerned, but he did not know the law and therefore did not know what to do. Apparently the process servers had called repeatedly on Lugg and Clark at their homes, but they were not in and could not be found. I said that Julian should tell them to come round to his bed-sit immediately and then he could accompany them to the Labour Hall to identify Lugg and Clark so that they could be served before they entered the meeting.

But by the time the process servers arrived and we all got round to the Labour Hall (only a few minutes' walk away) the meeting had started. This was a tricky situation because the vast hordes of barbarian Marxists in the huge upstairs assembly room of the Labour Hall would be none too pleased to have their meeting stopped. It would be like interrupting someone in the middle of an orgasm.

Obviously, it would be preferable if the matter could be dealt with discreetly without serving the Injunction in the middle of the meeting. I told Julian to go into the meeting, to inform the delegates of the existence of the Injunction and ask that they call off the meeting. Julian said, 'They probably won't let me speak!' I replied, 'Well, that's their look-out. Rise to a Point of Order: they have got to take a Point of

Order. If they won't listen you will just have to slump dejectedly out and we will be forced to serve the Injunction on them immediately. In that case you will have to open the doors for us. (The doors were locked by the Marxists to keep out the Press and any 'undesirables' — though most of the undesirables were already inside.)

Julian walked in to some heavy groans and remarks like 'Look what the cat's brought in!' He sat in his seat for a few seconds and heard Lugg say how pleased he was to be able to open this Annual Meeting and how the previous year had been an unhappy one but now everyone was more united and the disagreements were coming to an end. Julian stood up: 'Mr Chairman, on a Point of Order....' 'Shut up and sit down or get out!' Lugg bellowed at him. And with a great roar the Marxist chorus bellowed in unison 'GET OUT!' A number of them moved towards him to fling him out. Julian shrugged his shoulders in a despairing manner and dejectedly ambled towards the door and dispiritedly shuffled down the stairs. Sadly he opened the door — and in we came with the injunction!

I was the first in, closely followed by three process servers, with Julian bringing up the rear. We walked up the stairs at a very brisk and businesslike pace. At the top of the stairs were the swing doors into the meeting hall. We entered very smartly. I was impressed with the resounding 'thwack' as the doors banged together behind us. Down the other end of the long hall I could see someone speaking, a grumpy-looking man sitting behind a huge table and flanked by others on either side of him. It was the chairman, Lugg. The hall was packed full. And what a horrible sight! There were some terrible faces contorted with rage and hatred for everybody (I suppose they were 'alienated'). These were the class war warriors. It was a dingy, decaying building and it was now peopled with these absolutely dreadful characters. I was taken aback for a moment by the evil atmosphere. I felt I had walked in to a Witches' Sabbat in mid-session. I clutched the Injunction.

Then brandishing it aloft, as one might make the sign of the Cross, I took a deep breath and in a very loud voice I said the dire words:

'HAROLD FRANCIS LUGG! (at this eighty heads jerked

round) BY ORDER OF THE HIGH COURT OF JUSTICE
(at these words a terrible cry went up) IT IS ORDERED
AND DIRECTED THAT THE DEFENDANTS HAROLD
FRANCIS LUGG AND JOHN CLARK WHETHER BY
THEMSELVES THEIR SERVANTS OR AGENTS OR
OTHERWISE BE RESTRAINED FROM PROCEEDING
WITH OR CONDUCTING ANY BUSINESS OF THE
ANNUAL MEETING TO BE HELD ON 23 FEBRUARY,
1977.
   IF YOU THE WITHIN-NAMED HAROLD FRANCIS
LUGG OR YOU THE WITHIN-NAMED JOHN CLARK
DO DISOBEY THIS ORDER YOU WILL BE LIABLE
TO PROCESS OF EXECUTION FOR THE PURPOSE
OF COMPELLING YOU TO DO THE SAME.'

When I finished I could only hear a deafening, horrendous,
agonising howl and, on a higher register from some of the
harpies, a falsetto screech. Surely this was the voice of the
Damned? I expected any moment to hear a great flapping
of wings and to see the whole assembly fly off into the
night. No wonder Joan Lestor and Eric Heffer are worried
about witch-hunts!

4
Closing the Gap

While I had been reading the Injunction the professional process servers had served copies on Lugg and Clark. Even before I had finished reading it I had noted that a small knot of people had gathered around me. The face that sticks in the memory was that of Tom Jenkins, the teacher. It was contorted with rage. Every time I have seen him he has looked livid. I found that the people gathered round me were threatening to break my neck if I did not leave immediately. When we first came in someone had shouted out 'They've brought in the heavy mob.' It rather amused me at the time. I wonder who they thought we were?

Andy Bevan then got up and harangued the meeting. 'Don't leave, comrades. Let's continue with the meeting. We mustn't bow down before the Tory courts. This is an attack on the Labour Party. If you ignore the Injunction you'll have the full weight of the Labour movement behind you.'

Julian got up and shouted back, 'If you defy the Injunction you will go to prison.' (He was quite right. To defy a court Injunction is an extremely serious matter, because it is to deny the authority of the Law and the courts. It is more serious than an ordinary crime.) Councillor Wally Hurford then got up and advised everyone to abandon the meeting. Meanwhile Lugg had gone out and called the police in to eject us. But the police confirmed that the Injunction was valid and advised him to obey it. Bevan was all for continuing. He presumably thought that he was perfectly safe because he was not named on the Injunction. If Lugg and Clark could be made into martyrs by being imprisoned, so much the better: a lot of political capital could be made out of it.

I had by now warned many of the key persons about con-

tempt of court. Owen Ashworth came up angrily and said
'O.K. you think you're clever? We'll get rid of this Injunction
in half an hour and the meeting will continue. We're going
to phone up and get a judge here right now and get this
Injunction discharged.' He clearly knew something about
Injunctions; perhaps he had been involved with Kelly when
left-wingers in Newham South had got Injunctions against
some of the Moderates who ran the Newham South Labour
Party. I very much doubted whether they would succeed in
getting a judge out of his cosy country house in the home
counties to drive all the way to a derelict hall in East Ham
at 9.00 pm on a cold wintry night. But off they went while
many of the people milled around in the hall waiting for a
judge to turn up. It was like waiting for Godot.

I left them to it and went off to get myself a meal. I
thought I had earned something even better than the
Kentucky Fried Chicken I had foregone earlier in the
evening. I learnt later that the rump of the meeting had
stayed for a long time and the judge had not turned up after
all. Apparently Ashworth and Kelly had had a terrible time
trying to get on to a judge. At first they could not find a
telephone. Then they went to a pub where the public phone
was in continual use by beery working class characters
chatting to their girl-friends. They did not share our friends'
concern about this dire threat to the Labour movement and
refused to make way for them! Eventually they got to a
phone. Then, like the army officer in 'Dr Strangelove' trying
to phone the President to avert a nuclear war, they ran into
terrible difficulties. Their 2p piece got jammed and they got
cut off. They rang round solicitors, barristers and judges. No
barrister would listen to them until they got a solicitor. I
think they finally managed to track down a solicitor's clerk
before they gave up in disgust. It was a pretty forlorn
endeavour, because unless the judge who gave the Injunction
could be persuaded to discharge it there was very little hope
of persuading anyone else to do so.

The next day I read in the London evening papers of an
attack on us by Arthur Latham, left-wing MP for Paddington.
He had not been at the meeting but that did not stop him
denouncing us for behaving like 'hooligans' — which was
laughable, as well as libellous. He added that he was thinking
of reporting us to the Director of Public Prosecutions. I

thought of suing him for libel, I still could. Perhaps I will!

On the same day (24 February 1977) a meeting of the Party's Executive Committee was held. This EC meeting was completely invalid. What had happened was that late the previous evening after the Injunction had been served on the Annual Meeting, Lugg jumped up and shouted out to the rump of the meeting that there would be an EC meeting the following day. That did not count as a valid notification because some EC members had left, others were not there in the first place, some who were there did not hear, and no one was told what the meeting was to be about. But this standard of behaviour was what the Newham North-East Party had degenerated to since the left had taken over.

The invalid EC meeting made two big decisions. One was to spend the local Party's funds to pay for the defence of Lugg and Clark; the other was to set a timetable for choosing a new Parliamentary candidate. The Injunction had essentially blocked the Marxists from operating for the time being through the GMC, so they immediately sought to by-pass it by doing the same things through the EC.

In addition to the fact that the EC meeting was invalidly convened, it was also invalid for another reason. The EC was the old EC. Its members had gone out of office. No new ones had been elected because the Annual Meeting was stopped. There was no EC! Lugg and the rest were masquerading as the EC when they were nothing of the kind. And what a cheek to try to get their hands on the Party's money to pay for their defence! Why should the Party (that is, the 1,000 Party members, over 80 per cent of whom were Moderates and opposed to them) pay for their costs? It would mean that people like Julian and Alec Kellaway were helping to pay for the defence to the action they had brought! Why should the local Party pay for the expenses of Lugg and Clark who had broken the Party's Rules? Surely there was a much better case for the plaintiffs' costs to be borne by the Party — because they were trying to enforce the Rules?

Well, it is quite clear that another dose of legal action was required. People rushed forward to be plaintiffs; they were sick to death of the Marxists' tricks. Within forty-eight hours six people had agreed to become plaintiffs, including Freddie Bament, Daisy Turner and Councillor Wally Hurford.

In order to keep the costs down to the minimum I decided

that the case should be brought in person (without solicitors or counsel). I drafted the writ, summons and affidavits myself and I travelled down to the Law Courts in the Strand to help conduct the case. At the Law Courts I met Freddie Bament. He did not seem in the least intimidated that he, a retired working man, would have to conduct his own case himself (with only my help) even though he knew absolutely nothing about the law and had never set foot in a civil court before. He was game for anything, though he winced with pain if he had to sit down for too long because of his back, and he walked at a remarkably quick step for a man with an injured leg hobbling on a walking stick. He was doing all this out of a pure devotion to duty. There was absolutely nothing whatever in it for him except a lot of trouble and a tiring day. But he was as cheerful as anything, cracking jokes and telling anecdotes while we were waiting for the judge to see us.

After some time we were ushered into the presence of the judge (sitting in Chambers). The judge was the same one who had granted the first Injunction, Mr Justice Stocker, a kindly old gentleman who looked a bit like a bank manager. Mr Bament introduced us both and asked if I could speak. It is very unusual to let people who are not qualified lawyers and not litigants-in-person speak. However, I persuaded the judge to let me do so and I outlined the case. Then Mr Bament said he wanted to speak and the judge replied 'Yes, Mr Bament. You are the only one who is supposed to be speaking!' Mr Bament then launched into a long tirade about the left-wingers at Newham which was rather off the legal point but obviously very keenly-felt, and the judge listened to it patiently. At the end the judge said that he thought we were probably right and would win the case but that he was not going to grant another Injunction just now. I suspect that he had been dismayed by the hue and cry that went up from Labour left-wingers over the first Injunction because if he thought the case was very strong it was surely right to grant the Injunction?

When we came out Mr Bament was a little crestfallen. 'We didn't get it, did we?' he asked. 'Never mind, Mr Bament,' I said, 'we'll appeal.' So I went round with him to lodge an immediate appeal to be heard the next day. Then off he went back to East Ham and I to Oxford.

The following day I met Mr Bament again at the Law Courts. We found out that we were scheduled to go in at 2.00 pm. After lunch we made our way to the court of the Master of the Rolls. The appeal was to be heard by one of England's most famous judges, Lord Denning, sitting with two other Appeal Court judges. In the court were a large number of people including four bewigged barristers. Another case was in progress and they sat there just like an orchestra ready to strike up as soon as the conductor raised his baton. But our appeal took precedence and they had to wait for us. Mr Bament and I, clutching our mackintoshes, scarves, law books and papers, trundled in like a couple of émigrés. I was thinking as we came in what a marvellous thing it was that a humble citizen like Mr Bament was able within twenty-four hours to have the ear of one of the finest and most important judges in the country. The court officials we had dealt with the day before had indicated that we were wasting our time and that there was no chance of getting an Injunction – but at least we had the chance to put the case.

'Who are you?' said Lord Denning looking at me. I looked up at him, a man of nearly eighty with a wise and intelligent face. I looked at the two Lords Justices on either side of him and I felt for a moment that I had been transported to the eighteenth century. Their faces and expressions were just not modern twentieth-century ones. I said that I had come to assist Mr Bament and that I requested permission to speak. 'Oh,' said Lord Denning gravely, 'we don't like your sort here!' (He meant that it was against the conventions for advisers to address the court. Technically they are called McKenzie persons.) I boldly suggested that I could be regarded as an *amicus curiae* (friend of the court) rather than a McKenzie person. A flicker of a smile seemed momentarily to cross Lord Denning's face but he made no reply and turned with a kindly expression to Mr Bament and said 'Well, Mr Bament. What is this all about?'

Mr Bament explained that it was a battle between the left and right of the Labour Party because the left had broken the Rules. 'Which side are you on?' Lord Denning asked. Mr Bament said he was against the left. 'Is there anyone in the middle?' asked Lord Denning. Mr Bament said that there used to be but that since the left had taken over it was no longer possible to be in the middle: you were either for them or against them. Mr Bament added that the Party was being damaged by outsiders who had moved into the area and taken it over and that the local people were worried at what had been going on. He said that the left did not run the Party properly, did not give out the proper notice for meetings and had been using every trick in the book. The judges had obviously taken to Mr Bament: he was so obviously completely sincere, and they perhaps felt rather protective towards him also, especially Lord Denning who is noted for his sympathy for those from humble walks of life.

Mr Bament then launched into a long monologue (a little like Lucky's monologue in *Waiting for Godot*). I realised at once that he was talking about what had gone on when the left-wingers had taken over his ward, Kensington Ward; he said that things had gone upside down but that since Eddie Lee had been elected secretly there had been a great improvement. The trouble was that the case was about the Executive Committee, not Kensington ward. After a while this dawned on the judges and Lord Denning motioned towards me with his little finger and said, 'You'd better help him out.' I rattled through the legal arguments. At first there was resistance from the judges, who interrupted with pointed questions, but after a while I sensed that they were coming along with me. The judge on Lord Denning's right (I think it was Lord Justice Cumming-Bruce) showed that he was in agreement and encouraged me by making additional points in support. When I had finished Lord Denning announced that an Injunction would be granted, in slightly different terms from the one I had requested, to protect the funds of the Party from being misappropriated to pay the costs of Lugg and Clark.

Mr Bament was delighted and told the Press that we had succeeded in preventing the left from using the Party's money to finance themselves. We went off to fill in the details of the Order and after a time it came back with the Appeal Court's stamp on it. The Injunction was given to the professional process servers who had served Lugg and Clark before. One of them told me some time later that when he went round to Lugg's house Lugg opened the door, saw him, and said 'Oh, it's you again!' and would have banged the door shut but that he, quick as a flash, had his foot in the door and served Lugg (it sounded as though it was done quicker than you could say 'Harold Francis Lugg').

At the end of March 1977 the main hearing of the Falvey case (as it became known after Gerard Falvey, the first plaintiff) was to take place. The legal procedure is that you start with an interim hearing to resolve the immediate problem of whether or not an Injunction should be granted. We had had several of these just to determine whether it should be given, then whether it should be discharged, then whether it should be continued. The Injunction was still intact, holding the Marxists down, at the end of March. The main and final hearing was to determine who was right on the merits of the case and who should therefore win it. An order for a speedy trial had been made and it is record time for a final hearing to be arranged in little over a month (normally it takes at least a couple of years from starting the action to the final hearing).

I had arranged for feelers to be put out to the other side to settle the action. These met with a cold response. I was surprised. I thought that Lugg and Clark would be worried about the costs. Indeed, one reason why I offered a settlement was that I did not want there to be any hardship to individuals over the case. Lugg was a former milkman and though he was better off than many in Newham he was far from wealthy. John Clark, on a healthy £6,000 a year salary, was very well off by Newham standards, especially for a young man in his mid-twenties, but even in his case no one would be happy about incurring high costs. When we obtained the Injunction the cost was not very high − about £500 − but if they persisted in fighting the action it would rise very quickly. We were willing to write off our costs had they settled, but they insisted on fighting. At first, I was a little puzzled, but I realised why when I saw that Reg Underhill, Number 2 Labour bureaucrat, had sent in an affidavit to support them.

Underhill's affidavit was something of a shock to us. What was he doing falling over himself to support this gang of very left-wing people who had taken over in Newham? After all, was it not Underhill who had written the report on Marxist 'entryism' from which I quoted in Chapter 2? Underhill was not a Marxist, indeed his private views were Moderate. But we were beginning to learn that this was worse! A Marxist who does something the Marxists want is less dangerous than a Moderate who backs the Marxists. Such a man provides 'cover' for them: he lends respectability to them, and enables them to disguise their activities. People no longer realise that it is the Marxists who are calling the tune. They say, 'But Reg Underhill is a Moderate, surely you're not saying that he is a Marxist?' No I am not. But the fact remains, *Underhill is as Underhill does*. In politics what counts is not what reputation a person has, it is what he actually does. If he speaks 'right' but votes 'left' do you call him a right-winger? Underhill was talking Moderate but he was not acting as a Moderate. He was backing the left to the hilt, as was pointed out in the affidavits filed in support of the plaintiffs in this case.

The affidavits pointed out that, as a paid administrator of the Party, Underhill had to do what his political masters (Atkinson, Allaun, Heffer, Lestor, Maynard, Mikardo and the others) wanted because his job was on the line. When he wrote wrote his report on 'Entryism' he thought that something might be done to stop entryism into the Labour Party by political extremists. But he received two sharp snubs in quick succession. In December 1976 Andy Bevan, one of the leaders of Militant, the main entryism group, was appointed as a colleague of his at Transport House! In January 1977 a four-man committee was appointed to examine his report on entryism, which had been completely ignored for the previous two years. The four men were Hayward, Foot, Nick Bradley and Heffer, not the kind of people who could be expected to take any effective action against infiltrators. They duly recommended a slap on the wrist with a feather duster for the infiltrators in the form of 'informing' constituency parties about the dangers of infiltration (sic!) and 'urging' them to resist it; stating that 'members of the Labour Party should not join organisations which have secret methods to subvert the Party'; and pointing out that 'there are also fundamental reasons why as democratic socialists we do not agree with much of the doctrine of Communists and Trotskyites.' So far, so good — but what positive action did they propose to take? None. All the 'urging' and 'informing' added up to nothing. Everyone knew already, and those who were prepared to do something about it did not need any 'urging'. What they did need, however, was the active support of the NEC or at least not to be actively opposed by it. The Report came out firmly against 'witch hunts' and said that

'Trotskyist views cannot be beaten by disciplinary action.'
Maybe, but disciplinary action could certainly prevent the
Trotskyists from taking over one section of the Labour Party
after another. After all, it stands to reason that if the
Marxists are using a policy of 'entryism' the most effective
response is precisely the disciplinary policy of ejectionism.
If some trespassers came in through your back door would
you say 'Trespassing views cannot be beaten by disciplinary
action,' and 'urge' and 'inform' your neighbours about
trespassing — or would you take the simple action of kicking
them out?

Transport House decided that the Labour Party would
launch an appeal to pay the costs of Lugg and Clark and
if this did not raise enough they would pay all their costs
out of Labour Party funds. This was disgraceful. Transport
House and the NEC were supposed to be impartial — a bit
like the civil service. They were not supposed to take sides
in the battle between left and right. It would be like the
civil service and the monarchy coming out in open support
of the Tory Party. It was now brought home to us just how
biased Transport House and the National Executive
Committee were. One of the main reasons why infiltration
had proceeded so far was that they were in some cases
backing it and in all cases doing nothing to resist it. This
active hostility towards the Newham Moderates was in
sharp contrast to their former stance when the Marxists had
captured the Newham Party and sacked Prentice. Then they
posed as neutral. But now they launched an attack on us.
It had become clear what their policy was: when the Marxists
are winning, wring your hands in despair and say that nothing
can be done unless there are procedural irregularities; but if
the Moderates get on top, strain every nerve to stop them.

Lugg and Clark, feeling that they had an unlimited supply
of money from the Labour Party funds, lashed out and hired
Lord Gifford as junior counsel and an expensive Chancery
QC, Gerald Godfrey. We modestly stuck to a junior counsel
alone, Stuart McKinnon. Once again my offer was repeated
for an amicable settlement without a court hearing. I set out
a written scheme and it was presented to our opponents. It
stated that the scheme was negotiable. They turned it down
flat and refused even to discuss it. The judge suggested that
we reach agreement. Again they refused to budge an inch.

They thought they could hammer us into the ground and that, with Transport House, an expensive QC, and the funds of the Labour Party behind them, they would be invincible.

But they were wrong. We were extremely fortunate in having a very intelligent judge, Mr Justice Kerr, to hear the case. He was sharp enough to realise what had been going on and saw straight through the threadbare excuses put up by the other side. But I have never seen any person stretching over backwards so far to be fair. He was courteous, patient and extended every facility to both sides. It was a model performance. He was the only judge I have seen before or since who appeared to be *solely* influenced by strict points of law, unwavering in his desire to establish the truth, and keeping an open mind on the case to the very end.

I had widened the case, when it became clear that Lugg and Clark would not settle, so that two more points were raised. One was that the Executive Committee had extended the deadline for nominations and informed their side so it could take advantage of the extension, but had not informed the Moderates. The other was a far-reaching one. I had discovered that the trade union delegations had been wrongly calculated due to Transport House advice. Transport House, which has never shown much respect for the Labour Party's Rules and has tended to be a law unto itself, had advised constituency parties to take affiliation fees from trade unions upon the basis of the entire membership of the branch concerned but to calculate their delegate-entitlements only on the strength of that portion of their membership resident in the constituency. That might sound fair enough but it is not, for three reasons. First, the Rules say otherwise and they should stick to what the Rules say, not what they think reasonable. If the Rules are unsatisfactory they should be changed, not ignored. Secondly, the union secretaries have no records, in many cases, of the addresses of their members (often recorded, as in the case of the T & G, at regional office) nor of the constituency boundaries. It is therefore either a great deal of unpaid work for them outside their normal duties or it is virtually impossible for them to calculate which of their members live in the constituency. Therefore to do it on this basis leads to mere guess-work and presents manifold opportunities for gross cheating. Thirdly, if they take the fees for the full membership they have no right to disenfranchise a large portion of them. That is a case of taxation without representation. Transport House wanted to deprive the union members of their voting rights but collect the money for them just the same! I added this point to our case so that the question could be sorted out at the same time at virtually no extra cost for all concerned.

So the three counts against the defendants were insufficient notice, selective notification of the deadline extension, and miscalculation of the trade union delegate-entitlement. Any one of these would have invalidated the meeting.

The judge found we were right on all three counts. Despite all their advantages, Lugg and Clark simply had a lousy case and were completely in the wrong. They had thought they could smash us but had miscalculated very badly. They did not bother to lodge an Appeal; they were evidently advised that there was no hope.

Lugg and Clark, having blatantly broken the Rules, spurned repeated approaches for an amicable settlement, and had Transport House (quite illegally, in my view) guarantee their costs, then posed as persecuted martyrs! This was like someone trying to kick you, missing, hitting a wall and hurting his toe, and then expecting people to sympathise with him! The myth was built up that we had hounded a poor milkman with no money and a poor young man, John Clark, whose wife was having a baby. Yet it was they who had taken the offensive from start to finish. They never had to pay a single penny, they refused even to entertain discussions for an amicable settlement, and most of the money spent on the case was due to their insistence on having two very expensive lawyers! Eventually this myth grew to grotesque proportions and I dubbed the resultant story 'The Sad Tale of Poore John Clark'. It was a real tear-jerker for those who knew nothing about the matter: for those who did it was nauseating. It cut very little ice down in Newham. When one bleeding heart waxed eloquent about the 'plight' of poor old Harold Lugg, the former milkman, to one of the Newham bus-drivers he was shocked to receive the jovial response, 'Harold will have to sell a lot of extra pintas!'

After the judgement had been given, I wrote to Ron Hayward, suggesting that the NEC arrange to call the Annual Meeting. Lugg and Clark were proposing to call the meeting

themselves but as far as we were concerned they had had
their chance and we were not prepared to trust them again.
They maintained that they had acted in good faith. You will
have formed your own opinion on whether that claim is
credible. We had too. Of course I was far from happy about
Transport House supervising the election, but I thought they
would at least be an improvement on the local leftists.

So the task of making the arrangements for a new Annual
Meeting was entrusted to Reg Underhill, the National Agent
of the Labour Party. The Labour bureaucrats and the NEC
were thus given their last chance to turn over a new leaf and
redeem themselves in the eyes of Newham Moderates by
acting properly and fairly without taking sides between left
and right.

The Newham Marxists were now satisfied. They did not
expect Underhill to act against them. They thought that
they had a comfortable lead and that their position was
invincible. They accused us of 'wrecking' and 'time-wasting',
as if our purpose were merely to delay the Annual Meeting
for the sake of it. In fact I intended that we should win it.
Julian was very sceptical, thinking that it was impossible, but
I encouraged him to persevere. The problem was one of time.
We had less than three months left in which to undo what
40 highly active Marxists had achieved over a period of more
than two years.

We arranged for another 20 delegates to be signed up,
mainly from the trade unions. We were helped in this by the
third point in the *Falvey* case (the one about trade union
delegations) but it was not the most important factor. Many
of the new delegates would have been eligible under the old
system and I doubt whether the court ruling added more
than about 5 votes to our count.

It was most important to sign these people up without
alerting the left. It was obviously very suspicious that two
large T & G branches suddenly affiliated and proposed to
take up their full complement of delegates. (With the court
ruling this was 12: without it, it would have been about 8.)
The Secretary of both of these branches was Alf Deakin, a
staunch Moderate. He put us in touch with some very good
people. I told Julian to impress upon them the need to disguise the fact that they were Moderates and, if possible, get
them to pass themselves off as left-wingers. Some of them

took to this and had enormous fun in elaborate charades designed to trick the local Marxists into thinking they were on their side. It was done quite cunningly and an elaborate story was devised to provide them with cover. Obviously we could not get away with all 12 being regarded as Marxists so it was freely admitted that 2 or 3 were not. This subterfuge did not involve any lying or cheating — simply giving an impression of holding left-wing views and, by emphasising anti-Prentice feelings, letting the Marxists think that they were not Moderates. It took the Marxists in and they professed themselves very pleased with the 'Deakin delegates'.

It was amazing how much work was done in May and June between the ending of the Falvey case and the Annual Meeting which was scheduled for 13 July. During this time I was frequently being phoned by Reg Underhill to find out whether or not I would make an objection to certain delegates. I had gone through the list of delegates and challenged all the doubtful left-wing ones. As the convenor of the meeting, Underhill had enormous powers of discretion. His job was to confirm that someone was a member of the GMC, but this confirmation was not an automatic process. He had the power to disqualify. When the votes are very close victory can be a question of how many delegates the other side loses through disqualification.

I was disappointed but not surprised to note that, in using his discretion, Underhill came down very heavily against us. Very few of my strongest challenges were upheld, even when I was quite sure another tribunal would have decided differently. According to my calculation, 4 of our delegates were disqualified who should not have been, while the Marxists managed to retain 7 of their delegates who should have been disqualified. The net advantage to the Marxists from Underhill's use of his discretion was therefore about 11 votes. It is absurd really that the person who administers the system should be a person who has a vested interest in it. Now, however honest Mr Underhill considered himself to be (and we all greatly preferred him to the Newham Marxists) the fact that he had backed Lugg and Clark in the court case, worked as a colleague of Andy Bevan's at Transport House, and was an employee of an NEC led by Heffer, Atkinson, Mikardo, Lestor etc. did not inspire confidence. Even if he thought justice was done, we felt that it was not *seen* to be done. His decisions came out strongly against us, and we believed they were not correct constitutionally.

What could be done about this new factor in the situation — 'Underhill's Discretion'? I wondered whether we should apply to a court to remove him from the post or whether we should challenge his specific confirmations and disqualifications in the courts. However, I certainly did not want to encourage further legal action if it were at all avoidable. Legal action is an expensive and time-consuming exercise fraught with perils and holding forth uncertain outcomes. For me personally it involved a great deal of hard work. It kept me without sleep for days on end as I struggled to get all the documentation ready for the very tight deadlines imposed by the case that was being brought and by always having to use the emergency procedures. I decided to withdraw all my challenges as the Annual Meeting came near.

The reason why I did this was that I calculated that we would win anyway, despite the 11 votes lost through 'Underhill's Discretion'. The Marxists, on the other hand, were confident of an easy victory and Underhill was also confident they would win. They expected to win by about 10 votes, but of course they believed that 10 of the 12 Deacon delegates would vote for them. Even with 'Underhill's Discretion', if those Deacon delegates were to vote the other way then we would be 10 votes ahead. Now I knew perfectly well which way the Deacon Delegates would vote because we had recruited them, so I could afford to waive the 11 votes that Underhill had deprived us of by exercising his discretion against us. It was not an easy decision to make — to say goodbye to 11 votes in a closely-fought contest — but if I had persisted with the challenges it would have been used as an excuse to delay the holding of the Annual Meeting and leave Underhill in charge virtually indefinitely. It is interesting to speculate whether 'Underhill's Discretion' would have broadened to deprive us of 21 votes had it been known that the Deacon delegates were really on our side.

The Marxist strength stayed constant. There was no fourth wave of infiltration in 1977 because they thought they had it sown up. I had chiselled off a handful of their GMC delegates by exposing them as invalid, and Kelly himself had left the constituency, so actually they were very slightly weaker than they had been at the end of 1976. They had virtually reached their high water mark, and unless they drafted in another battalion of outsiders there was little they could do. They had never converted one Newham local to support them, so there was little prospect of winning any supporters at all. They had found GMC seats for most of their existing personnel, but it was not technically possible to find a GMC place for every single one because there was a shortage of pegs for their hats. There were only so many ward places and socialist places and once they had exhausted these they could only advance through the trade unions. But they had very little trade unionist support and some of their people were not eligible for a trade union place. It is very fortunate that the National Union of Teachers is not affiliated to the Labour Party: this meant that the NUT members could not be returned as trade union delegates.

Our position was potentially much stronger. They were conducting a *blitzkrieg* to capture the constituency. It was essential for them to tie it all up quickly. On the other hand the longer we had, the more certain our victory. We had a virtually inexhaustible reservoir of support: 800 out of the 1000 members were potential supporters, most of the trade unionists supported us, and the vast majority of Labour voters supported us. We were joining up new members to the Party, encouraging lapsed members to rejoin, getting new trade unions to affiliate, old ones to increase their level of affiliation, and dormant ones to take up their full delegate-entitlement. We were starting to find some very good people. Our problem was time.

The new breed of people we were bringing in were very different from the dodderers of the past. We were bringing in tough, militant moderates — middle-aged trade unionists used to tough negotiation, not easily frightened, but with a profound distaste for communists whom they had generally seen at first hand within their own trade unions. Although there were a number of very good people among the old stalwarts most of them were getting on in years, and it is undeniable that a number of them did not want to get involved in a struggle and would have been prepared to lose rather than fight.

One of the new breed was Patrick Milsom, a bus driver. He had been an active trade unionist for many years but had not

become a Labour Party member. He had a wife and kids. He
took a bit of persuading to become involved but once he had
been persuaded he became very keen. One of his bus garage
mates had said, 'If you can get Pat interested the Commies
won't know what hit them! He's not afraid of anyone: he
even tells the Gaffer where to get off!' Mr Milsom was just
the kind of man we needed. He was quite a character, with a
lot of guts.

The problem now was to work out our ticket — whom we
should put up for what positions. There was no problem over
the 6 trade union delegates for the Executive Committee.
They were easy to find because we had so many good trade
unionists to choose from. The problem was over the officers.
Who should be Chairman? Julian and I discussed this over the
phone at some length. We could not be sure what our lead
was. I put it at about 10 votes in my calculation, about 12 at
the maximum and about 6 at the minimum. We thought of
putting Mr Milsom up for chairman. He seemed tough enough
but he was new, we did not really know him, and he had had
no experience. I decided that we would probably put him up
the following year. Unfortunately we had very few people
to choose between. John Pagett had indicated he did not
want to stand for Chairman. He was a very jovial busman and
I do not think he really liked the unpleasantness of these
meetings. Eddie Lee clearly had the qualities of Chairman: he
had the poise, the experience and the intelligence. We both
agreed that he would have made an excellent Chairman (or
Secretary) in normal circumstances but I was unsure of his
willingness to go along with the tough measures that would
be needed. I knew that if we won we would be in for a rough
ride. He had nearly resigned over the Kensington *coup* back
in 1976 and my view was that the last thing we could afford
to risk in the Chairman was a resignation.

The obvious choice seemed to be Ray Massey. I had met
him once for a couple of minutes at the end of the Falvey
case. He had backed us solidly, cooperated steadily, and
had become a plaintiff, which indicated the requisite toughness of character. He was an uneducated man, but he seemed
to have his priorities right and would be a tough chairman. I
would have liked to have made Julian the Chairman but
unfortunately he had an 'anti-vote' and it was too risky to
put him up because our lead was not high enough. Even a

12-vote lead would be wiped out completely if just 6 people voted the other way.

So Ray Massey was to be Chairman, Eddie Lee and John Pagett were to be Vice-Chairman. That left the Treasurer, Secretary and Assistant Secretary. There was no problem over the Treasurer: Alec Kellaway was the obvious choice. We needed someone who would not fiddle the books and disgrace us (!) or make a mess of the accounts. Alec's integrity was beyond question and he had studied economics at Oxford. I was working out the respective merits of various candidates for the Secretaryship when I heard from Julian to my great dismay that Hart was going to stand. My own opinion was that he had already done great damage to the Moderate cause. While we had been trying to save the situation, he had been driving at twenty miles an hour down the fast lane obstructing the ambulance.

I asked Julian to see if anyone could dissuade him from standing. He was obdurate. I do not know precisely what his motivations were. He talked on about 'reconciliation' and 'bringing the Party together' and ending the battle between factions. It is all very well to talk of reconciliations in broken-down marriages but how can you reconcile yourself to the enemies of democracy? I do not think Hart had any real conception of what the Marxists stood for and what sort of people they were. Julian thought his main motivation was to stay as Council leader. He did not seem to care whether the other Moderates won or lost and did nothing to support them. He knew that by insisting on standing he could ride to office on our backs, deriving over 80 per cent of his support from our work and our people while at the same time dissociating himself from us and attacking our use of legal action.

Hart had only really become involved to save Prentice. I think he had been worried about the effect of the influx of Marxists on the Local Establishment and had backed Prentice in 1976 for that reason, but that by the end of 1976 he had given up and moved over to a policy of all-out appeasement. Once Prentice appeared finished he said that he no longer saw the need to continue the battle. He had always seen it as a fight for Prentice. In my view Prentice was merely the occasion not the cause. The fight was not about Prentice personally. It was about democracy and only con-

cerned Prentice in that he appeared to be its flag-bearer in
Newham North-East and there was no other flag-bearer
available.

Then there was the problem of Sylvia Jones. Julian told
me, and so did she, that she wanted to be Vice-Chairman.
My fear was that she might resign, and for the Vice-Chairman
to resign would be a disaster. In the end she want forward
as candidate for Assistant Secretary.

So now our ticket was complete. At the lower levels it was
fine: it had such good solid characters on it as Daisy Turner
and my favourite of all of them Freddie Bament. One newcomer who looked very promising was Ken Kilsby, a slow
and thoughtful man. He was very cautious in committing
himself and used to ask to have everything explained. He
listened and took it all in. He was clearly weighing it up
very carefully. He said that he was opposed to the Marxists
but that he had little time for some of the people on the
Newham Council who had let the constituency get into such
a shambles. He was not exactly a fervent supporter of Reg
Prentice's either, though I do not think he was particularly
hostile. Most important of all he struck us as a man of
integrity who could be trusted.

A special meeting of our leading candidates was called
before the nominations were finalised. I was apprehensive
that some of them might do a Thomas Beckett on us and
say 'Thank you very much, Goodbye!' as soon as they were
elected. Our main concern was that the newly-elected
Moderates did not continue to follow the strategy that had
got them elected they would very soon be turned out and all
the work would be wasted. At the meeting both Julian and I
hammered these points home. We explained that it was
useless to win only to be turned out a few weeks later and
that if our team won it would have to stay united. Success
was not a question of individual enterprise but of uniting
round a consistent strategy. I had worked out the terms of an
agreement which were that, as in the past, I was to devise the
strategy for beating the left and they agreed to follow it subject to two conditions. These were that if it went against
their conscience they would abstain (a standard recognised
procedure in any civilised institution: discipline must not
crush the individual conscience) and that it only applied to
measures necessary to beat the left in Newham; on all matters

of local and national policy not directly relevant to this they reserved the right to vote as they chose.

I agreed to prior consultation where feasible. It was also agreed that the discipline would be a temporary measure until a new MP was chosen and that it would be relaxed after about nine months. No one can possibly say this was an encroachment on anyone's rights: it was a perfectly reasonable thing to agree to. However we said that we did not want simply to take a majority vote on it; we wanted each person to accept it individually. I added that it was a sad necessity to insist on even this minimum degree of disciplined voting but that united and pre-planned action was essential in view of the fact that the Marxists were organised in this way and had been from the start. For our people it was quite different. Even a small degree of organisation of this kind worried them as taking away their individual judgement. I often think how much of our time we spent arguing the ethics of various procedures: how simple it would have been to be Marxists and not bothered by such qualms.

We went round the room asking our people for their comments. The first to be asked was Ray Massey. He agreed with alacrity and expressed no doubts at all. Eddie Lee was not happy with it, and I am not sure in the end that he ever agreed to it. Daisy Turner was asked, and she made a little speech in favour saying that the left do all sorts of things but don't like it when they are on the receiving-end. Then Freddie Bament was asked and he replied with his favourite saying that 'We must fight fire with fire.' Ken Kilsby sucked on his pipe and thought long and hard. He asked a few questions. Then after what seemed like an eternity he said he would give the undertaking. Alec Kellaway and Mr Milsom delivered strong speeches in favour. All the others also agreed.

We then had a very pleasant chat and agreed how nice it would be if the friendly and jolly atmosphere of this meeting were to be the norm for Labour Party meetings. Daisy Turner said they used to be very pleasant affairs until the Marxists came in and ruined the friendly relationships and created an atmosphere of bitterness and hatred. I remember that Julian once went along to give a talk to one of the Moderate women's sections and he reported that they all listened attentively, asked incisive questions and took a serious interest in

matters of policy. He said that it was a very happy atmosphere. 'That's what Labour Party meetings ought to be like,'
he added.

The Annual Meeting was practically upon us. It was to
take place on 13 July — it would be an unlucky day for
somebody. I had forebodings as the day approached. I had
said to Julian several weeks earlier that if Transport House or
the NEC found out about the real loyalties of the Deakin
delegates and saw that they would lose they would call the
election off. He had replied that he did not believe they
would have the nerve to do such a blatant thing: it would
look too bad and would expose them as completely cynical.
I said I hoped he was right but I would not put it past them.

Then disaster struck. On Sunday 10 July 1977, the
Observer, in an article clearly inspired by the Newham
Marxists (this can be inferred from the intrinsic qualities of
the article which exhibited knowledge that was privy only to
them and made their characteristic points) declared: 'When
the embattled Newham North-East Constituency Party holds
its reconvened annual meeting on Wednesday it is expected
to discover that Mr Reg Prentice's supporters are again in a
majority on the management committee.' The article pointed
out that until February 1977 there were about 94 delegates
on the GMC, but now there were about 124. The extra 30
were our men. Clearly the Marxists had begun to tumble to
what we had been doing.

It is interesting to note that in July 1975 there were less
than 60 GMC members (Prentice was defeated by 29 votes
to 19), by July 1976 there were around 90 GMC members,
and by July 1977 there were over 120. The GMC had more
than doubled in two years. In the six months we had been
in Newham we had had about 5 Marxists disqualified and
added about 45 delegates to the total. My calculation at this
time was that the 124 contained about 40 Marxists, 10 left-
wing sympathisers, 50 of our supporters and 5 unknowns. The
remainder were 'wet Moderates' who supported Prentice
personally but could not be relied on to stand up against
pressure from the other side.

The problem was, of course, that the Marxists and their
friends would achieve something approaching a 100 per cent
turnout whereas not all our people would be able to come,
and some who would promise to come would not bother.

Of the wet Moderates (numbering about 20) I did not expect more than 12 to turn up. In the event only half of them came.

We crossed our fingers and hoped that the *Observer* article would not change anything, but I told Julian that I would not be surprised if Transport House cancelled the meeting. Julian said he was sure they would not dare, just two days before the election: it would look so bad publicly. Well, nothing happened on Monday and I was beginning to think we were all right. Then on Tuesday morning I was dragged out of bed half asleep from my late night calculations on the voting. It was Julian. 'Guess what?' 'What?' I said 'I hope it's important or I won't thank you for dragging me out of bed at this time in the morning!' 'They've cancelled the election!'

I did not really believe it. Even though I had half-expected this to happen, it was so bad that somehow I did not really believe it would. I felt like going back to bed but I realised that some fast action was needed, so I immediately set about getting an Injunction. I told Julian to find some plaintiffs. Within half an hour he had found 8 plaintiffs — Mrs van Haeftan, Freddie Bament, Gerard Falvey and his mother, Ray Massey, Mrs Threadgold, Alec Kellaway and Julian himself. Many others offered themselves. Everyone was outraged.

What had happened was that a meeting of the Labour Party's Organisation Committee had been held on the afternoon of Monday 11 July. Ten members turned up. They included Nick Bradley, Eric Heffer, Frank Allaun, Norman Atkinson, Joan Lestor, Ian Mikardo and others. They voted to cancel the Annual Meeting of the Newham North-East Party. Underhill appeared most embarrassed by this because he had given his word to us that there would be no jiggery-pokery. He was not available when I repeatedly phoned him but when Julian got through he just said 'I am directed to say that ..., I am directed to do this' and so on.

As the enormity of the act sank in, the outrage in Newham increased. The Organisation Committee was an official Labour Party committee which consisted of 2/3 of the NEC. *An official Labour Party committee had cancelled the Annual Meeting of a Constituency Party because the local Marxist infiltrators* were expected to lose the election. Not only was this indefensible, it was very worrying. If these people could cancel a local Labour Party's election because their Marxist friends were going to lose, what would stop them from cancelling a General Election if they got to power? The contempt for democratic processes that they showed on this occasion indicates their real feelings towards democracy. It is my honest belief that the people who voted for the cancellation of this local election *would* cancel a General Election if they were in power and expected to lose it. You cannot find any greater enemies of democracy than those whose instinctive reaction is to cancel elections which they expect to lose.

From 11.00 am on Tuesday 12 July I worked solidly on the legal case. We needed to go for an Injunction immediately and the courts shut at 4.00 pm, or 4.30 pm by special appointment. I phoned the London solicitors who had been our London agents in the Falvey case. They were very efficient. I had two secretaries with dictaphones connected with me over the telephone and, using my two phones alternately, I dictated the affidavits, the writ, the major cases and legal points and the other necessary documents. These were then rushed round to our barrister, with whom I had a hurried consultation, and then he went in to arrange the case in court. And he argued it very well by all accounts. We were given an Injunction in this *ex parte* application.

The following day Underhill appeared with a barrister and solicitor to try to get the Injunction discharged. I do not know by what authority he was thus pouring Labour Party money, not his money any more than it was mine because it belonged to all Labour Party members collectively, down the drain. It really was preposterous that he had the nerve to come to court and spend Labour Party money to support an attack on Labour Party democracy of which he seemed ashamed — as he certainly ought to have been.

What excuses were offered for cancelling a meeting two days before it was due to take place? Actually it was worse than that. The decision had been rushed through as an emergency motion on the Monday, so the six missing members of the Organisation Committee did not know it was coming up. Why an emergency motion? Because the *Observer* article reached them only the previous day and there was no chance to notify the members. What made it even worse was that it was decided to keep the cancellation decision *secret*. Underhill was told not to let anyone know the meeting was cancelled but to turn up at 8.00 pm on Wednesday 13 July to tell the 100 or more people who had gathered there, having waited weeks for their Annual Meeting and having rearranged their shifts and private lives to accommodate it, 'Sorry folks — it's all off!' It was an appalling way to act, and it showed a deep contempt for the ordinary Labour Party members in Newham. The cancellation was to be kept secret in order to avoid damaging publicity or legal action. The only reason that we knew of it was that we were tipped off by a journalist, whose identity I must keep secret to protect him from retaliation.

Can you imagine, as I put it to the court when these matters came up, a greater instance of political skulduggery than cancelling an election, cancelling it behind the backs of over 1/3 of your committee, cancelling it when you don't have the power to cancel it, and cancelling it secretly so as to put everyone to the inconvenience of turning up only to be told that it will not take place? I told the court that I had come to realise that we were not dealing with people who play by the normal rules but with the political equivalent of crooks. I told the court that they had made what might politely be termed 'excuses' for cancelling the meeting but these were actually a pack of lies.

What were the 'excuses' which the barrister appearing for Underhill put before a sceptical Mr Justice Caulfield, who quite obviously did not believe a word of it? He said that certain 'irregularities' had emerged and therefore it was necessary to call off the election. There was 'some doubt' about the trade union delegates. No doubt the judge bore in mind the following points: If the reason for cancellation was the alleged 'irregularities', why did the motion passed by the Organisation Committee say that 'no useful purpose would be served by holding an election because of the continued existence of the dispute between the two sides'? That is the epitath the dictator writes: 'No useful purpose would be served by continuing with democracy.' Surely the very purpose of elections is to resolve disputes? If there were no disagreements or disputes then they would be unnecessary. Obviously the Labour bureaucracy had changed their story between Monday when the motion was passed and Wednesday when they came to court. Presumably they were advised that legally 'irregularity' was a stronger line to pursue than 'no useful purpose'. Next point: Underhill himself was in charge of the election! So why were there irregularities in the first place? His defence was that he had botched the election! This was absurd. He had spent nearly three months working solidly on it. There had been challenges from us and from the left. He had taken legal advice on it. Everything was checked and double-checked. In accuracy of delegates' credentials it was probably the best convened meeting that had ever been called in the history of the Labour Party. Next point: Who complained about the irregularities — and when? Next point: Precisely what were the irregularities? Next point: Were they discovered on Sunday night or Sunday morning? Next point: Was the *Observer* article a pure coincidence? Next point: Why could not the irregularities, if they existed, be put right on Monday and Tuesday without cancelling the meeting? Next point: Why, if there was nothing to hide, was the cancellation kept secret?

The judge indicated that he was not at all impressed with their case. They saw they would not get the Injunction lifted. It was now about 5.00 pm on Wednesday and the meeting was due to start in Newham in three hours' time. I had advised that telegrams should be sent to all the 125-odd delegates so that they were in no doubt that the meeting was *not* cancelled, because the High Court had granted the rare mandatory Injunction overriding the cancellation and ordering Underhill to proceed with the meeting. The telegrams cost over £700 but our Solicitors had agreed they were necessary. (We are still arguing with the other side over who should pay for these telegrams: I think they will have to pay in the end.) However, now, at 5.00 pm, Underhill's lawyer started to argue that the terms of the Injunction should be changed slightly. He wanted a change in the wording so that the meeting could itself vote to adjourn. I was not able to be in court, which was unfortunate as I might have grasped what they were up to. The judge granted their request. Our lawyer had no reason to oppose it. It seemed to have no significance. The judge stood up, the hearing was finished. The lawyers went home. Underhill hurried off to take the chair at the Newham North-East Annual Meeting.

I arrived in Newham about 7.00 pm and busied myself with preparations before the meeting. Julian was responsible for organising transport for the delegates and badgering them to make sure they turned up. Soon it was 8.00 pm and the meeting was about to start. It began rather late because of the careful checks on delegates' credentials at the door. Transport House had sent several officials down to assist Underhill. I waited outside, where I was roundly abused and threatened by a group of Marxists. I identified some of them later as belonging to the Workers' Revolutionary Party. There were also a couple of Communist Party members and one or two Socialist Workers' Party people. They were all very nasty people. I became involved in a shouting match with them after one of them had shouted that I was a 'fascist'. I pointed out to him that he would have been at home in the Nazi Party because he believed in the politics of hate, the exaltation of violence, the crushing of democracy, dirty tricks, and State control. One or two of these people were clearly mentally unbalanced. One of them was literally foaming at the mouth. He was later arrested after an altercation with the police. I taxed these people with the question: 'What are you doing concerning yourself with the Annual Meeting of the Newham Labour Party when you are not even members of the Labour Party?' One person said that I was being paid by the CIA to destroy the Labour Party. I merely laughed at such nonsense. I wondered what kind of mental universe these people existed in? What dark phantasms peopled their frenzied minds? There really was no point of mental contact between us: their mental processes were as impenetrable as a Black Hole in space.

I became aware that the time was passing and still there was no news. Surely there ought to be some results by now? Julian had promised to send someone to tell me as soon as the officers were elected so that I could release my prepared Press Release. I had prepared one that anticipated a clean sweep for us — a complete victory — and commented on that basis. Then, after they had all been at the meeting for over an hour, someone came down to say that the election had not started! Andy Bevan had got up and had proposed a motion that the Annual Meeting adjourn and hold no elections. So *that* was why Underhill wanted to make sure the wording of the Injunction permitted an adjournment motion. This point came up in a later court hearing. Underhill swore that 'Mr Bevan came to me before the meeting and asked

whether I would accept a motion to adjourn if he moved it.
I said ... I would accept it in view of what Mr Justice
Caulfield had said. When he moved the motion, I accepted
it.... [If it is implied] that I put Mr Bevan up to this, or what
we somehow conspired together to get the meeting
adjourned, I deny it emphatically. Any party official who
tried to manipulate a meeting in this way, would be betraying
his professional responsibility and inciting [sic] dismissal.'
Oh, yes, Mr Underhill, I can just see Eric Heffer, Joan Lestor,
Norman Atkinson, Frank Allaun, Nick Bradley, Alex Kitson,
Uncle Tom Cobleigh and all, dismissing you for helping Andy
Bevan, the man they appointed as National Youth Officer.

That was Mr Underhill's account on oath. Ours was
different. We found it difficult to believe that Andy Bevan
left it until minutes before the meeting before raising this
point. We suggested to the court that he and Underhill had
had their little conversation (or 'conspiracy' in Underhill's
own word) *before* the court hearing on Wednesday, probably
on Wednesday morning. This would explain why the issue
was raised in the court hearing; otherwise it would have
been an extraordinary coincidence for Underhill to make an
issue of it then and for Bevan to raise the issue quite independently immediately afterwards. Our contention to the court
was that Underhill had done precisely what he described as
improper behaviour for a supposedly independent official of
the Labour Party. Underhill said he was 'disappointed' that
we suggested this. We were a long way beyond the stage of
'disappointment' with him.

It was now nearly 10.00 pm. The meeting should have
been over but the elections had not started. The debate on
whether or not the meeting should adjourn went on for
about an hour and a half. Underhill should never have permitted this gross abuse. I suppose Bevan's idea was that,
even if he did not succeed in getting the meeting called off,
perhaps some of the Moderates would leave after an hour's
acrimonious debate on whether the Annual Meeting should
take place and then his faction would win a majority. But
this time the tactic did not work. Finally a vote was taken.
The news was brought down to the waiting crowd of photo-
graphers, newsmen, interested Moderates from Newham
South and Newham North-West, the Communists, Socialist
Workers and so forth who stood outside: Andy Bevan's

motion had been defeated by 54 votes to 50. The margin was smaller than I had hoped. I later learned that Jack Hart had voted for Andy Bevan's motion! Hart has a lot to answer for. I suppose he was trying to make himself popular with Transport House. He voted for the Moderate slate in the actual elections. A couple of our supporters who were not too bright voted the wrong way. They had no written material to guide them and they did not understand what the vote was about. Perhaps Bevan had also counted on this 'bamboozle factor' — getting people to vote the wrong way through confusion.

And now, late at night, came the good results that we had all been waiting for. The Labour Party's Press Officer, Percy Clark, announced the following results: Massey 59; Lugg 49; Hart 58; Bradbury 47.

This meant we would sweep the board by an average margin of about 10 votes, and that is what happened. The special representation of the Socialist Societies and the Co-op on the Executive Committee meant that our majority would be smaller on it. The election for the Executive Committee produced 14 Moderates and 12 in the Marxist camp. So we had a working 2-vote majority. But one of those 14 Moderates was Jack Hart. If he voted the wrong way it would be 13 all, with Ray Massey having the casting vote. The same applied to Sylvia Jones. The third man to watch was Eddie Lee: he would not betray us but he might resign if he disagreed with some tactic or policy.

The position on the Local Government Committee was very unsatisfactory. Underhill had adopted a representation system (a system of apportioning seats to different Party units and affiliated units) which had the effect of disqualifying a number of the people we had nominated. Had we known that this system would be adopted we would have made different nominations but it was sprung on us in the course of the Annual Meeting after 10.00 pm when the Marxists shouted to Underhill to adopt this particular system. The Local Government Committee selects the councillors, so it was an important committee. We took about half the places, the Marxists got the other half.

When the dust settled it was seen that we had scored a major victory. For a few days the Labour bureaucracy huffed and puffed about declaring the meeting invalid and then went quiet. Needless to say no one ever heard another word about those alleged 'irregularities'. Underhill decided to concede the case we had brought and later I extracted an admission from his solicitors that there was nothing whatever invalid about the July Annual Meeting. So much for the 'irregularities' which were used in court in sworn evidence to justify cancellation of the meeting.

5

The Big Battalions

Well, would we now have peace at the last? I very much doubted it. I told Julian that the Marxists would never accept a democratic verdict and that now we were in the saddle we could expect the local party to turn into a 'bucking bronco'. He agreed but thought there might be a lull before the storm.

It was a very brief lull. I had hoped to take a holiday in August, at least to the extent of going to the beach and taking life easy. I had become acutely conscious of the fact that I was in for a long haul and that this victory would not be the end, but, at best, only 'the end of the beginning'. Seeing the summer drifting by before me it became harder than ever to stay on the treadmill. It was a rude awakening in every sense when Julian phoned to tell me that Jack Hart had called a meeting of the officers and a meeting of the Finance and General Purposes Committee. 'This isn't going to please you...' Julian began. It didn't. Hart, as usual, was the fly in the ointment. When the Marxists were on top he used to turn up to the Executive Committee after pleading with Sylvia Jones to accompany him for 'moral support' and then he would sit, quiet as a mouse, hardly ever raising a voice in protest. Now that the Moderates were on top, no thanks to him, he had sprung to life again.

What was he doing now? The answer seemed to be the one given to the court when this matter came up, that Hart had become Transport House's front-man in Newham and was taking his orders directly from Underhill. So we still had not got rid of Transport House. With the Marxists beaten in the election, Transport House immediately turned to the newly elected secretary, Hart, and sought to control the Party through him. He was in very frequent contact with them. Again the question arises: what on earth was Transport

House up to, interfering in the affairs of this constituency party? *The Transport House and Regional Office bureaucracy had clearly become the permanent and active allies of the Newham Marxists.*

Hart announced to the meeting of the officers that he saw himself as the constitutional adviser to the Newham Party. He banned Julian from the meeting because he was not an officer. There was no constitutional provision for officers' meetings — it was invented to by-pass Julian and me.

So we had a fine situation in prospect — Hart running the local party but taking his orders from Underhill who was taking his orders from the National Executive Committee which was run by the Lestor—Heffer—Atkinson—Allaun—Mikardo faction which was backing Andy Bevan and the other Newham Marxists. We might as well not have bothered with the election!

We had to resolve the question of tactics immediately. It would be hopeless for the Moderates' position if meetings were called invalidly after we had made so much fuss about this. Nothing would discredit us more. Also, from a tactical point of view, if Hart called meetings as and when he pleased and we could not get our people to turn out, the Marxists would try to force our officers to resign through 'No Confidence' motions. I wanted to make sure that the Party was run properly and strictly according to the Rules. We had to be whiter than white because so many were waiting to trip us up. Otherwise Hart could, if he chose to, deliberately call an invalid meeting and provide the NEC with an excuse for suspending the Party. They were continually dropping hints to the Press that suspension was imminent and they were still smarting from their humiliating defeat in court.

So when I heard that Hart had called a couple of meetings in August (when the Party does not meet anyway) I decided we had to have an immediate showdown. I told Julian to ask Ray Massey to tell Hart to call the meetings off and remonstrate with him for acting unilaterally and calling meetings without the permission of the Chairman. Massey said he would, but reported that Hart had said the meetings should go ahead. Hart added that he would not talk to either Julian or me on the subject. 'Very well,' I said to Julian 'we must ask Massey to issue notices cancelling the meetings and pointing out that Hart did not have the authority to call them.

Julian went to see Massey and late at night he rang me up to tell me that Massey had shouted at him and virtually flung him out. When I phoned Massey the following day he ranted on about 'Lewis' instead of talking about 'Julian' as he usually did. I told Massey that in my view he was honour-bound to cancel these meetings and that I explicitly advised it as a vital measure if Hart, who had voted for Bevan's motion to adjourn, were not to succeed in both disgracing us with invalid meetings and dislodging us through Marxist-packed meetings. I reminded him of the undertaking he had given, to work together with the Moderates on our agreed strategy. When he announced that he refused to cancel the meetings and had decided to back Hart I thought back to his eagerness to give that undertaking. He had been the first, the quickest, and the most enthusiastic. Now his former behaviour appeared in a different light. Julian remembered his question to him when they first met: 'What's in it for you?' We remembered his characteristic phrases 'To be quite frank ... To be honest with you ....'

When this matter was raised in later court hearings the judges asked why Massey had defected. Was he not a Moderate? Massey said that he had disagreed with us and agreed with Hart. This was absurd. Hart had consistently opposed legal action from the start (I think he genuinely disapproved of it) but Massey had been a plaintiff against Lugg and Clark and also in July against Underhill. Massey said that he was not 'going to be told what to do'. This also was absurd, when he had given an undertaking quite voluntarily, as had most of the other candidates, to follow the common strategy for beating the left. If he did not like it he did not have to agree to it. He was elected on the basis of that undertaking.

Why had Massey turned against us? Ambition no doubt played a part. He had become Chairman, and perhaps he calculated that he no longer needed us. He wanted to get on the Council, and Jack Hart as Council Leader might have seemed a better star to hitch his wagon to now that he had gone so far with us. The judges were also told, in answer to the question of why Massey had turned against us, that Ray Massey lived in a council flat and was very anxious to move into a council house, and that Hart as

Council Leader had great influence in such matters. Hart
countered this by swearing that, though he had met Massey
and discussed this point with him, he emphatically denied
any wrong-doing or showing any special favours and had
merely helped Massey as any good Councillor would help
any member of the public who approached him. This had
all been occurring, we discovered afterwards, in August
1977. If Massey had alienated Hart he might have thought
this would affect his chances of a council house, and our
contention to the court was that this was the main reason
for Massey's defection. All the other Moderates were disgusted with him.

It was quite clear that Massey was not going to cross Hart.
In these circumstances the only thing to do was to ask him to
resign. When it became clear that ordinary persuasion would
not work I telephoned him and pointed out that, as he had
broken the terms of the agreement whereby Julian had
indemnified him in respect of the *Falvey* case and the *Van
Haeftan* case (against Underhill), the indemnity no longer
held and his liability for costs was not covered. I offered to
talk to Julian and persuade him to reinstate the indemnity
provided Massey put his resignation letter in by first post
the next morning. I told him to send one copy to Eddie Lee,
the Vice-Chairman, one to Hart, the Secretary, and one to
me. In reality he was in little danger of having to pay costs,
since we had won the *Falvey* case and Underhill would
certainly have waived costs in the *Van Haeftan* case.
However, the mind that calculated the difference between a
council house and a council flat was very much alive to the
possibility of having to pay out any money, and I was
gratified to receive, post-haste, the resignation letter.

If Massey stayed on as Chairman and voted with Hart and
the Marxists then the score would be 13:13 on the Executive
Committee with Massey having the casting vote. But if he
resigned it was 13:12 to us. I could see we were going to be
in for a battle like a tough endgame in chess where every
pawn is worth its weight in gold.

Soon afterwards Julian came up to visit me in Oxford. He
brought the news that Massey had 'withdrawn' his resignation
and that Hart had returned his resignation letter.

Mr Milsom was perhaps the most angry of all at Massey's
betrayal: he had not liked the look of Massey to start with.

'How can he withdraw his resignation? I've never heard of such rubbish,' said Mr Milsom. 'How are we going to nail him?' I replied that if the worst came to the worst we would have to get an Injunction against Massey to keep him out of the Chair, but perhaps he would see reason. We agreed that the problem appeared to be that Massey had some intellectual difficulty with the concept of finality inherent in his resignation.

Mr Milsom wanted to write to him to spell out the consequences of resignation at a simple level of comprehensibility. His letter was a gem of simplicity:

Dear Ray, What on earth is your game? ... You were dithering around for a fortnight before finally handing in your resignation, but now you've gone you are wasting everyone's time by trying to undo what's already been done. I came into this thing to hammer the left — but if you get up to the same tricks I'll hammer you too.... 'Can't you grasp the simple fact that once you have resigned YOU HAVE RESIGNED, and since you *have* resigned, that's it, that's your lot. Finis. The End. Caput. And thank God for that! Goodbye!

The letter asked Massey for an undertaking that he would not attempt to take the chair and indicated that it would be a matter for the solicitors if he persisted in trying to act as Chairman. It ended:

I'm damned if I'm going to spend my leisure time turning out for hours at a time to meetings and then find out later that it's all been wasted because your presence messed up the legalities of them, to say nothing of the botch-up this would make of the Party's affairs. I hope I have made myself clear.

Well, this was a sordid unhappy incident; but looking back on it I do not really see how we could have acted differently. Perhaps it was not very nice to push Massey into resigning in the way I did but I think it was the right thing to do. He had defected completely. It was not simply that he backed Hart, he had completely changed allegiance. Indeed in his own ward, Kensington, he started to vote *with* the Marxists

against the Moderates and he threw in his lot with them
completely. He continued to claim he was Chairman and was
going to seize the chair physically.

The Constitutional position was tricky because there were
two Vice-Chairmen, Lee and Pagett. When Massey had first
resigned Hart had hoped to turn Pagett into a puppet and had
written to him inviting him to take over. But when Pagett
wrote back indicating that, unlike Massey, he intended to
honour his word, then Hart returned Massey's resignation
letter and persuaded him to stay on. All this time Hart was in
close touch with Transport House.

When Milsom brought a High Court action against Massey
to prevent him taking the chair (if he did our meetings would
become invalid because he was no longer legally the Chairman) and against Hart, for treating Massey as the Chairman,
Transport House put their solicitors in to support them and
guaranteed all their costs. This turned the issue into a major
battle. By what right was Transport House taking sides again
and spending Party money to help them to manipulate things
in favour of the Newham Marxists? The Massey problem
would never have arisen if Hart had not defied the Moderate
majority by pushing Massey into staying. The truth is ines-
capable: Hart was acting in accordance with the wishes of
Transport House, and Transport House was desperately de-
voting time and money to destroy us politically. They
wanted to crush us because we were the only people who had
ever beaten the Marxist infiltrators, and Transport House
had, out of fear and in some cases out of sympathy, thrown
in its lot with the extreme left of the Labour Party. Hart and
Massey were being used by Transport House in an attempt
to destroy our position so that the Moderate group would
crumble and the Marxists could be reinstated. Massey
followed Hart, Hart followed Transport House, Transport
House followed the extreme left-wing majority faction on the
NEC which backed Bevan and the Newham Marxists; and
Massey now voted *with* the Newham Marxists, so the circle
was complete.

The Labour Party's solicitors now wrote to inform me that
Massey was withdrawing from the action against Underhill.
It struck me as extraordinary that the Labour Party's
solicitors should agree to represent Massey in the *Milsom*
case at a time when Massey was still a plaintiff, against their

client, Reg Underhill, in the *Van Haeftan* case and that the Labour Party solicitors should write to inform us that Massey was now withdrawing from the *Van Haeftan* case.

The most disturbing aspect of this episode, though, was that a number of the Labour bureaucrats appeared to think that they had the right to use huge sums of money from the Party's coffers to support one side in an internal Labour Party battle against another.

An Injunction was obtained against Massey. The judge accepted that he had resigned. I had written a memorandum on different types of resignation and this was what was called a categorical resignation which was unilateral and took effect whether or not it was accepted. With Massey out of the way, would the elected Moderates now be permitted to get on with running the local Party without further attempts by Transport House to unseat them? I knew that Transport House was planning its next offensive, which was to suspend the Party when some trumped-up excuse could be found. So we decided to start to organise resistance. We now had to deal with Transport House, the National Executive Committee, the Newham Marxists, and Hart.

A meeting of the Executive Committee was due to be held on 8 September 1977. I had worked out the terms of a series of motions designed to curb Hart, to resist the National Executive Committee, and to put a stop to Marxist fiddles. They included provision to set up a fighting fund to defend local party autonomy from NEC and Transport House interference and a series of investigations into areas where the Marxists had cheated or were suspected of having cheated. There was also a motion of censure against Hart, not calling for his resignation but instructing him not to usurp the powers of the Party committees again and attempt to run the Party as a one-man show. Eddie Lee took the Chair and did rather well, but the meeting was subjected to a prolonged filibuster by the Marxists and Hart. A Labour bureaucrat, Bill Jones, the Regional Officer, came down and had plenty to say for himself. Jones kept on intervening on the side of the left — just as a spectator might invade the field and start to join in the game to assist one of the sides. He talked as though he was the embodiment of the Labour Party and his word was law. I rather liked Bill Jones as a personality but he was another one of those 'moderates', like Underhill, who saw which way the wind was blowing, buckled under, and became enthusiastic in supporting the new status quo within the Party. These people are much more help to the Marxists than a Marxist could ever be.

The filibuster prevented the EC from carrying out any business whatever until the meeting had to close at 10.00 pm. We had a majority but not the necessary 2/3 majority to suspend standing orders and continue past 10.00 pm. So these two hours were wasted with people saying the equivalent of 'Rhubarb, Rhubarb'.

It was like climbing a mountain. Everything the elected Moderates attempted to do was opposed *a l'outrance.* The filibuster is a well-known tactic. I do not regard it as an illegitimate one in the same way that many of the Marxists methods were, but it indicated that they were not going to let anything go. I advised that a special meeting of the Executive Committee should be called, that the 21 motions should be the only items of business for it, and that in view of the filibuster all 21 motions should be composited into a single one.

The special EC meeting was called for 21 September 1977. I decided to attend it to make sure that the local Moderates were not intimidated or bamboozled and to ensure there were no procedural irregularities which could be used to overturn the decisions made by the meeting. Our people were in very good shape. Andy Bevan and Tom Jenkins objected to my being invited to attend it but the meeting voted to admit me. Bevan and Jenkins then walked out of the meeting leaving just one of their supporters to monitor it. Seeing we were in a majority they gave up and left us to it. And what a pleasant meeting we had without them! Every courtesy was extended to the solitary representative they had left. No attempt was made to harrass or humiliate him or interrupt him or cut him short when he spoke against the motions. He was among civilised people. How different it would have been to be a solitary Moderate among a bunch of Marxists. The meeting went like clockwork, as a good Labour Party meeting should, without raucous voices, threats, jeering and bitter rows. I was told by a couple of the old stalwarts present that it was like it used to be in Newham before the Marxists had come in and spoilt everything.

This meeting passed the 21 motions on a composite, appointed Julian as Party Steward and myself as the Party's Constitutional Adviser (two posts which I had considered necessary in the circumstances of Newham at this time) and postponed an invalid General Management Committee meeting that Hart had taken it upon himself to call for 28 September 1977. The EC was furious at Hart's action because Hart had not informed all GMC members of the meeting; he had not provided an up-to-date list of GMC delegates so no one knew who was eligible to attend; he had made no arrangements for stewarding the meeting; he gave insufficient notice; and there were various other irregularities. The meeting was therefore invalid and it would reflect badly on the new Moderate regime to hold an invalid meeting after complaining when the Marxists had done so. The Moderates would be blamed for Hart's unilateral act. Hart must have known he was breaking the Rules. I wonder why he called the meeting in that way?

The Moderates who attended that EC meeting were very determined people. John Pagett was suffering from flu but he struggled on with the meeting. A new mood of determination had set in. We had very good people on that EC and the Marxists were not going to find it easy to brush them aside. In a secret ballot they all voted for all the motions. Hart was completely isolated among the Moderates: not one of them supported him. In a secret ballot they all voted to censure him. We had no hold over them at all. We had no carrots to tempt them with, no sticks to beat them with, and no means of even knowing who it was if someone defected in a secret ballot. Only the invisible strands of honour and integrity and an unselfish concern for democracy held these people together. We had twelve very good people. The thirteenth was Sylvia Jones whom I was very wary of.

Underhill intervened once again with a long detailed attack on the 21 motions saying that they should not have been passed and that the Executive Committee had no right to consider them. Underhill was wrong constitutionally. He kept telling the Newham Party what the constitution required and his interpretations were usually wrong. It made a farce of local Party democracy when the Labour Party's National Agent intervened weekly to tell the Party what motions it could pass and what ones it could not. He certainly did not do that for any Marxist-run constituencies. What a sharp contrast between this detailed concern with the Party's affairs and the blind eye that Transport House had turned towards the gross irregularities when the Marxists were in control in 1975 and 1976.

One of the 21 motions praised Newham South 'for its stand against Marxist infiltrators'. The Newham South Labour Party had expelled four extreme left-wingers from membership because they had caused disruption, broken Party rules and infiltrated the Party and conspired to take it over. The four immediately responded with legal action; and *Transport House and the NEC supported them to the hilt.* One Transport House official was asked why Transport House had condemned Newham North-East Moderates for taking legal action and had paid for the Marxists' legal costs against them, but had not criticised the Newham South Marxists for taking legal action against Newham South Moderates and had refused to contribute one penny towards the Moderates' costs. He lamely replied, 'Individuals are free to take legal action. We can't stop them.' Of course not, but the contrast between Newham South and Newham North-East is not to be explained by an objection to legal action on principle. The principle here is 'Marxist Legal Action, Good: Moderate Legal Action, Bad.'

On 28 September 1977 the Newham South Labour Party held a GMC meeting to consider the question of the expulsions. John Keys (head of the London Regional Office, a Labour bureaucrat ranking below Underhill but above Bill Jones) attended. In an affidavit, Dora Lovejoy, one of the most vigorous fighting Moderates in the whole of Newham and a delightful woman, said:

> John Keys told this meeting of Newham South General Committee that 'he personally didn't care one way or the other if we took these people back in or not. But he was directed to say that, if we did not, the National Executive Committee would expel every member of Newham South from the Labour Party.' He said that 'we' (meaning thereby the NEC) would close the whole of Newham South down, and would take it over and start from the beginning again.' He added, apparently by way of an incentive, the following: 'You could take them back now.

Perhaps next week' (that is, after the Party Conference at which the National Executive Committee is elected) 'we will have another NEC, and then you would be able to expel them again.'

Of course it is not only in Newham that the Labour bureaucrats have been aiding and abetting the left (which includes Marxist infiltrators). The Membership Secretary of a ward in Islington North constituency, John Barnes, gave an affidavit in our case in January 1978 in which he swore:

In North Islington we too have been suffering from a concerted campaign by Trotskyite Communists and their associates to capture control of the local Labour Party ... This campaign has involved abuse of Party positions, the bending and breaking of Party Rules and procedures, refusal to keep order at meetings or to obey rulings from the Chair, and interminable procedural delays by the far-left to sabotage business whenever the Moderates are in a majority ... From what I know of the events in Newham North-East the state of affairs there is a mirror-image of what has been happening in Islington North ... The most significant difference in the two cases is, however, that in Islington North it is the Far-Left which has taken legal action, and not the Moderates, and this has been done without so much as a murmur of disapproval from the National Executive Committee .... I regret to say that the role of the National Executive Committee in all this, so far as it relates to my own constituency, leaves very much to be desired. It has done nothing to prevent the systematic harassment and attempted takeover by the extremists, but has been quick to intervene whenever the Moderates (who have not yet lost control) take steps to try to protect themselves.

Mr Barnes added that the Islington North Party had been threatened with suspension by Bill Jones and concluded:

There is no doubt at all in my mind that the National Executive Committee is strongly in favour of the attempt by militants to capture the North Islington Constituency Labour Party, and is prepared to use such purported powers as suspension, reorganisation, and disaffiliation to prevent us, as Moderates, from mounting an effective defence against it.

Hart refused to notify the GMC delegates that the EC had decided to postpone the GMC meeting because it had been improperly convened and to recall it as soon as the irregularities had been put right. This would probably be about three weeks later. John Pagett, as Vice-Chairman, therefore sent a note to all delegates informing them that the meeting was postponed and explaining why the EC had taken this decision. Hart in turn sent out a letter to all GMC delegates informing them that the meeting *would* take place and that he was going to ignore the EC's decision.

Why did Hart decide to defy the EC? He knew that by provoking this confrontation he was surely going to bring about more legal action. Yet he went blithely ahead, completely unperturbed about the thousands of pounds for which he was putting himself at risk. This would have been very uncharacteristic behaviour. Later we discovered he had not taken any risk. Transport House had guaranteed all his costs and put the case into the hands of the Labour Party solicitors. So the Labour Party bureaucrats were putting Hart up to it again and throwing thousands of pounds of Labour Party money behind him. Their desperation to finish off the Newham Moderates had reached unprecedented levels. Once again we were put on the defensive by an onslaught from the Central Labour Party bureaucrats. Transport House had even gone to the lengths of giving Hart the Labour Party solicitors and paying all his costs in a private libel action that Julian had brought against him.

We were now in a very tricky situation. Hart had insisted on pressing ahead with a patently illegal meeting. Transport House was behind him. So, of course, were the Newham Marxists. Motions were tabled to 'elect' a new Chairman. This was unconstitutional for a start. When the Chairman dies or resigns the Vice-Chairmen take over; that is what Vice-Chairmen are for. It would be absurd, as well as unconstitutional, if some poorly-attended, unrepresentative meeting could install a new Chairman perhaps of the opposite political persuasion to the rest of the officers who had been elected at the well-attended Annual Meeting. There were also motions down to sack the Vice-Presidents (who had only been in office for six weeks) and to remove a number of Moderates from the Council Panel.

So it had to be legal action once again. Mr Milsom was adamant that he wished to bring a case to stop this illegal meeting and, of course, to stop the decisions it would have taken. We knew that most of the Moderates would not turn up. Some had not even been informed of it in the first place, others had been informed of it too late to attend, and, of course, all had been told that the meeting was off. All that would take place would be a gathering of the Marxist rump calling itself a meeting of the General Management Committee and attempting to exercise that Committee's powers, and also attempting to exercise some powers that even a proper Committee meeting did not have. An Injunction was applied for and obtained. I worked out the basis of the legal case and did most of the legal work on it. Unfortunately, however, I was not able to be in court as I was tied up in Oxford teaching.

The Injunction was obtained without difficulty from Mr Justice Lawson. Mr Milsom's solicitor and his assistant, from a firm in Romford (the biggest firm in East London), filled in the details of the Injunction and gave the Injunction over to their usual process server. The Injunction named Hart and various prominent leftists who were cooperating with him in organising the meeting. They were Andy Bevan, Tom Jenkins, Owen Ashworth, and John Rowse.

I arrived outside the Labour Hall shortly before 8.00 pm on 28 September 1977, having hurried there straight from Oxford after finishing my teaching. I was dismayed to find that the meeting was taking place after all. What had happened about the Injunction? I tried to enter but there were several Marxists guarding the door which they slammed shut and locked against me. Several Moderates were locked out. Then after a while Julian came down and also Mr Milsom and a Moderate trade union delegate, Mr Champion. They explained that the Injunction had not been served. We went to phone the solicitor immediately at his home to contact the process server. What had happened, apparently, was that the Marxists had had someone posted at the Courts in the Strand and as soon as they heard about the Injunction they had all gone to ground. The process server had called on each

of the defendants twice at their homes and none of them
were to be found. At one address the people lied and said
it was not the address of the person concerned. The Marxists
had decided to defy any Injunction, evade service of it, and
use force to exclude anyone attempting to serve an
Injunction or in any way interfering with their purposes.
They had posted guards on the doors. Julian had been physically excluded from the meeting until there had been a vote
to 'elect' a Chairman. Andy Bevan was 'elected'. The meeting
consisted of all 40 Marxists and probably one or two extras
who should not have been there, Hart and a few wets, and
about 8 or 10 Moderates who had gone along as observers.

Most of the Moderates boycotted the meeting. For those
who attended it it was a terrifying ordeal. Some of the
Moderates wanted to leave but as one said 'did not think she
would be allowed to'. The doors were locked, bolted and
guarded. The Marxists themselves had broken into the
premises to open them up to start the illegal meeting. The
Moderates present were too terrified to speak against the
Marxist proposals for they were in no doubt they would have
been beaten up if they had. The meeting continued in this
vein for nearly an hour and a half, the time it took the
solicitor to contact the process server and the process server
to return with the Injunction. When he arrived and saw the
Marxists guarding the doors and heard what happened, he
was too frightened to serve the Injunction. He pushed it into
our hands, ran to his car and drove off rapidly. I told Mr
Milsom, Mr Champion and Julian how to serve the Injunction
and said that I would attend to assist them.

We knew that nothing short of a sledgehammer and para-
troopers would get us through the front door, which was
well and truly secured and guarded by a contingent of
Marxist thugs. However, there was another way in, up the
fire-escape at the back and then through a door into the back
of the hall. That would bring us to within a few yards of the
Chairman's table. The meeting sat facing that table with its
back towards the windows that looked out over the High
Street and from which the Marxist look-outs had been
watching us.

Julian had informed the meeting of the Injunction but he
had been shouted down and Andy Bevan had said the
meeting would ignore the Injunction. They were from this

moment onward in contempt of court. The meeting had been opened by Bill Jones. What was this supposedly impartial national Labour Party official doing opening an illegal meeting in Newham? The whole thing was, of course, a put-up job by Transport House.

It was now 9.20 pm and time to serve the Injunction. We tiptoed up the back-stairs, Julian very quietly turned the key in the lock and we stealthily entered through the first door. A few paces away was the second door, which was not locked. This exit was of course, hardly ever used by anyone. We entered quietly and briskly and with a few paces we had reached the Chairman's table. There was Andy Bevan in the middle, Hart on one side of him, and Bill Jones on the other. Our entry was swift and silent. The Marxist guards had relaxed their vigil because, of course, it was now nearly an hour and a half since the meeting had started. The Injunction was served on Andy Bevan. He held it aloft and with a grand and exaggerated gesture ripped it in two and tossed it over his shoulder.

At this point there was a mass attack on the four of us by about twenty of the Marxists. They were vicious — kicking and punching. Chairs were sent flying. One person tried to pick up a chair to use against us and was only restrained by the fact that his chair was connected to all the others in his row. Bevan sat there smiling, though any proper Chairman would have tried to stop the attack and restore order. Bill Jones and Hart did nothing to intervene either. I was forced out through the back entrance and nearly knocked down the stairs. From inside the hall I could hear some terrible thuds and thumps and bangs. I told Dora Lovejoy to call the police as we had been violently assaulted and the three still inside were in danger. I then went up the stairs again to try to assist them, but the Marxists who had pushed me out had locked the door against me.

In a matter of minutes about five squad cars with sirens going à la Kojak had screeched their way round to the Labour Hall. By this time Julian, Mr Milsom, and Mr Champion had been ejected through the front entrance and joined us and a large contingent of police on the pavement of the High Street. We looked up and saw the Marxist look-outs staring down on us. The Marxists, in defiance of the Injunction, had continued with the meeting. After I had

explained the position to the police they decided to enter.
Mr Champion had been badly kicked and was limping about
most uncomfortably and we were all the worse for the treatment we had suffered. Mr Milsom, Mr Champion and Julian
were members of the GMC so by what right they were
forcibly ejected from the meeting I do not know. One of the
people ejecting Julian told the *Newham Recorder*: 'He was
lucky. If we hadn't got him out he would have been torn
limb from limb.' The police ascended the back stairs and
banged on the outer door — still locked.

The Marxists inside hurried on with the meeting racing
through the agenda faster and faster as the knocking became
louder and more persistent. After knocking for over five
minutes the police broke the door down and entered.
Immediately they did so the meeting ended and everyone
rushed to get out. The first man to try to rush out past us
was none other than Jack Hart who said, 'Please let me pass.
This has nothing to do with me'. Mr Milsom shot his arm
out and said, 'This little man isn't going anywhere. He's in
it up to his neck!' We all entered the main hall. Mr Champion
went to identify his main attacker but the person concerned
was shielded by a large group of Marxists and the policeman
said later that he had to withdraw because it would have
provoked a fight to try to arrest him under those
circumstances. The police did not want to procecute; we
were after all in the East End, the territory of the Krays,
where the threshold of violence required to promote police
action is very high. They said that as no one had bled it was
a case of assault rather than actual bodily harm — though
what one normally understands as bodily harm had certainly
been done — and it was not their policy to prosecute assault
cases.

It had been a very hectic couple of hours:

7.45 pm Hart meets Andy Bevan outside the Labour Hall;
they confer, and the two with several others
disappear down the side alley leading to the back
entrance.

7.50 pm The door to the main hall is kicked open by the
Marxists breaking the padlocks. (Mr Bament objects
to this act of vandalism and a Marxist tells him
'Never mind. The doors were weak anyway!')

7.57 pm The meeting starts. It is opened by Bill Jones.

8.01 pm Andy Bevan is installed as Chairman.

8.05 pm Julian informs all present of the High Court Injunction.

9.15 pm The process server arrives with the Injunction.

9.20 pm We serve the Injunction and are attacked.

9.40 pm Police have to break in to the premises whereupon the meeting disbands.

We went back into court on 29 September and Mr Milsom's counsel informed Mr Justice Lawson of the fate of his Injunction — which he was not too pleased to hear! He granted another couple of Injunctions forbidding various persons from acting on the basis of motions carried out at the illegal meeting.

Soon after this I wrote to Mr Sam Silkin, the Attorney-General, asking him to take action in respect of the defiance of the High Court Injunction and the assults on process servers serving the Injunction and the Defendants. Mr Milsom's solicitors wrote a short note agreeing with my letter and requesting action. Silkin ignored my letter completely at first (though he replied to solicitors who endorsed my complaint). He also refused to discuss the matter. Finally, when he was pressed, a letter was sent back saying that the Attorney-General did not think it appropriate for himself to take action. No reasons were given. He was busy at this time with the Labour Party Conference. When I wrote to him I hardly thought it likely that he would prosecute the National Youth Officer of the Labour Party, Andy Bevan. Silkin's previous record in the *Gouriet* case and on civil liberties was hardly one to inspire confidence and he is arguably the worst Attorney-General this century.

The 1977 Labour Conference had met from 3 to 7 October and had approved massive changes in the Rules for Constituency Labour Parties. These changes, the most important in the Labour Party's history, were brought about by our Newham campaign. The official NEC report on the 1977 Annual Conference under the heading 'Newham North East Constituency Labour Party and Amendments to the Rules for Constituency Labour Parties' (p 9) gives a history (rather tendentious in places) of the legal actions in 1977. It claims that 'the normal annual meeting was

convened for 23 February 1977, in accordance with the
rules of the constituency Labour Party,' which is nonsense.
It was *not* in accordance with the rules. The report makes
no mention of the fact that only two days' notice was
given. With distortions and omissions such as these one
wonders whether ordinary Labour Party members have a
clue what is going on in their Party. They are fed this 'official
misinformation' and they believe it because they have no way
of knowing what rubbish it is. They are at the mercy of their
paid administrative servants, the Labour bureaucrats, who
manipulate them ceaselessly.

Surprisingly, the embarrassing motion passed concerning
the July meeting was printed in full: 'That in view of the
continued existence of the dispute within the Newham
North-East Constituency Labour Party, this Committee
does not believe that a useful purpose would be served by
having the Annual Meeting ....' The NEC recommended widespread Rule changes to the Annual Conference, which
rubber-stamped them. The report said that the reason for
these changes was to strengthen and clarify the Rules to
prevent legal actions challenging them, as had been done
over the trade union delegate-entitlements in the *Falvey* case.
In actual fact the rule changes were cunningly designed in
such a way that they would promote Marxist takeovers in
constituency Labour Parties. It was made easier to censure
and remove officers and delegates, (thus approaching the
'recall'). The NEC was given the power to impose a
Parliamentary Candidate on a local constituency Party without even consulting it (this was done so that, if we retained
control, the NEC could impose a left-wing candidate on the
Party, and could do the same wherever a similar situation
arose). The NEC was also given powers to seize the properties
and assets of Parties that were dissolved, enabling them to
threaten local constituency parties with expropriation. These
powers were to be exercised by a hopelessly undemocratic
and unrepresentative NEC which was not directly elected by
anyone but picked by half-a-dozen trade union bosses who
had been elected by around 10 per cent of their own
memberships (perhaps for life) and by left-wing constituency
activists with political views similar to those of the Newham
Marxists.

On 6 October there was a court hearing in the two cases

that Mr Milsom had brought. One was the Chairmanship action against Massey and Hart and the other was the invalid 28 September meeting action against Hart and a number of Newham leftists. Mr Justice Forbes, looking very sprightly and sharp, was the judge. He had evidently read the affidavits very carefully. Our barrister did not need to say anything and he hardly spoke a word. The judge turned to the defence counsel who was the Labour Party's regular barrister and made him squirm by a series of devastating questions. 'The defendants did not know the Injunction had been granted,' said the barrister at one point. The judge robustly replied, 'I don't believe a word of it. Are you trying to tell me that an Injunction was granted before 4.00 o'clock and four hours later nobody in Newham knew about it when the process server had called on five addresses a couple of times and people who knew of the Injunction had talked to their friends and acquaintances. Such news travels by the grapevine.'

'The Chairman was elected unanimously at this meeting, so this proves that all the Newham Party members were united and wanted him,' said the defence lawyer. 'Sounds like a Soviet election to me,' snapped the judge. The judge then ripped his legal arguments to shreds, pointed out a series of factual errors, and no matter how much the defence counsel twisted and turned he remorselessly pinned him down. The judge's performance was outstanding; he left the Labour lawyers gasping and I saw Lord Milner, the Labour Party solicitor, visibly slump down further and further in his chair as the case proceeded. Mr Justice Forbes had really got the measure of the Newham Marxists and their tricks and he saw straight through them at once. He showed how a sharp, tough-minded and intelligent man with a grasp of political realities can get on top of a problem like this in a very short time. After all the pussy-footing and euphemisms we had been plagued with it was a real delight to sit back and watch this judge shred their case to pieces in such a devastating fashion that at the end the barrister was virtually left speechless. I wish it could have been recorded. I have never seen such an embarrassing exposure of our political opponents. The judge, without prompting, continued the Injunctions, widened the Injunction against Massey who, he said, had broken his undertaking to the Court, and delivered an excellent and well-reasoned judgement which upheld all the legal points I had raised and even a couple which I had not thought of.

As we walked out of the Court we were very happy that at last someone had come down fully on our side. Mr Justice Kerr and Mr Justice Caulfield and Mr Justice Lawson and Lord Justice Shaw and Lord Denning's court had each upheld the legal arguments I had put forward but they had done so on technical grounds. They had either not fully grasped or not wished to comment upon the perfidious and unsavoury nature of the Marxists and their allies whom we were fighting against. It was good to find that someone at least had shown he was fully aware of this.

Sylvia Jones resigned when Prentice joined the Conservative Party on 8 October. When she had been put up for office on our ticket I had vetoed her for Vice-President and only very reluctantly permitted her to stand as Assistant Secretary when Julian said she had promised that she would not resign under any circumstances. This was important because constitutionally no EC member could be replaced. So it was like a game of football without substitutes. Fortunately Sylvia's resignation, which could have left us in the lurch, was counter-balanced by one of those fortunate little incidents which happen too infrequently. One of the leftist women had been made pregnant and had resigned, and when one of the leftists, Alan Howarth, tried to come in to replace her as the ward delegate on the EC I was able to stop him because it was unconstitutional. Still it was worrying the way our EC people had been going down. The EC was contracting rapidly in size: first Massey, then the pregnant woman, then Sylvia Jones had gone off in the space of about six weeks. When I thought of our precarious EC position with its one-vote lead, before going to bed at night I used to hum to myself the little rhyme:

Ten green bottles hanging on a wall
Ten green bottles hanging on a wall
And if one green bottle should accidentally fall
There'd be nine green bottles hanging on the wall.
Nine green bottles ... etc.

Eddie Lee was a bottle that had been teetering on the edge. For personal reasons he had almost resigned on several occasions and once gone as far as writing out a resignation letter. Fortunately Julian managed to persuade him to stay, but we were hanging on by the skin of our teeth.

However, by mid-October we were thoroughly on top of the situation. Hart had been countered and his powers curbed. Massey had been put out of the way for good and held down by an Injunction which prevented him occupying the chair before the next Annual Meeting. The Executive Committee was firmly in control of the convening of GMC meetings and the day-to-day running of the Party and we had a 12:11 majority on it. Even if one of our people was missing we still had the casting vote of one of the Vice-Chairmen, Eddie Lee or John Pagett, to fall back on. One Marxist appeared to have moved out of the area, so we probably had a permanent 2-vote lead in fact. We had got down to the real flint. All the mud and rubbish had been sloughed off — Massey had gone, Prentice and his personal followers had gone, Hart had gone, all the faint hearts and bleeding hearts, the wets and sentimentalists, the feeble-minded and the wiseacres, the frauds, the opportunists and the time-servers, all these worthless specimens had either fled or slunk over to the opposing camp. We were left only with those who had the mark of quality stamped indelibly upon them. And in Kant's phrase, they were shining like a jewel in its own light.

Our twelve people on the Executive Committee belonged to that rare breed, the public-spirited Moderate activist. They had been through thick and thin with us. None of them was after anything for himself. All were motivated by a desire to see democracy prevail over its enemies. Some were old stalwarts who had been in the local Party for forty years or more like Councillor Wally Hurford, Daisy Turner, and Bert Simpson. Some were veterans of the Prentice resistance who had swung solidly behind us, like Alec Kellaway. One, of course, was Julian Lewis himself who had worked enormously hard in unpleasant and frustrating circumstances. Some, like Patrick Milsom, Eddie Lee, John Pagett and Ken Kilsby were the new generation, the people in whose capable hands the Party would rest when our task of removing the Marxists was complete. And I must not forget my old favourite, Freddie Bament, who never missed a meeting. They were all authentic loyal Labour Party members, but they recognised that democracy was even more important than the Labour Party, and that the Marxists spelt death to democracy.

Now that it was clear that we could not be toppled from within, it became more likely than ever that the National Executive Committee would try to remove us and displace the Moderates by administrative action. Just before the National Conference, the NEC had resolved to set up an 'Inquiry' into the Newham North-East Party. We knew what this meant. It was to be the Inquisition that preceded the burning at the stake.

It is important to remember the lengths to which our opponents had gone to remove us and reinstate the Marxists. First cheating had been tried. Then the election had been cancelled. Then Hart was used as a Trojan Horse. Then Massey had been induced to change sides and support the Marxists. Then an attempt had been made to install Andy Bevan as Chairman. Finally the Marxists had resorted to terror to control meetings, had defied a High Court Injunction, torn it up, attacked the process servers, and locked the police out. But as Gladstone once said, in a famous phrase, 'The resources of civilisation are not yet exhausted.' All these vicious and underhand challenges had been surmounted and defeated. We were not going to back down however great the assault upon us. Having got into the driving-seat of the Party we were determined to stay there and complete the journey. Bits were dropping off it, other vehicles were trying to bash into us and knock us off the road, some of the passengers had fallen out as we went along, and we had nearly gone over the precipice a couple of times; but we kept the accelerator down, and if we lost our tyres we were going to keep driving on our rims.

We were not going to be intimidated. If necessary, I was prepared to hold a GMC meeting in the Labour Hall with myself sitting beside the Chairman, and Julian directing the stewards. If any Marxist thugs interrupted the proceedings or threatened anyone they would be removed. The Transport House commissars would be excluded, and if necessary a hundred policemen would be hired as stewards, as at a football match, to protect the Moderates against the Marxists, who were like the Nazis in the German Reichstag in the 1930s. The Marxists were beginning to be disheartened as they realised that we had got the upper-hand over them.

They saw that, against all the odds, they were being beaten.

But then disaster struck. Mr Milsom had decided to bring contempt of court proceedings himself, and we agreed with this decision. He had been shocked and outraged by threats by one of the Marxists at the meeting to injure his wife and children, who had taken no part whatever in the Labour Party. He was also very angry that Mr Champion, who had volunteered to help serve the Injunction but knew nothing about it and had never been involved in any of the legal action, had been hurt and badly bruised by the cowardly and vicious Marxist attack on him. We were all sorry about Mr Champion and we felt a bit guilty that he had become involved, though we had not expected the attack. We were all particularly struck by the fact that the whole thing had been premeditated and prearranged and was not a spontaneous outburst of violence. But I suppose the two most important reasons were that if no action was taken to enforce the Injunction, then any future Injunctions would be mere scraps of paper, and that as the Marxists had now clearly resolved on a policy of trying to control meetings by force, threatening delegates, deciding who could come in and who could not, physically ejecting Moderate delegates and by a show of physical violence frightening people off from coming to meetings — this had to be stamped on immediately before it escalated to the point where someone was seriously injured, as could have happened on 28 September 1977.

Of course, we did not want to manufacture martyrs for the Marxists. We did not expect them to be sent to prison and we intended to make a plea for clemency if the judge indicated he was going to put them away for more than a few days — not that they did not deserve to go to prison, but in order not to make martyrs out of them. Our main concern was to deter. Bevan had incited people to ignore the February Injunction. We had taken no action then. In September his conduct was even worse. It is unfortunate that the only legal procedure that can be taken to enforce an Injunction is one called 'a motion of committal to prison for contempt of court'. The Marxists said that we 'wanted' to put them in prison but this is the standard procedure, indeed it is the only procedure. What we wanted was a stern reprimand, an Injunction against harassment or intimidation, and a warning that further conduct of this kind would lead to immediate imprisonment. That would probably have cured them.

On the morning of 26 October 1977 I caught the early train from Oxford. I was coming up to the Law Courts in the Strand for the contempt charges brought by Mr Milsom against Hart, Andy Bevan, Tom Jenkins, Owen Ashworth, John Rowse, Alan Howarth and Philip Bradbury. When I alighted from my taxi outside the Law Courts, I was amazed to see a huge demonstration with hailers, placards and the rest. These people were chanting: 'Free the Newham Seven! Tory Courts out!' I felt a little odd when I looked at one huge placard and saw *my own* name on it! It was held high in the air and said 'McCORMICK AND LEWIS — RIGHT-WING EXTREMISTS'. I saw that what I had once predicted had occurred: we had now, in the demonology of the left, moved up into the stratosphere together with General Pinochet, Vorster, Ian Smith and Hitler. I thought to myself 'surely I'm not that bad!' When this Rentacrowd outfit saw me it started jeering and howling. I had been standing there for a while until it suddenly dawned on them who I was and that the person standing a foot or two away from them was one of the arch-villains they were demonstrating about! I smiled at them good-naturedly and ascended the steps to the court.

When I located the court I was dismayed to see that the judge who had been picked to hear the case was Mr Justice Peter Pain. Mr Justice Peter Pain, like all judges, is incorruptible, perfectly just, above suspicion, has no ideological motivations whatever. But there was a man called Peter Pain who, before he became a judge (whereupon he immediately became pristine and pure), was renowned for his extremely left-wing views. I would put his views at that time as being similar to those of Atkinson and Mikardo. He took many trade union cases and was virtually a trade union lawyer for a long time. If I remember rightly it was he who was vehement in his opposition when conducting cases in Sir John Donaldson's Industrial Relations Court. I believe he once marched out of it. He was active in the Haldane Society — an organisation of left-wing lawyers which often promotes Marxist talks. He was appointed a judge by the Labour Government in 1975. In view of his past associations and views it is very surprising that he was chosen for this case and surprising he did not disqualify himself. How he was chosen is a mystery. Was it just a coincidence? Some of the Newham Marxists afterwards went around publicly saying that they were bailed out by higher authorities to save political embarrassment. They said that it had been a great mistake on my part to write to the Attorney-General because this alerted people to the imminence of proceedings. I do not know, if they knew something or were merely speculating. They are, of course, great believers in conspiracies. I simply do not know whether or not it was a mere mischance that we got Mr Justice Peter Pain.

There is another reason why the judge should certainly have disqualified himself from the case. You will remember that Andy Bevan was the protégé of Tony Benn. Andy Bevan had been a leading figure in Benn's own local party, Bristol South-East, before moving to Newham. Benn was the only prominent Labour politician to endorse Andy Bevan for the job of Labour Party National Youth Officer. He did more than endorse him — he campaigned for his appointment and paid him a fulsome tribute. Benn's public support for Bevan was splashed across every newspaper in the country. So Andy Bevan became publicly known as Tony Benn's protégé. Just think how gravely embarrassing it would have been for Tony Benn if Andy Bevan, whom he had forced into this crucial Labour Party post against the wishes of all his Cabinet colleagues, were to be convicted of contempt of court, especially in circumstances where there were allegations of premeditated defiance and violent assaults on fellow members of the Labour Party. This would have cast doubt on Benn's judgement and damaged his political career.

None of this should matter in the slightest to a judge hearing the case, who should be strictly impartial. But was it not a little difficult for Mr Justice Pain to seem to be impartial as a relation of Tony Benn's? They are first cousins. Tony Benn's left-wing political views are very similar to those held by Peter Pain before he became a judge.

He showed his hostility to Mr Milsom's case right from the start. On the first morning he muddled up his affidavits and then said that Mr Milsom had not fulfilled his undertaking to the Court to get them sworn — 'if the undertaking is not complied with the person who is giving it [that is, Mr Milsom] is himself in contempt of court.' Throughout the case he interjected sarcastic and hostile comments towards

Mr Milsom, Julian and myself. He interrupted us when we gave evidence. Sometimes he was so quick to jump down our throats that he slipped up, as in this exchange:

Mr Justice Pain: Now look, that will not do, Mr Lewis, you must try and answer counsel's questions. He asked you what did you think the meeting of the Local Government Committee was going to do?

Mr Edwards QC: The Management Committee

Mr Justice Pain: Oh, I beg your pardon, I am sorry, in that case then ... No, I am sorry, I withdraw my remark.

The judge said that from his own recollection in earlier years of the Labour Party Rule-Book certain posts did not exist, and started to criticise the constitutional practice in Newham North-East. This was irrelevant to the proceedings which concerned whether or not a court order had been breached and process servers assaulted. When I objected to one question as irrelevant Mr Justice Pain snapped back, 'Now it is not for the witness to raise questions on relevance.' In his judgement he went out of his way to criticise Mr Milsom, Julian and myself. He said of me that 'it may be because his speciality is philosophy I know not, but he seemed to be quite unable to deal with short questions of fact by the succinct answers they should be dealt with.' (I later went through the transcript and discovered that several Marxists had given much longer answers than mine: he did not criticise them for this at all).

Mr Milsom was disgusted at the judge. There were seven people on trial and he released them as they were acquitted. After several had been released, Mr Milsom said in a tone of real disgust 'He's letting them go, one by one.' A friend of mine who sat in the court said to me that she had never seen such a strange performance from a judge and pointed out, what Julian and I had already noticed, that the judge frowned when points were made in our favour and smiled when they were made against. Then, on the fourth day Mr Justice Pain looked very pleased with himself. He had clearly been having great difficulty in seeing his way to disposing of the case and letting everyone off. I had drafted the Notice of Motion and it covered all the breaches of the Injunction, Bevan's incitement to defy the Injunction, and the assaults in such a way that it was very exhaustive.

But Mr Justice Pain saw a short-cut. He suddenly launched into a diatribe describing Mr Milsom as 'a deplorable liar'. He could not point to any specific lies he had told, but said it was 'a judge's impression'. There had been one misunderstanding over Mr Milsom's evidence. This is not surprising. I found it difficult to make sense of some of the QCs's questions myself. An ordinary uneducated and rather inarticulate man like Mr Milsom was at a great disadvantage in a court of law, and this was cruelly taken advantage of. (The same was done when Mr Bament gave evidence — and the judge was very sharp with him.) The judge stated that if Mr Milsom had lied then he was in contempt and if he were in contempt he could not proceed with his contempt action against the defendants. He had tried this gambit on the first day over the affidavits. Now he called Mr Milsom a liar and tried it again. If he really thought Mr Milsom had lied he would have sent the papers to the Director of Public Prosecutions. But he shrank back from doing this — he said that he would not do it because Mr Milsom was a 'pathetic little character'. However, the judge had got his law badly wrong: an applicant in a committal case is not a plaintiff seeking equitable relief but he is like a person laying a criminal information. His own character and conduct is immaterial and his contempt (if any) cannot be set against the defendants' contempt. In any case it would have been perjury, not contempt. Bad luck, Peter Pain! It is worth noting that in courts the smooth-tongued easily get away with murder and the slow-witted and inarticulate can be made to look like fools or criminals.

A witness in court can so easily be pushed into saying something he does not want to say in an aggressive cross-examination, or he can be confused and then painted as a liar. Mr Milsom's barrister said to the judge about Mr Milsom that there was a 'lack of sophistication' in the way he gave his evidence and added 'but certainly listening to him I found it difficult to put my finger on anything which seemed to me to be false as opposed to just confused'. Just for the record in view of the abusive and unfair attack on Mr Milsom, I should like to state that, from what I and the Newham Moderates know of him, Mr Milsom is *not* a liar. He is a very public-spirited man and he and his family were very hurt and offended by this attack on him which was repeated in the papers and on television. He has no redress against this blackening of his reputation. The judge is privileged from libel proceedings. I think Mr Justice Pain realised what Mr Milsom thought about him for he said, when he let Mr Milsom leave the witness box, 'He may feel that this unsympathetic Judge's Court is not a very nice place to be in.' What made this worse than ever was that many of the Marxists were lying throughout the trial and I cannot understand how the judge saw a non-existent mote in Mr Milsom's eye when there was a huge beam in theirs.

For example they said we were drunk when we came in. They said we sent chairs and tables flying. They said we attacked them. One Marxist girl came up when Julian was pointing out Phil Bradbury as one of his attackers and said, 'We saw him attack you Phil.' They carefully concocted a couple of false accounts. At first they said that we attacked them. When this appeared implausible — a meeting of fifty people being attacked by four, with Julian wearing glasses and one of the four being Mr Champion, a mild bystander — they changed their story and said that the people who attacked us had been trying to protect us from the rest of the meeting! I passed Julian a note which commented on the unlikelihood of twenty people rushing forward to defend us from their fellows. It said: 'The mild men rushed forward to protect us from the angry men who sat seething in their seats.'

There were some points of high farce in the proceedings. The first incident to receive careful attention was when Tom Jenkins, the teacher, barred the door and refused to let Julian into the meeting at the start — even though he was a member. Jenkins had appointed himself a steward of the meeting and arrogated to himself and a few cronies the right to decide who could come in. When Julian asked him by what authority he had been made steward and by what authority he was obstructing him from entering Jenkins replied, 'On the authority of the working class.' The second incident was when Julian was grabbed by the throat by Philip Bradbury and kicked and kneed by a number of others. Several witnesses described this as a hostile and vicious attack. The Judge chose to interpret it as Bradbury comfortingly laying his hands on Julian in order to protect him from the rest of the meeting: 'It may be in the course of that that his hands went near Mr Lewis's neck or on Mr Lewis's neck ... but I am quite satisfied that there was nothing in the sense of an attack on Mr Lewis's neck.' Did the judge think for a moment, leaving aside the fact that I, Gerald Falvey and Mrs Clayden all identified Bradbury in a vicious attack on Julian grabbing him by the throat, that proceedings would have been brought against anyone who was really trying to protect us. But the judge failed to get the facts right. He claimed that Mrs Clayden had *not* identified Bradbury with his hands round Julian's neck. Mr Milsom's barrister interrupted to say that he and the defendants' barrister 'both agree that Mrs Clayden did identify Mr Bradbury.' Mr Justice Pain said: 'Oh do you, thank you very much. Very well then, if you both agree with that then, of course, I accept that. It must be a point that had slipped my attention.' The third incident was when Champion was kicked. He identified Tom Jenkins as his assailant. Identification was not the issue: Jenkins admitted being with Mr Champion but said Mr Champion had attacked him! Listen to this cross-examination by Mr Milsom's barrister (Mr Eady):

Mr Eady: Are you in fact an irascible person?

Jenkins: I don't know the meaning of that word.

Mr Eady: You are a teacher, aren't you?

Jenkins: Yes.

Mr Eady: And you don't know the meaning of the word irascible?

Jenkins: No.

Mr Eady: Are you a person who is easily moved to temper?

Jenkins: No.

Mr Eady: Violent?

Jenkins: No.

Mr Eady: Didn't you kick Mr Champion in the crutch?

Jenkins: Not at all.

Mr Eady: Did you see anybody else kick Mr Champion in the crutch?

Jenkins: No, I didn't.

Mr Eady: So that is something on which Mr Champion is telling a straight lie, is it?

Jenkins: Mr Champion might have hit himself or he might have got the injury some other way, I don't know, he might have knocked himself against a table or fallen over outside, but I didn't see any person in that meeting inflicting any injury on anyone.

(at this point I passed a piece of paper to Julian with the comment: 'The Strange Case of the Aggressive Groin.'). Mr Milsom complained bitterly over lunch about Marxists like Jenkins being in a position, as teachers, to teach his kids. Julian dubbed the two assailants 'Fingers Bradbury' and 'Jenkins the Boot'. Of course, there were many other assailants whom we could not identify because of the large number that had attacked us.

At the end of the six day trial Mr Justice Pain let the remaining defendants off. Bevan was acquitted of defying the Injunction, having ripped it up, because it did not have its penal notice filled in. (This is the part that reads, 'If you fail to … you will be subject to process of execution, etc.' and most unfortunately our solicitors had neglected to fill it in.) Hart was acquitted of defying the Injunction, and also Ashworth, because they said they did not believe the Injunction had been granted. Bevan was acquitted of inciting people to defy the Injunction because it was said that he had only expressed a personal view and not tried to persuade others to defy it. Howarth and Rowse were acquitted because of the missing penal notice. Bradbury was acquitted because he had been trying to protect Julian Lewis, not attack him (Julian and the rest of us had made a terrible mistake. Perhaps we ought to apologise to Phil Bradbury). Jenkins was acquitted because, although the judge said his evidence was unsatisfactory, he was 'not ... satisfied, with a sufficient degree of certainty ... that the assault took place'. Mr Champion's bruise, attested by a medical certificate, was presumably an imaginary one. Or perhaps, as Jenkins suggested, he did hit himself in the crutch after all. Having implied he was a liar the judge then called Mr Champion a very reliable witness!

An appeal was filed on Mr Milsom's behalf claiming that the judge's behaviour had given rise 'to a reasonable suspicion of possible bias' (you can't say he was biased, we were told, even if he were). The general impression was that the judge had got it all sewn up neatly in a way that made it largely appeal-proof because Appeal Courts, not having the witnesses before them, are reluctant to overturn a judge's findings of fact based on his impressions of the witnesses. However, the judge had clearly made a number of errors in law. I thought that if the law were strictly applied we would win on appeal. A couple of QCs who looked at the papers agreed that we would probably succeed on at least one of the various counts for the appeal.

I felt appalled at having seen at first-hand a political trial where justice went out of the window and I think that Mr Justice Peter Pain should never have been given this case in view of his associations and interests before he became a judge. Justice, at the least, was not *seen* to be done. Out of the twenty hearings on the Newham question in which I was involved, this was the only one of which I could say this, though I did not agree with a number of the decisions in the others. The judge ended his judgement by implying that if we brought other cases other judges should adopt his assessment of the witnesses (i.e. that our leading people were unreliable) and said, 'I would like to conclude by expressing the hope that this is the last time that the Courts have heard of the Newham North-East Labour Party.'

One of the points that was raised in the trial was where we were getting our money from. Julian explained that he had given a personal indemnity to the plaintiffs in Newham backed by promises from certain sources which had to remain anonymous. I have not said anything about this so far. I have little to say now. If people promise money and ask for their identity to be kept confidential then we will naturally respect that confidence. As private individuals we are not obliged to divulge our sources. All I will say is that there have been several sources and they are all perfectly respectable sources in a legal and moral sense. People may think that 'he who pays the piper calls the tune' but in our case I think the tune has been idiosyncratically and authentically mine and I have decided what to do on all the points of strategy. When we came into this fight we were using our own money — indeed it cost both Julian and me a considerable sum from our own very meagre resources — and we have never recovered this, so we are now worse off financially than when we started. The idea that anyone could buy our services for some ulterior purpose is preposterous, and I know perfectly well that, whatever purposes have been pursued, they have been mine, and nobody else's. We would not take money from anyone — certain sources would be ruled out — but the important thing is the use to which any money is put rather than the source from which it derives. You don't, if you are collecting for cancer research, conduct an Inquisition on prospective contributors, so why should this be regarded as a crucial factor when conducting a battle for democracy? Unfortunately, this was and is the main area of interest of the Press. They do not pester the Trotskyists and their friends, who derive vast sums (many times anything we have managed to raise) from very dubious sources, yet they do pester us incessantly with the question 'Where is your money coming from?' We alsways answer 'No comment.'

On 26 October, 1977, the first day of the contempt of court trial, a motion had been moved at the National Executive Committee meeting by Nick Bradley. Nick Bradley, if you have forgotten, is Andy Bevan's accomplice and a fellow leader of Militant. He is after the Newham North-East seat for himself too. He was the Young Socialists representative on the NEC. He appears to have had a hand in Bevan's appointment as National Youth Officer. Once these Trotskyists get in they beaver away and, like Queens on the chessboard, they are worth nine of everybody else. Bradley's motion was:

That the National Executive Committee suspend the General Committee, Executive Committee and Officers of the Newham North-East Constituency Labour Party ... and authorise the National Agent to conduct ... the affairs of the Constituency Party ... and ... convene the next General Committee meeting of the ... Party.

Note that the wards were not suspended, because the Marxists controlled the majority of the wards. Translated, this motion means: 'Suspend the Party so that the Moderates elected in July are removed, install Underhill as a dictator to replace local democracy, and then make sure that he calls the next GMC meeting so that he exercises the powers of deciding who is eligible and ruling on Points of Order. This should put the Marxists back in control.' The NEC also passed a motion agreeing in advance to pay the legal costs of the Marxists who had committed contempt of court – irrespective of whether they should be found guilty or not guilty of it.

An 'Inquiry had been set up by the NEC in September into the Newham North-East Party. The Inquiry was proposed by Alex Kitson (who around this time made a name for himself by his speeches in praise of the Soviet way of life on a visit there) and it was seconded by Ian Mikardo. The persons who were elected to the Inquiry were Eric Heffer (who likes Eurocommunism and voted for Andy Bevan's appointment), Harold Hickling (whose vote in the early stages clinched Bevan's appointment), and Tom 'Uncle Tom' Bradley MP, the token tame Moderate who swims along furiously with the tide (he had sat on the committee which considered the report on Entryism and decided to do nothing positive to stop it). Two other people were to sit on the Inquiry and do all the administration. Very independent they were – Bill Jones and Reg Underhill! 'Don't even bother to go along,' advised Councillor Wally Hurford. 'I've been to lots of these Transport House Inquiries. They are a farce. They've always decided what to do to start with and they're just going through the motions.'

The Inquiry was indeed a farce, an Inquisition for the few Moderates such as Eddie Lee, who went along. It did not even invite me or notify me of its existence, but it recommended that I be suspended from the Labour Party, and

Julian too. It also recommended that the Newham Party's Officers and Executive Committee (where we were in a firm majority) should stay suspended until their period of office expired, that a special meeting of the GMC should be called, controlled, and chaired by Underhill and should put through (i.e. rush through ahead of time) the constitutional changes passed by the Annual Conference so that we would be deprived of a number of our trade union votes. Translated this means 'Knock out McCormick and Lewis by suspending them from the Labour Party; knock out the elected Moderate Officers and EC members by suspending them from office until their term of office is finished; manipulate the GMC in order to change the Newham Party's Rules for the sole and specific purpose of dislodging the Moderate group in Newham.' They were prepared to go to any lengths to put the Newham Marxists back in control.

On 14 December the NEC voted to accept these recommendations. We pipped them to the post on the question of our suspension. I arranged for proceedings to be brought and an Injunction was obtained, some twenty minutes before they were going to vote to suspend us, ordering them not to. They then turned round and said that, though it was on the Agenda, though a large number of them had previously voted for it at a meeting of the Organisation Committee (the NEC's sub-committee) on 5 December, they had no intention of voting to suspend us! Underhill swore on oath that this was true.

The votes to suspend the Party and pay the Marxists' costs taken by the NEC on 26 October 1977, and the vote to call a special meeting to change the rules while keeping the elected officers and EC suspended taken on 14 December 1977, were unanimous. Whatever happened to Shirley Williams and the other self-styled Moderates on the NEC? They had all voted *for* these motions. Why? Sheer political cowardice. In late 1977 Shirley Williams commented on us and said we should operate 'by persuasion, not legal action'. How do you 'persuade' a man who has grabbed you by the throat or is trying to kick you in the groin, who wants to cancel elections if you look like winning, who cheats, cheats and cheats again, who intimidates your supporters, and who is a fanatical believer in some off-beat religion called Marxism? Is this not rather silly? But I doubt if she even believes it herself. She knows they are beyond persuasion. So her advice is 'Lie back and enjoy it,' or 'Put your head in the sand and perhaps they'll go away.' Thanks to people like her it is much more difficult to defeat the Marxists. Her attitude sabotages the fight. Because she and the others voted *for* the motion it undermined our argument in court that it was a partisan measure. If she had voted against with other Moderates the judges would have accepted it as partisan and granted an Injunction against it. But when Labour Marxists and the Labour Establishment present a united front it is going to be a very brave judge indeed who would be prepared to say 'Yes it is a partisan measure and these Moderates are only voting for it because they are afraid not to.'

Callaghan singled us out for attack after I had made a broadcast on the 'World at One' threatening that if the Newham North-East suspension was not lifted we would investigate other Labour constituency Parties from which we had been receiving reports of gross irregularities by Marxists. In another 'World at One' programme at the beginning of January 1978 Callaghan was asked if he was worried about Trotskyist infiltration. He replied by saying he was very worried about *us*! He said that we had been tripping up local Party officials conscientiously trying to do their duty by catching them out on tiny technical errors. He must have known this was false. A *Daily Telegraph* editorial on 4 January 1978 entitled 'Callaghan to the Marxists' aid' commented: 'Having remained ingloriously mute while his Cabinet colleague Prentice was fighting for his political life, the Leader of the Labour Party found his tongue as soon as the Moderates fought back. True, he has found a pretext, that to bring in the law would frighten off amateurs and perhaps cost them or their party money if they inadvertently transgressed party statutes. But this is as laboured as it is transparent, quite apart from his characteristic desire to deprive citizens of access to the law. For one thing, the entryists are neither innocents nor amateurs. Secondly, those who innocently infringe regulations can easily make amends thereby obviating lawsuits.'

The criticism of us by Shirley Williams and Callaghan was combined with a left-wing onslaught upon us. Joan Lestor, Labour Party Chairman, went out to speak at a rally in East London against us. Norman Atkinson, Labour Party

Treasurer, was reported in the *Sunday Times* (18 December 1977) as saying that if any Labour Party members provided financial support for us 'they faced expulsion for bringing the party into disrepute.' This orchestrated attack on us obviously made it more difficult for the courts to uphold us on points of law arising out of the dispute.

Of course, we vigorously challenged the suspension of the Party in the Courts. The case went before Mr Justice Michael Davies in January 1978. Our argument was that the suspension was contrary to natural justice because no hearing had been given to the people suspended. We had a very powerful precedent to support us on this point. But unfortunately the judge made it clear that he, like a number of judges, did not believe in natural justice (some judges are hostile to it, others are very keen on it — it is a contentious legal doctrine). We also argued that the NEC had no powers to suspend or dissolve a Party, only to disaffiliate it. Although our QC agreed with me and with our junior that this point was very strong indeed the judge did not seem impressed by it. There were other points too but these were the main ones. We were at a grave disadvantage because the other side had put in a huge affidavit running to over a hundred pages and providing a very tendentious and unfair account of the history of the dispute. A large number of Transport House people and their legal advisers had worked round the clock on this.

We appealed to the Appeal Court where the case was heard by Lord Denning, Lord Justice Ormrod and Lord Justice Geoffrey Lane. We made no criticism of the trial judge: he was perfectly fair and not biased against us in any way, we simply argued that he had got the law wrong and misread a major precedent. In the Appeal Court we almost won. We came within a whisker of it on the third day. But in the last days it went against us. Lord Denning was by far the most sympathetic throughout and I think he wanted to come down on our side; the other two judges were against us. Lord Justice Ormrod was another judge who had little time for natural justice, so our strongest point did not move him. Lord Justice Lane was rather sharp with us and I fear he was alienated during the course of the trial. He made it clear that he did not like Julian. But also he did not seem to have any understanding of political realities. At one point he asked 'What is Trotskyism?' Obviously it was difficult for him to understand the Byzantine intrigues of the Labour Party Establishment and the fanaticism of the Marxists we were fighting because he was rather out of touch with ordinary political life. I would not want to criticise Lord Denning, a great man and a good judge, who was always polite and helpful. He was far and away the most intelligent of the three judges and he was the only judge of the three to understand some of the more complex legal points that I had prepared for the court in a short written draft. Unfortunately I was not allowed to speak on this occasion and our QC had to go over to another case, so Julian had to conduct his case, turning to me every couple of minutes for legal points and observations — a very unsatisfactory way of proceeding. Julian spoke very well and I do not think he can fairly be criticised, but he was in no way an expert on the law. Still it was very disappointing for me that Lord Denning finally came out against our case. His account of the facts supported our position but he supported the other side on the legal points.

Why did we lose? We lost the first hearing partly because Transport House delivered about ten times as much evidence as we had. We lost the Appeal Court hearing partly because having lost the first hearing we were at a disadvantage — we had to prove that the previous judge had got it wrong, so the presumption was in favour of the defendants. This made it an uphill task. But there were two main reasons running through both hearings. The first and most important was that the people holding high positions and calling themselves 'Moderates' like Callaghan, Shirley Williams and Reg Underhill had backed the Marxists against us and supported the suspension of the Party. Lord Denning said in his judgement that we would have got the Injunction if we could have proved that the NEC had acted with an ulterior partisan motive to support one faction against the other, but he said that there was not sufficient evidence to prove this. How could there be when Shirley Williams and the other Moderates on the NEC had voted in favour of suspension and Callaghan had attacked us? How could there be when Underhill submitted an affidavit in which he stated on oath: 'It is utterly and fundamentally false ... that the NEC is a left-wing body that has deliberately shown favour to attempts by Marxists ... to gain control of the affairs of Newham North-

East.' And again, 'I know [it] has been alleged ... that many people of extreme left-wing views, acting in concert, moved into Newham North-East and gained control of it in February 1976.... But there is no sufficient proof or evidence of it to justify taking action.... The suggestion that the NEC has knowingly tolerated a take-over of Newham North-East ... is wrong. My enquiries and investigations into the matter have never produced evidence that would enable me to recommend to the NEC that remedial action should be taken.' And again, 'The appointment of Mr Bevan as Youth Officer [has been used] as evidence of the left-wing tendency of the NEC .... But the fact that he was appointed does not show that a majority of the NEC sympathise with his political views. He had excellent qualifications for the post.' And he said that Julian had been 'inhuman' for sueing Lugg and Clark and being 'indifferent to their suffering'. He concluded, 'From my observations of the Organisation Committee and the NEC I believe they have behaved neutrally in the affairs [of Newham North-East], their sole interest being to see that the rules and practice of the Labour Party are adhered to. I have myself attempted to behave throughout with scrupulous fairness and impartiality.' Once Underhill had sworn this the judges would be virtually calling him a perjurer if they had concluded that the NEC *had* acted in a partisan fashion. Is it surprising that they recoiled from this?

The second reason why we did not prevail was that we simply had insufficient resources. By staying up for two days and nights on end I did manage to produce a long affidavit in answer to Underhill's, but still they had the edge in the volume of evidence. They could call on a huge legal team, thousands of pounds, fifty typists, fifty researchers, and an army of bureaucrats. They opened Transport House over the weekend while the case was continuing and banged in another long affidavit on Monday morning which we never had an opportunity to answer. We put up a valiant fight and almost made it, only Underhill and his associates know how close they were to defeat and at one time they were really desperate. But in the end the superior resources triumphed.

Had we been able to take it to the House of Lords ... but the money had run out. About £70,000–£90,000 had been spent as a total for both sides in the battle and the sources had been bled dry. Consequently Julian was unable to further indemnify anyone, including himself. What had finally stopped our car was that we had run out of fuel. Nothing else would have stopped us.

Epilogue

January 1978, Ward Meetings: After the Annual Meetings of the wards and a frantic last minute Rule change, and partly as a result of a much more liberal dose of 'Underhill's Discretion' and partly as a result of unconstitutional action which we now have no money to challenge in the courts, we find that Underhill has disqualified well over half our delegates! But we had anticipated this and decided to boycott the Annual Meeting called by Underhill. He had become Party Dictator: there was no longer any local Party democracy, it had been suspended until the Marxists were reinstated.

February 1978, Annual Meeting: Hart, perhaps having finally recognised that the Marxists would sweep the board, stands for the Chairmanship and wins a derisory 17 votes. He is also easily beaten for the Vice-Chairmanship. Massey, in a desperate and wild lunge for power stands *against* Hart *and* the Marxists for the Chairmanship and polls 3 votes. Alan Howarth (one of the 'Newham Seven' and one of the earliest entrants to the Party) is elected unopposed as Secretary. John Clark (of whom Underhill's affidavit said that because of the legal action against him 'I do not believe he will stand for party office again and this is unfortunate' *does* stand and is elected unopposed as Treasurer. Young Michael Brown, the teacher, who had said we were destroying the Labour Party is elected as one of the Vice-Presidents. The other Vice-President is ... Andy Bevan! The new Chairman is ... Philip Bradbury! Who better to keep order at meetings than a man who will comfortably rest his hands on your throat to protect you? The Marxists have swept the board. Mr Underhill comments: 'Twelve months of unnecessary hell for the party are now over.' It is peace at the last. The chaos that had worried the judges has ended and the order that they yearned for has been restored. The short honeymoon period, those halcyon months, when the Moderates were in control and there was no cheating and no intimidation whatever — has

been cruelly ended. Normality has been restored. The NEC
has suspended local democracy and brought the 'Prague
Spring' to an end. For the 'Forty Thieves' on the GMC and
for the 10 per cent of Marxists in the local Party as a whole
it is a day to celebrate — but for the rest of the Newham
people it is a sad and bitter dénouement to a brave and
exhausting fight that they had won — until they were suspended by the NEC.

Summer 1978

The Marxist-dominated Newham Party draws up a short-list
for Newham North-East. Not surprisingly the short-list is
composed of left-wingers. Nick Bradley (the Trotskyist who
proposed the motion to suspend the Newham Party to
remove the Moderates) applies for the post for himself and
secures twenty votes. But a former Chairman of the Tribune
Group, James Dickens, is chosen with thirty-seven votes.

April 1979

Still determined to get Nick Bradley in, the Militant faction
of the Newham Marxists work to undermine the new man,
Dickens. Even he is not left-wing enough for them. When he
puts forward his election address for the May 1979 election
only two of the six officers and less than half of the General
Management Committee are prepared to endorse it. He sees
the writing on the wall — and immediately resigns. This
causes acute embarrasment and electoral damage to the
Labour Party at the height of its campaign. In this election
left-wing extremism in the Labour Party is one of the main
issues.

May 1979

At the General Election on 3 May, the voters reject the argument from a number of pundits and academics that there is
no need to worry about left-wing extremism in the Labour
Party, and that in any case, Jim Callaghan and Shirley
Williams have everything under control. If Shirley Williams
had publicly gone on the offensive over left-wing extremists
in the Labour Party instead of trying to 'persuade' them, and
if she had publicly associated herself with our fight in
Newham instead of opposing us, then she might have won
public esteem as a woman who does not compromise with

enemies of democracy, and she would probably have saved her seat. The Labour Party as a whole pays the price for infiltration as it is defeated on a huge swing of over five per cent — the biggest in recent times. But the Labour Party's defeat now opens up the way for the left to strengthen its position steadily over the next five years. Tony Benn is soon to launch himself on a bid for the leadership arguing that the Annual Conference, rather than the Parliamentary Party, should elect the Leader. Whatever his fortunes, the left in the Labour Party is bound to grow in strength.

Also at the election Reg Prentice (who had been sitting until then as the Conservative MP for Newham North-East having changed sides since originally being elected as the Labour MP for Newham North-East) is duly returned as Conservative MP for Daventry (a safe Tory seat). Soon afterwards he is made a Minister again — this time under a Conservative government. He becomes Minister of State for Social Security with a brief to cut down on 'scroungers'. One of his fellow MP's in the new Parliament is the new left-wing Labour MP for Newham North East, Ron Leighton. Ron Leighton is to the left of James Dickens so this is a welcome development for the Newham Marxists. Needless to say the selection procedure once again infringed the Labour Party's own rules. He secured 22,818 votes and swept in with a majority of over ten thousand. This proves yet again that because people vote for a party and not a person, those who can capture the party label in a safe seat are assured of victory, however unrepresentative their views may be.

How strange that both Mr Prentice and his opponents, the Marxists, should have achieved simultaneous success. Does this mean that 'Everybody won and everybody must have prizes'? Well, not quite everybody. There is an empty place at the feast. Those who fought not for themselves, not for a position or a prize, those who fought simply for democracy, those to whom this book is dedicated — are left out in the cold ... and forgotten.

6
Marxist Methods

In this book reference has been made from time to time to various methods used by the Marxists. I want to look at this more systematically. A pattern emerges when you start to collate information. It is not an accident that Marxists use certain characteristic methods, because these methods are peculiarly appropriate for them. Time and time again in Oxford, Newham and elsewhere I came across the same methods being used. I have now drawn up a brief summary of them in the form of a *Twenty-Point Tactical Technique*. This lists the secret weapons of the Marxists. These weapons are quite often out of sight as if in a hidden arsenal. But when they are needed they are brought into the battle. Whenever the going gets rough for the Marxists, whenever they face serious, organised resistance, these weapons are brought into play.

The first group of methods comes under the heading of *INTIMIDATION* -- 'Putting the Frighteners on'. It consists of violence and physical threats, psychological intimidation, and victimisation.

Violence and physical threats
This frequently accompanies Marxist takeovers of local Labour Parties. In Newham North-East there was virtually none up to 1975, but when organised resistance got underway in 1976, and even more so when it was successful in 1977, this technique was brought into operation. I myself was variously threatened by several Marxists with 'having my neck broken', being 'flung down the stairs', being 'done over' and so forth. Such threats were made on several occasions when I visited the constituency. Once I was told,

'Get out of Newham and don't come back or you'll get beaten up.' Julian Lewis was threatened by one Marxist that he would have 'his arms twisted off' if he did not do what the Marxist told him. Mr Milsom had to arrange police protection of his home when he was threatened with the words: 'Your cards are marked. We've got your number, mate. My family will come over and do your family tonight.' These threats against Julian and Mr Milsom are supported by affidavits. John Pagett was threatened over the phone that he would be beaten up. One delegate was told at a meeting, 'Sit down or I'll beat you up.'

Sometimes it went beyond threats to actual violence. I was ejected from a meeting and nearly knocked down the stairs. Julian Lewis had his hand injured and incurred extensive bruising to his legs from being kneed and kicked by Marxists at a meeting. Mr Champion gave evidence in court how he was kicked very hard on the thigh by a kick aimed at his groin. He was limping about for quite a long time afterwards. Julian had a brick hurled through his window on one occasion. On another occasion the brakes on his motorcycle were tampered with. At Newham South some members of the GMC were intimidated by a 'picket' of their meetings by various Marxists. One Moderate lady was spat upon. At Islington North the Moderate Labour MP, Michael O'Halloran, was attacked by members of a group of 40 extreme left-wingers who were, and are, trying to kick him out as the MP, who had burst in to his constituency 'surgery' without an appointment at about 8.00 pm on 11 March 1977. This is a classic instance and I will quote the MP's own words to describe the incident:

Between 8.00 and 8.30 pm most of the demonstrators had occupied the Party building, and about 40 of them burst into my interview room, chanting such slogans as 'Out with O'Halloran.' The crowd was accompanied by a photographer, who jumped on to my desk. He started taking photographs ... the flash bulbs were going off. One or two others tried to hood my left arm and put a piece of wood into my right hand and to force my arm above my head in order to take a photograph of me apparently attempting to assault members of the demonstration. I suddenly became conscious that someone, I do not know who, had

my left arm twisted up behind my back. I tried to escape
from the room but was blocked by several people. Several
punches were then received by me. I was kicked and
badly bruised, and my trousers were ripped to pieces. I was
finally rescued by some of those attending the meeting
upstairs. Following the blows I had received on my head,
I collapsed on the stairs leading to the ground floor and
had to receive medical treatment.

I was especially interested by the aspect of the photographer.
When I waited outside the Labour Hall in Newham North-
East for the July 1977 Annual Meeting I received exactly the
same treatment. One of the Marxists came up to me as I
stood on the pavement and, only inches away, took one
photograph after another of me, circling me and using flash-
bulbs. He must have taken ten or fifteen pictures. It was
clearly an attempt to intimidate me. I said drily, 'I suppose
these pictures will go on your files of enemies of the people,'
and he replied darkly 'That's right.' The Marxist photographer can not only record people for the files; he is also on
hand to provide photos to compromise people, as the MP
pointed out. Also, the mere repeated flashing of flash-bulbs
in people's eyes and the knowledge that they are being pin-
pointed and recorded is itself intimidatory. My enquiries
have revealed that this 'aggressive photography' technique is a
common Marxist tactic.

Psychological intimidation

This is one of the more effective Marxist weapons. At
meetings it takes the form of 'the Marxist chorus' — a
cacophony of jeers, shouting and interruptions if a Moderate
speaks in a manner they disapprove of. My objection, as an
organist and choirmaster, is chiefly on musical grounds. But
for many people it is very intimidating to be subjected to a
barrage of noise, and especially prolonged mockery and
jeering. Of course, in the Marxist countries, especially China,
this technique is perfected and the aberrant individual is subjected to campaigns of mockery and abuse as a form of
'criticism and self-criticism'. At Newham North-East
meetings, jeering and shouting were commonly used in this
way and superadded to torrents of verbal abuse. Many
people, especially ordinary, relatively uneducated and in-

articulate people like the Newham working-class Moderates, dread any form of public speaking and feel most uncomfortable. To subject them to this treatment is a form of mental cruelty. I know of several brave and tough-minded people who found these meetings a real ordeal. It was very difficult to get Moderates to speak at these meetings for this reason.

Another standard technique is the 'spotlight confrontation'. An individual is collared or cornered or obstructed by a small group of Marxists who try to extract some concession from him. Thus the spotlight is put on him, he is put in an isolated and vulnerable position; he may be obstructed from leaving the building, and he has to face the pressure of interrogation from several angry people surrounding him. Perhaps they want him to sign a petition or vote a certain way, or perhaps they are trying to extract information from him. It is the weaker Moderates and the waverers who easily succumb to this approach. It has the special requirement of being *ambiguous* − although the pressure is felt by the person at the receiving end, it is not always obvious even to bystanders. Consequently it evokes little opposition or backlash, and the person himself, having no proper excuse for succumbing, tends to pretend, even to himself, that he was 'persuaded' rather than 'pressurized'.

More recalcitrant individuals were subjected to the crude technique of being followed in the street by a number of Marxists on their way to or from meetings. This is still more frightening. Most Parliaments have special immunities to protect members on the journey to and from Parliamentary debates, because this is a particularly vulnerable moment when they are separated from their home base and family and also separated from their colleagues at the meeting. In both Newham South and Newham North-East I came across a number of complaints of this kind of harassment.

One of the most frightening experiences can be the anonymous phone call. A number of Moderates had these inflicted on them as the battle between them and the Marxists reached crisis points. Alec Kellaway tells me that Reg Prentice had to go ex-directory after being pestered in this way but that as soon as he informed people of his new phone number the Marxists printed it. Councillor Wally Hurford, who was rung at 3.00 am, pointed out that it was no joke to receive this kind of treatment when you are eighty years old and have a sick wife. A number of Moderates in Newham North East had to go ex-directory. The scars of those days are still with them: I notice it still, when I phone some of them up, in the apprehensive, tentative and suspicious way they answer the phone and the immediate relaxation when they realise it is not a Marxist.

Most frightening of all to many people is the 'anonymous after-midnight phone call'. I received a few of these but they did not bother me in the slightest, because I am always up and around in the early hours of the morning. When I pointed this out to the heavy breather at the other end I received no more of these calls. But for many people, especially those with children in the house, it can be very annoying, and for some it can be terrifying. Take the case of Mrs Dora Lovejoy in Newham South. She is a middle-aged lady with several kids and a heart condition. She was perhaps the firmest resister of Marxist incursions into Newham South Labour Party, and in their view she was clearly in need of political education. She got it. It came in the form of the anonymous phone calls. Over a period of eighteen months she was plagued with these calls. The phone would ring at 1.00 am. She would race down the stairs to answer it, panting with the strain on her heart. The phone would be hung up. She would go back to bed. She would start to go back to sleep. The phone would ring again. She was phoned in this way several times a week between 1.00 am and 4.00 am, often three times within the hour. The calls did not come from a call box but a private subscriber. At the other end there was only silence. Additionally she was subjected to the occasional obscene phone call during the daytime. The phone call campaign started on the first day she was alone after coming out of hospital following a major heart attack. The shock of it, and her weakness in her convalescent state, made her collapse. There is no escaping the horrifying inference that the Marxists were putting her through this ordeal in the full knowledge that it could kill her. Even in a hard East End neighbourhood, which abounds with gangsters and big-time crooks, there is a code of honour, and even the ruthless villains of the area would hesitate to treat a defenceless woman in this way. In the Communist countries, of course, you are spared the late phone calls: you get the 'Midnight Knock' instead.

In Newham North-West one person, whom I do not wish to identify for fear of causing him further suffering, was mercilessly hounded by the Marxists. He received the 'telephone treatment' in addition to many other techniques of psychological warfare. This virtually brought on a complete nervous breakdown. He also has had a heart attack. A number of Newham people tell me that they think he was also blackmailed over his private life. A leading figure in Newham South Labour Party received a 'home visitation' from the Marxists on one occasion. It was a terrifying experience for him and his wife. They were subjected to an horrendous din, banging on their windows and doors, and a great deal of abuse. They were greatly upset by the incident. They also underwent 'aggressive photography'.

It is not surprising that such techniques took their toll. There was a veritable catalogue of resignations on the Moderate side. A resignation in the middle of a term of office indicates that something is amiss. In normal organizations a resignation can result from such things as promotion, illness, family troubles, overwork, and so on. Sometimes resignations are used as a political tactic. But in Newham one repeatedly came across the 'resignation under pressure'. Time and time again Moderates elected to positions at an Annual Meeting were hounded out of them, often not long afterwards, by a sustained Marxist campaign to make their lives a misery. I also came across an example of how this worked in Oxford, when a Moderate President of the Balliol Junior Common Room was hounded out of his office. At Newham many offices in the Labour Party were 'won' by frightening the Moderate incumbent out of them; then a Marxist would step into the vacancy that had been artificially created for him. When landlords do it to get a tenant out it is called 'winkling'. This happened in several Newham North-East wards: it also happened in Newham North-West.

One Moderate Labour MP under attack from the Marxists experienced a particularly diabolical ploy — fortunately one of their rarer techniques. You have heard of the 'poison letter'. Well, this was the 'poison cartoon', a hideous caricature of his mentally deficient daughter sent on a greetings card and a caption to the effect that he was mentally deficient, hence his political stance. Just imagine how ghastly it would have been for the family if the little girl had herself stumbled across it. It was bad enough as it was.

Victimisation

Funnily enough the Marxists often whine about victimis-ation, while being among the main practitioners of it. A standard technique is to damn the principal figure of the opposition as 'Public Enemy No. 1'. It is a technique designed to isolate the victim and deter others from associat-ing with him. All the hate is channelled on to one figure (or group) who is singled out for massive obloquy. Councillor Wally Hurford got this treatment in Newham North-East in 1975. The Marxists have an unerring instinct for picking on the figure who represents the greatest threat to their schemes. The idea of creating a hate-figure or arch-demon is itself abhorrent. Trotsky got this treatment in Stalinist Russia: the 'Gang of Four' are getting it in China. After Wally Hurford, it became McCormick and Lewis in Newham North-East and Dora Lovejoy in Newham South. I once remarked to Julian that we had moved up into the stratosphere in the demonology of the left. We were being talked about and depicted as though we were the Devil Incarnate. Everything that went against the Marxists in Newham was blamed on us even if it had nothing to do with us — just as Snowball was blamed in 'Animal Farm' for everything that went wrong and was accused of having sabotaged it. This is a ridiculous way to treat someone like Wally Hurford, a leading local Labour Party member for half-a-century. It is a ridiculous way to treat the two of us who were merely trying to restore democracy and not trying to impose our own (pretty ordin-ary) views on topical matters of policy.

The second group of methods consists of various methods of *CHEATING*. It includes bogus voting, notification abuses, and surprise business.

Bogus voting

This takes many forms. I came across 'Personation' (impersonating another person and casting his vote) in Oxford. Two cases have also been reported to me in recent years in Islington North, though I did not meet it in

Newham. It is not one of the strongest techniques because of the danger of being caught red-handed. 'Ballot-stuffing' by Marxists (i.e. adding false votes) also occurred quite frequently in Oxford. It was suspected that it had occurred in Newham, but I am not satisfied that this has been proved. The most usual method of acquiring bogus votes in Newham North-East was to lie about the number of members an organisation had, thereby inflating its delegate-entitlement, and this happened frequently. Make a 'mistake' (as in 'Monopoly': 'Bank error in your favour: collect an extra £200') about the basis for calculating delegate-entitlement ('Collect an extra 4 votes'); return as accredited delegates those who are disqualified on residential or other grounds from being delegates; or, most crudely of all, simply send along delegates surplus to entitlement and have them march in and start voting. Cheating over delegates was rife in Newham North-East. It obtained many extra bogus votes for the Marxists and was a decisive factor in their success. It is a most blatant form of cheating.

The technique also works in reverse. *Bona fide* Moderate delegates can simply be refused the right to vote on some trumped-up challenge to their accreditation. A variant on this technique is to 'suspend' them. There is no authority for the EC of a Party to take this step against Party members who have not broken the rules. Yet in Newham North-East two Moderates in Kensington ward were 'suspended' in this way. Never mind that it is hopelessly invalid: it works for a while until action is taken to rectify it. A combined tactic of disqualification of genuine voters and the enfranchisement of ineligible voters and the casting of spurious votes is very effective.

Notification abuses

This was one of the favourite techniques. If people are to attend a meeting they must know when it is. They must know well in advance in order to keep their diary free for that day, arrange baby-sitters and so forth. The purpose of notification of meetings is to alert them to make the necessary arrangements. The proper notice is one sent out in good time in accordance with the Rules, giving each Committee-member the same clear information as to the date, time and place of the meeting. What did the Marxists do?

First they provided a 'differential notice'. They warned their own people weeks in advance through the grapevine of particular meetings and then only sent out the official notification some time later. Consequently their people had the unfair advantage of an early warning system. The Marxists knew, say, 6 weeks ahead that the meeting would take place at a particular time: the Moderates were only told, say, 1 or 2 weeks in advance.

Secondly, 'insufficient notice' was often given. The Rules might stipulate 14 days' notice, and instead only 6 days would be given. This always had the effect of producing a net disadvantage to the Moderates for two main reasons. In the first place many of them did shift-work in the evenings when meetings took place in Newham. They had to give the foreman 2 or 3 weeks' notice to change their shifts and fix up a replacement. The other reason was that Moderates tended to be less willing to re-arrange their schedules. The workers had less free time and, being less fanatical than the middle-class Marxists, were less willing to cancel other arrangements than they would have been. At its most scandalous, 'insufficient notice' became 'excessively late notice'. A classic example was when only 2 days' notice of the 1977 February Annual Meeting of Newham North-East was given instead of the required minimum of 2 weeks (as related in the account of the *Falvey* case and sworn in many affidavits).

Thirdly, the worst abuse of all is 'selective notification'. The Marxists simply omit to send notices to a number of Moderates, despite the fact that they are fully entitled to attend the meeting and that there is a duty to inform them of it. This happened on a large number of occasions in Newham North-East. It was always Moderates who were overlooked in this way. It was a great help to the Marxist voting figures.

Surprise business

Anyone who knows anything about meetings knows that the proper way to conduct meetings of committees is to send out the agenda in good time before the meeting which sets out clearly what items of business it is proposed to transact — for example, what motions have been put forward to be debated and voted upon. This procedure is clear, open, and fair. It is therefore anathema to the Marxists. They have mastered the technique of evading the protections built into this system by springing surprise business on meetings. The Moderates present are not prepared for it and are caught on the hop. More important still, many Moderates are absent because they did not realise that the particular items were to be dealt with.

The 'surprise business technique' takes many forms. First, there are 'inconspicuous items'. On long and complicated Agenda it is fairly easy to tuck away some important and contentious item so that it does not catch the eye of the more casual Moderate when he glances through his agenda. These tucked-away items work on the same principle as the use of the 'small print' in contracts — and are sometimes printed in small print.

Secondly, there are the 'disguised items', which are described in such a way as to mislead the recipient about the real nature of the item concerned. Sometimes this is achieved by general headings which give no clue as to the specific business to be transacted, sometimes by descriptions which are wholly misleading. The idea is to pretend that some dull, routine matter is to be dealt with, and instead deal with some important and highly controversial matter. For example, 'Item 4: Motion in Secretary's Report' would give no indication whether this was some completely routine, innocuous motion, or a censure motion on the Secretary calling for his resignation because of hostility towards his report.

Thirdly, items of business can be deliberately left off the main agenda and then put on 'supplementary agenda' which can be circulated at the last minute. This has the same sort of effect as differential or insufficient notice of the meeting, except that it applies to a certain portion of the business rather than the holding of the meeting. Alternatively you can simply have 'late circulation of the agenda' which achieves the same effect for all the business of the meeting.

Fourthly, and worst of all, certain items can be omitted entirely from all agenda sent round. They can then be introduced at the meeting itself under 'Emergency Motions' (this is an abuse of the emergency motion procedure) or under 'Any other business' (an abuse of this procedure). The Marxists have informed their side that the item would come up: many Moderates have not turned up. The 'surprise business technique' was used frequently at constituency party and ward level in Newham North-East. It was very effective and helped the Marxists a great deal.

The third group of methods covers *FALSIFICATION*. It includes the stage-managed inquiry, the poisoned grapevine, the defamation campaign, corrupt historiography and mendacious misdescription.

The stage-managed inquiry

The purpose of a proper inquiry is to elicit the truth and perhaps make recommendations for action. Members of any Inquiry should be unprejudiced, should enter the inquiry with an open mind, should avoid having preconceptions, should operate in an open manner, make available all relevant documents to all sides, and evaluate the evidence in a critical manner. A Marxist-inspired inquiry, however, is quite a different matter. They do not like genuine inquiries for the same reason that a Russian Communist criticised free elections: 'The trouble with your elections in the West is that they are so unpredictable.' For them the purpose of an inquiry is to provide an impressive and official endorsement of an answer previously arrived at through other means. The inquiry is not to discover but to convince. A further purpose is to go through the motions and complete the formalities of an inquiry in order to satisfy legal requirements of natural justice.

One long-standing Newham Councillor said, 'I have given up going along to Transport House Inquiries because they are such a farce.' I do not agree. They are not a farce. They are brilliant showpiece exercises greatly to be admired for their technical virtuosity — though nothing else. In the three cases concerning the suspension of the Newham North-East Party, myself, and Julian Lewis, the Transport House Inquiry, which was dominated by Eric Heffer MP, came under severe attack. The court was told how a very careful pre-selection screening process had been devised to ensure that even though the Marxists were in a minority they provided the lion's share of the witnesses invited. The way to do this is to see where the Marxist strongholds are and then to devise some specious principle for artificially dividing them off from the Moderate strongholds. This works in the same way as 'gerrymandering'. For example, if the Marxist strength is in the big-membership wards, invent some principle for inviting only the big wards; if it is in the small-membership wards do the reverse; if it is in the high-turnout-for-meetings wards then have some principle geared to this. In Newham North-East the Marxists had their strength in the wards: the Moderates chiefly in the trade union delegations. Consequently no trade union delegates were invited at all. Only the very acute and percipient with knowledge of the Labour Party will appreciate how things of this kind can be rigged; the average person will easily be taken in by what looks to be reasonable on the surface just as a skilful gerrymander deceives people very easily.

Next, witnesses can be easily led by 'leading questions' and 'leaning questions' (i.e. questions which 'lean' on them, such as 'Surely you're not so naive as to think...' or 'You don't really believe that...' which put people on the defensive). This is especially good for bullying the weak and submissive Moderates and those who desire to appear 'reasonable' and 'helpful'. They can be pushed by a succession of tiny degrees into saying something they did not really mean. As soon as they do so, it is pounced upon and recorded. Then there is 'hostile questioning' for the Moderates, 'benign questioning' for the Marxists. It is also easy to take advantage of witnesses who are not very fully informed. Suggestions are put to them with which they half-heartedly concur because they are not sure of their ground, and again their answers are pounced on and recorded as though they were genuine opinions.

The terms of reference of the inquiry are either specific and pointed towards the area of interest that favours the Marxists, or are non-existent and invented as the inquiry proceeds so the Moderates do not know what is coming up. Most important of all, witnesses' contributions are summarised very selectively. Any anti-Marxist bits are omitted, and heavy weather is made of anything favouring the Marxists. Remarks are torn out of context and summaries are carefully phrased to favour the Marxist side. There was a complaint from one witness at the Autumn 1977 Newham North-East Inquiry, a Mr Norris, a member of the Labour Party for twenty-eight years, who swore an affidavit saying:

On page nine of the report an account of my testimony
is given. It states 'Mr Norris said it was a democratic Party
and during his many years of membership he had seen
both left and right come and go.' This is a total mis-
representation of my evidence. ... No mention is made
of the concern I expressed at communist infiltration
of the Party, and I regard the report as a deliberate
attempt to twist what I said to the Inquiry members,
because I spoke up for the Moderates.

The scope for twisting, omitting, rephrasing, exaggerating,
toning down, tearing out of context, confusing and misleading that is available to the inquiry members is
tremendous. One of the most essential principles in any
inquiry is that its members should be of the highest integrity
and of acknowledged impartiality, and that no one should be
a judge in his own cause — *'Nemo iudex in re sua'*. This does
not apply in Marxist-run Inquiries. Another delightful ploy is
for Marxists to include a wet token Moderate or two, who
can be bullied, politically-bribed, or conned into sitting on
the inquiry team and giving it still more respectability.
Marxists always manage to find some Moderates to do their
work for them.

One technique I thought quite effective was for 'hostile
witnesses' to pose as 'friendly' witnesses which gives a false
impression of a genuine spread of opinion. Thus Owen
Ashworth posed as a Moderate when he attended the
inquiry. His recorded testimony begins: 'He considered himself moderate on some issues but not on others.' The court
had to be told that he was renowned for holding very left-
wing views.

In our society, fortunately, there are few opportunities for
Marxists to hold trials. Occasionally 'kangaroo courts' are
held by Marxists in trade union branches. But in a Marxist
society the 'show trial' is a well-known piece of household
furniture. It is very interesting to read how in the 1930s vast
numbers of socialists, liberals and conservatives in England
and America were completely taken in by Stalin's show
trials. Only the most acute and perceptive saw through the
subterfuge. Marxist-run inquiries similarly fool a large
number of people. The Transport House Inquiry into
Newham North-East fooled a lot of people, including even

judges who are trained to be sceptical.

The poisoned grapevine

The Marxists have an extremely well-developed and pervasive grapevine which forms a most efficient communications system. It enables each Marxist to make instant comments on matters far removed from his immediate sphere of activities. There is thus a Marxist 'version' of almost everything, especially of topical events. This version is often hopelessly, and usually deliberately, false with regard to some of the facts and the overall interpretation of them. Yet the presence of some correct facts, and above all the pretension to knowledge of the matter, gives the Marxist an enormous advantage in debates. Hitler used to say that the politician should tell the 'Big Lie' and pointed out that lies are very effective at public meetings: you can only check up later on, the damage has then been done, and few people bother to check up anyway. A combination of lies, half-truths, and truths is the most devastating combination of all, especially when pitched against the ignorant and uneducated. This is what the 'poisoned grapevine' furnishes each Marxist with.

The technique enables prominent figures to be brought into play to make instant comments on matters of which they have no direct knowledge; they are fed the information through the poisoned grapevine. Thus when the Injunction was served to stop the February 1977 Annual Meeting, a version of the incident was fed to Arthur Latham, MP for Paddington and a prominent Tribunite. He came out with a statement, which was splashed across the front pages of the London papers, condemning the serving of the Injunction. The report (London *Evening News* 24 February 1977, front page) stated:

A Labour MP today called on the Lord Chancellor, Lord Elwyn-Jones, to order an immediate inquiry into the behaviour of court officials at the annual meeting of the Newham North-East Labour Party. Mr Arthur Latham (Paddington), immediate past-chairman of the Tribune Group, said: 'There must be a full-scale inquiry ... the inquiry must consider the uncouth behaviour of the court officials who burst into the Newham North-East meeting without warning, with no prior notice, and in a totally uncivilised manner, terrifying particularly some of the women in the audience.... This goes far beyond the 'dirty tricks brigade' ... and this hooligan behaviour by the court officials is beyond belief.'

This description of four men quietly walking through a door-way is a typical example of the most unadulterated rubbish. It was not only wholly false, it was absolutely preposterous. As Mr Prentice said, 'We were surprised when they came in, but there was no hooliganism.' This kind of fictitious non-sense can be very damaging politically.

The Marxists use the technique of the poisoned grapevine and they engage 'Rent-a-voice', often a prominent public figure, to peddle their intentions. How can one guard against the systematic inventing and peddling of a damaging tissue of complete lies as a deliberate and calculated tactic for political advantage? I wondered what the grapevine link was with Latham. *Latham was not there*, yet he spoke as though he knew the facts. Some of the Newham Leftists evidently primed Latham within hours of the event so he could give an account of what may have taken place and make his instant comment on that.

The defamation campaign

In any kind of dispute it is not unknown for tempers to flare and harsh words to be spoken. Less frequently, people rush into print with careless words, leading to a slander or libel action. But this is not what I am discussing here. I am dis-cussing a 'defamation campaign' — a cold-blooded, calculated, systematic campaign of character assassination to deter, punish and discredit individuals who stand up to the Marxists and organise opposition to them. I know all about this because I was at the receiving-end of just such a campaign when I stood against a Communist for the post of President of the Graduate Society of Balliol College, Oxford, several years ago. Many other people have been victims of this Marxist tactic in the three Newham constituencies and Islington North. Sometimes it takes the form of a 'whispering campaign', sometimes of printed, or more usually duplicated, material.

In Newham an eight-page leaflet was circulated among Labour Party members. It was a 'libel leaflet', devoted to personal attacks on Moderate Labour councillors and officers in the three Newham constituencies. I say it was a libel leaflet because it was devoted exclusively to vicious attacks on people's private lives and was designed to ruin their reputations. It accused people falsely of having affairs, causing untold misery to their families. Some people were accused of being crooks. Stuff about the people concerned was often invented in surprising detail, though if you checked up on it you found it to be completely false. A lot of trouble went into these attempts at character assassination: they were cunningly devised to sow discord and misunderstandings, implant suspicions and cause agonising embarrassment and distress to their victims. The leaflet was called *Tupp'enny 'Orrible* and it lived up to its name. The Moderates used to dread the appearance of the next issue. They could never do anything about it. The first issue gave the address of its printer and publisher: it turned out to be a boarded-up house that had been empty for some time. The second issue gave as the address that of a prominent Moderate councillor. One issue gave details of some monstrous sexual perversions that were attributed to two prominent Moderates. Sometimes it would include true reports to make the rest of the stuff convincing, though even what was true still represented a gross intrusion upon privacy. One issue of this magazine containing a despicable attack on a respected Moderate Councillor came out the week he died and caused great distress to his family.

Corrupt historiography

The Marxists are good at distorting history, turning prominent politicians into 'unpersons' if they take the wrong side. In Russia such people are expunged from the history books. The men on top have the books rewritten to put them at the centre of the historical stage when in reality they had been sulking in the wings. There is a marvellous description of this in *Animal Farm* where Napoleon, who was in reality bloodied by a stray pellet when fleeing from the scene of the battle, re-emerges in the history books as the hero of the hour.

It is early days for the Newham North-East story to be rewritten but in due course it will be. In the meantime we can see the coalescing of the myth. The Newham North-

East Labour Party saw before anyone else that Mr Prentice
was a Tory-in-disguise and for this reason got rid of him. The
Tory Press organised a hate-campaign against them, but they
had the support of most local Labour Party members. The
Party was then infiltrated by Oxford University elements
tied in with the intelligence services and various extreme
right-wing groups with a large slush fund of money that had
come from the CIA. These 'infiltrators' were working to
destroy the Labour Party; they fooled a few of the older
residents who did not understand what was going on and
they tried to use the courts to bankrupt the Labour Party
and put those who opposed them in prison. They were
completely ruthless and cynical manipulators, exploiting
the Rule-Book for their own advantage and determined to
do down those who were working selflessly to solve
Newham's housing problems. Marxist historians will write
up the 'Shrewsbury Two' as though they were the twentieth
century 'reincarnation of the Tolpuddle Martyrs' when in
reality they were a couple of violent thugs. Corrupt Historiography is when you write up stuff knowing perfectly well it
is untrue and misleading. It is a terrible form of intellectual
dishonesty.

Mendacious Misdescription

It is not only mendacious misdescription; it is malicious misdescription. It is a Marxist speciality. Marxists elevate the
'slogan' to the forefront of politics, though the slogan is in
itself an inaccurate, over-simplifying, shorthand type of
political argument. George Orwell satirised a typical slogan
as 'Four legs good: two legs bad.' Our Marxists in Newham
did not get far beyond that level.

The slogan itself is only a very mild form of this technique.
The worst form of it is 'false labelling', especially when it
becomes a 'political libel'. A 'political libel' is not necessarily
a libel in legal terms. It is not an attack on the reputation of
the individual but a smear on his political associations and
connexions. For example, Julian and I were accused of taking
money from the CBI. Allegations like this were completely
wild and no evidence was offered. This is one of the most
damaging allegations that can be made against a member of
the Labour Party, but, because it is not an attack on
character, it is not legally a libel.

Allegations of this kind flew thick and fast, not just against us but against many of the other Newham Moderates. The law offers no protection whatever against them — but they are singularly damaging. Did you know that you could be accused quite falsely of being 'a police informer' and you could not bring a successful libel action? These kinds of allegations are based on the maxim 'Fling enough mud and some of it will stick.' We were even smeared with being connected with the National Front — a vicious and ludicrous allegation.

Organisations like clubs and associations can be 'libelled' too. The CRD (Campaign for Representative Democracy) was called a 'CIA front'. There is no remedy for this kind of unjustified attack even though it weakens the organisation considerably.

Next on our list comes *PROVOCATION*, with its techniques of aggravating grievances and engineering confrontations.

Grievance — Aggravation

The aggravation of grievances is part of the Marxist repertoire. The Newham Marxists specialised in aggravating industrial disputes (some were connected with Fords at Dagenham), student disputes, race relations problems, lack of adequate housing and so on. They did nothing constructive to assist those who were grappling with the problems; instead they went out of their way to open old wounds and put salt in them. Of all the grievances they aggravated I think they had most success with the racial ones in Newham. The National Front were, of course, doing their bit of aggravation on the other side of the fence.

Confrontation — Engineering

Marxists also find the engineering of confrontations very useful. The technique works like this. First they do something to their advantage which is quite impermissible, and if the Moderates ignore it they do it again, or do worse, and collect all the advantages from it. They go on doing this until finally the Moderates are forced to respond. This response is depicted as authoritarian and ruthless and a number of Moderates are alienated. The Marxists go on producing these confrontations knowing full well they are forcing the Moder-

ates either to admit defeat or to respond in a way that will
alienate a substantial portion of their number, even if it is the
only way to save the situation.

For example, in Newham North-East the Marxists resorted
to all sorts of illegal and sometimes violent methods. This
engineered a confrontation and even a mere war of words
turned the stomach of some of the Moderates who fell from
the field slain by a boomeranging sharp word from other
Moderates. When legal action had to be used, further Moderates were alienated and fell by the wayside. So the Marxists
cheated and cheated and cheated — each time obliging the
Moderates either to give up or go on with one legal action
after another. Each successive one was depicted by the
Marxists as more 'extreme' than the one before and more
and more Moderates felt it was 'going too far'. The Marxists
provoke confrontation after confrontation hoping, usually
rightly, that the Moderates will lose their stomach for the
fight and be frightened off at the escalation of the conflict.

Sometimes Marxists try to provoke the police or authorities into an over-reaction. They then pose as persecuted
martyrs, like a stunt-man who runs across the road and
pretends to have been hit by an oncoming car, which really
has just missed him. His accomplice then steps forward to
demand compensation. One of the Marxists in Newham on
one occasion engineered a false row with a Moderate
councillor, hit him, and then fell clutching himself as though
he had been hit and demanded to be rushed off to hospital!

The final group of methods comprises those concerned with
MANIPULATION. It includes tedium, procrastination,
hypocrisy, siphoning of funds, honeycombing, adjusting
minutes and suppression of information.

The tedium weapon: 'boring out'

This is a well-known Marxist technique. A large number of
people may turn up at the beginning of a meeting. They are
then 'bored out'. The tedium weapon is turned on them.
Marxists deliberately haggle over every tiny detail and engage
in interminable monologues until they have literally bored
many of the Moderates out of the meeting. They have been
known to drag out meetings for hours and hours until most
of the Moderates have left before they deal with the impor-

tant business of the meeting.

At Oxford I became very familiar with this technique. At Newham, however, it had a much more limited scope because the Rules limited meetings to 2¼ hours maximum, though there was still room for the calling of extra meetings. The protection of the Rules, and the possibility of legal enforcement, did largely prevent this technique from wreaking its customary havoc. If only there were similar protection against all the other techniques! The only trouble with this protective mechanism was that it made Moderate-controlled bodies vulnerable to the 'filibuster'. The Moderate-dominated Newham North-East EC suffered a massive filibuster in September 1977.

Procrastination

This was much more successful. The Marxists at Newham characteristically procrastinated rather than refused. An 'indefinite procrastination' amounted in reality to an 'outright refusal' but it did not look so bad. This technique was applied to all sorts of things. If someone was entitled to vote once he obtained his Labour Party card, they would simply delay giving it to him for weeks, and often months, on end. If someone applied to join the Labour Party he could be 'stalled' for ages. It took Mr Milsom several months and threats of legal action before he could be admitted as a member of the Party. Many of the Moderates recruited to the Labour Party suffered interminable delays in the processing of their memberships by the Marxists. The motto was: 'Don't say No; Just say Wait.' The same technique, if it can be dignified with the term, was applied when it came to surrendering documents. For example, if Moderates were elected to replace Marxists, the Marxists delayed handing over the files. They figured, often rightly, that the Moderates would have been driven to resignation or otherwise forced out of office before they could be forced to surrender the files. Without the files, the job of the Moderate was often difficult, sometimes impossible.

Organised hypocrisy

Marxists are masters of the 'double standard' and the technique of 'organised hypocrisy' is frequently used. In its most characteristic form it consists of condemning others for

doing what you do yourself. The most striking example in
Newham was the fact that we were repeatedly and strongly
attacked for 'bringing the law into politics', having 'the
courts interfere in private Labour Party business' and so
forth. The Marxists' attack on us simply for using the law
reached a crescendo – until we began to wonder whether to
use the law made us some kind of criminal. Yet, having
based their whole case on opposition to the principle of
using the law, they applauded the Newham South left-
wingers for taking the Party officers to court to get themselves reinstated; and they applauded Joan Lestor's
Injunction against several Newham Moderates depriving them
of their political rights. This appalling Injunction, which I
described at the time as the equivalent of a South African
'banning order', was granted to the very person, Miss Joan
Lestor MP, extreme left-wing Chairman of the Labour Party,
who had been one of our most vocal critics for using the
courts.

Siphoning of funds

Marxists acquire their money from diverse sources, often
foreign ones. One of their favourite techniques is siphoning
off the funds of some official or non-partisan body and
applying the money to their own purposes. We saw earlier
how Militant's official policy was to use the youth wing of
the Labour Party (the Young Socialists) to provide funds for
their Marxist faction. It is a commonplace for students'
union funds to be siphoned off and applied to Marxist causes.

A variation on this technique is to siphon off paid time
(this amounts to siphoning off money because time is money
when it is paid for by a salary or wages). This takes the form
of spending working hours on Marxist pursuits. It can be
done 'officially' by getting an official or non-partisan body
to adopt Marxist policies or 'unofficially' by simply taking
time out to devote to Marxist pursuits. State-funded law
centres are often hotbeds of Marxist activity. A number of
the Eleemysonary charities devote part of their time or
budget to Marxist politicking. It is very bad when they
become infiltrated by Marxists who divert them to some
extent from alleviating poverty and suffering to promoting
social and political systems that will destroy people's liberties
and do little or nothing to alleviate the poverty. A consider-

able amount of siphoning of money or paid time goes on in some of the trade unions and trades councils too.

Honeycombing of organisations

Marxists strengthen their impact enormously by using their personnel over and over again in different organisations which are all interlocking. They do not usually declare themselves as Marxists but claim to be working for the ostensible aims and objects of the organisation concerned. Marxist 'cells' are built in all these different organisations and the net effect is a honeycomb-like set-up which is devoted to Marxist pursuits. There are very many of these different organisations that are either set up specially by Marxists or taken over by them. They tend to go especially for industrial relations, race relations, feminist, youth and pacifist organisations, and to a lesser extent for ecological, anti-poverty and educational organisations.

Adjusting the minutes

One form of manipulation that I came across quite frequently in Oxford and Newham was 'adjusting the minutes' of committee meetings to distort what had really taken place. Usually it was done by omissions: it is amazing how much you can distort a record simply by missing important bits out. However, the adjustment often went beyond that to saying that certain things were 'agreed' when they were not agreed at all.

Suppression of information: 'unofficial secrets'

'Knowledge is power' in many circumstances and the person who controls access to knowledge exercises power. Sometimes this power is grossly abused. The Marxists put the Moderates at a serious disadvantage by denying them information that they were entitled to have. 'Suppression of the lists' was one technique. Moderates in Newham found it impossible in many cases to find out the list of members for their own ward! The Marxist who was the Secretary refused to provide the information and treated membership as a closely guarded secret — to be guarded from his fellow members. The Marxist had the advantage of the lists: he could canvass, check that no Moderate non-member voted and so on. The Moderate could not canvass the members and had no way of discovering whether Marxist non-members were voting. Marxists often treat the Rule-Book as a state secret — except that it is often better kept than many state secrets.

In Newham North-East many areas of the Party were a completely closed book to most members. Where the Marxists had got into firm control of certain wards an 'Iron Curtain' had been erected against not only members of other wards but even the ordinary member of the ward itself. The files were treated like gold-dust, not to be scattered among the plebs. Indeed, if any ordinary ward member had the temerity to ask to see the list of his fellow ward-members he would get a reaction rather like that of Oliver Twist when he went up for a second helping of soup. To treat vital information that should be freely available to all members in an open democratic Party as 'unofficial secrets' is a powerful technique for perpetuating control. It makes a mockery of an election if one side does not know who the electorate is.

So much then for Marxist methods. Of course, I recognise that certain of these tactics may be used from time to time by non-Marxist groups. However, the significant political fact is the existence of a *distinctive Marxist method* consisting of the deliberate, sustained and systematic use of a whole range of these techniques as a calculated device for political advantage. It amazes me that so few people have noticed this most important political phenomenon. I have described the characteristic methods of Marxists when infiltrating the Labour Party and operating within the Labour Movement. I have built up this picture directly from my own experiences in, or knowledge of, four Labour constituencies and university student politics at Oxford. I do not believe that my experience is atypical. It would be extraordinary if Marxists behaved like this in the three Newham constituencies, Oxford University and Islington North — but nowhere else. But it is useful to point out how this experience fits into the overall picture when one looks at other higher education institutes and also at Marxist countries.

The methods I have examined are not methods of civilised politics. They have no place in a democratic society. Intimidation, cheating, falsification, provocation and manipulation are the quintessence of Stalinism. In Newham, it should be remembered, they have been used chiefly against ordinary working-class people who have been members of the Labour Party for between twenty and fifty years, most of them fairly elderly people. These people should never have been subjected to such methods. The Marxists must stand condemned for the Marxist methods they have used. Even if this were the only point that could be made against them, it would be bad enough. But it is not.

Since this chapter was written further evidence has emerged of Marxist terror tactics on an organised national basis. Scunthorpe in Lincolnshire is a long way from Newham, but the familiar Marxist methods crop up again. Mr Cyril Nottingham was a Labour Councillor for seventeen years and is a former Mayor of Scunthorpe. But in 1974, when he was leader of the Labour group, he revealed documents showing that left-wing extremists were trying to infiltrate the Labour Party nationally. He became known as a strong-minded Moderate. He was expelled from the Labour Party on the accusation of 'bringing it into disrepute'. His troubles did not cease on being expelled; he has been persecuted ever since. He had to leave Scunthorpe and live in a nearby village. In an editorial entitled 'Marxist Mafia' on 11 June 1979 The Sun *stated:*

> '*The hounding of moderate politicians by left-wing extremists is nothing new. But events in Scunthorpe suggest that some of these fanatics are now prepared to use Mafia tactics against their enemies. Mr Cyril Nottingham ... has been the victim of a vicious campaign. He and his family have received countless abusive telephone calls, vehicles belonging to his firm have been damaged and a slab of concrete was put through the plate-glass windows of one of his shops. [This was the third time within three months.] So frightened has Mr Nottingham become that his shops have now been fitted with hot-lines to the police station. And his wife has been put on tranquillisers. The Marxist Mafiosi of Scunthorpe might be proud of themselves. But their conduct will not win them a single vote from democratic citizens — of whatever party.*'

7
Conclusions

Newham North-East is not unique. What happened there
could happen anywhere. Indeed it already has happened in
many other constituencies.

Newham North-East is the most famous example of a
new trend in British politics — Marxist takeovers of constituency Labour parties.

Over the last decade there have been a number of cases
where moderate Labour MP's were ousted and replaced by
left-wingers. For example, Desmond Donnelly in Pembroke
was replaced by left-winger, Parry; Dick Taverne in Lincoln
was replaced by left-winger, Margaret Jackson; Eddie
Griffiths in Sheffield Brightside was replaced by one of
Labour's most fervent Marxists, Joan Maynard. Among the
most recent cases were Hammersmith North where Frank
Tomney was replaced by a left-winger and Liverpool Edge
Hill where Sir Arthur Irvine was driven out in sad circumstances which, his election agent said, helped to bring about
his death. So widespread was the local revulsion that this
formerly safe Labour seat was lost at a by-election in March
1979 to the Liberals. A very strong attack was made from
1977 to 1979 on Neville Sandelson, the moderate Labour
MP for Hayes and Harlington. Left-wingers took over his
constituency — they tried to drop him in 1977 but after
the personal intervention of the Prime Minister and Michael
Foot, he survived by four votes. Despite this rejection of
their attempt to drop him, the local left-wingers did not
accept the verdict and in March 1979 they tried again
(having increased their GMC vote by over 50% in the meantime) and this time were successful by 31 to 25 votes. But
it was too late at this stage to drop Sandelson for the May
1979 General Election.

If it were a question of MP's being dropped for personal reasons then there would be no discernible trend in the *dismissing* or in the *selecting*. In other words, one right-winger would be replaced by another, one left-winger by another left-winger, centrists would replace centrists, sometimes a left-winger would replace a right-winger, but sometimes it would be the other way round.

But this is *not* what has happened. Only one left-winger has been sacked in recent times — Eddie Milne. He was sacked for his integrity in exposing corruption, not because of his left-wing views. But he was replaced in Blyth by another left-winger, John Ryman. Maureen Colquhoun, MP for Northampton North, is a left-winger and she came under attack. But this time Labour's Nation Executive Committee jumped into action and saved her.

So there is a very clear principle at work: *Right-wing Labour MP's are sacked and replaced by left-wingers*. This is the steady trend. There is no reverse trend. All the evidence shows that this is the direction in which things are moving. Remember that when seven Moderates are dropped and replaced by seven left-wingers — the total advantage to the Marxist camp in Parliament is fourteen votes. This represents a major advance for the Marxists.

But it is far too slow for their liking. So they support the left-wing Campaign for Labour Party Democracy (President — Frank Allaun, Vice-President — Joan Maynard) which has been beavering away to change the Labour Party Rules in favour of compulsory reselection. This would mean that for each General Election the candidate is chosen afresh instead of the MP automatically becoming the candidate. It would make it very easy to get rid of moderate MP's and replace them by Marxists because you would no longer have to sack a moderate MP. His candidacy would automatically lapse and someone else would be chosen next time round. Consequently it could all be done more stealthily without the full glare of publicity involved in a big row between the MP and the local left-wing activists.

This move has already been very successful. Although it did not go as far as they demanded, the Marxists were nevertheless pleased with the major step forward when the 1977 Annual Conference (i.e. half-a-dozen union bosses plus the left-wing constituency activists) voted to approve automatic reselection in principle. The 1978 Annual Conference made the necessary changes in the Labour Party Rules. This means that after the 1979 General Election for the first time all Labour MPs will have to be reselected.

In the space of just four years (1973—1977) the Marxist camp gained twelve votes through dropping six Moderates and replacing them with left-wingers. I see no reason why it should not gain at least twenty-four votes (if not many more) by dropping twelve Moderates over the four years after the 1979 General Election. It has been suggested by several Labour MP's that there are twenty to thirty Labour Moderates 'at risk' now that automatic reselection has been introduced. This could mean a net gain to the Marxist camp of up to sixty votes.

The removal of a Moderate by a motion to deselect him is a 'political sacking' (i.e. a sacking for political reasons, rather than a 'personal sacking'). But this is only the tip of the iceberg. Much more serious, insidious, and extensive is the stealthy replacement of a Labour right-winger who has died, retired, taken up another occupation, withdrawn through illness, gone to the Lords, or departed for some other reason, by a centrist, or still worse, by a leftist, or worst of all, by a really hard-line Marxist.

All of these tilt the balance more towards the extreme left. For example, the moderate MP for Vauxhall, George Strauss, the Father of the House, had a successor for the 1979 General Election; Dr Stuart Holland, the Marxist intellectual. Similarly, Ernie Roberts, who was banned from standing as a Labour candidate for most of the period since 1945 because of his very left-wing views and his association with the Communist *Daily Worker* (now *The Morning Star*) is the successor to the moderate Labour MP for Hackney North. The very left-wing Denys 'Reg' Race, former student radical and NUPE Press Officer, took over in May 1979 the safe Labour seat of Wood Green from Joyce Butler (centre-left) who retired. The 1979 crop of very left-wing candidates also included Ken Livingstone (Hampstead) and Ted Knight (Hornsey).

Other changes are more mild — but still tilt the balance to the left. For example, Roy Jenkins, a right-winger, was succeeded by Terry Davis, a centrist. For over a decade the Labour Party has been losing many of its most able and strong-minded social democrat MP's — Woodrow Wyatt, Desmond Donnelly, Roy Jenkins, David Marquand, Reg Prentice, Brian Walden, Dick Leonard, Dick Taverne, John Mackintosh. There is no-one to take their places.

Let me illustrate the nature of the changes by referring to the Parliamentary position as it was in April 1979 prior to the General Election. At that time the Parliamentary Labour Party was composed as follows:

Left-Wing	Centre	Right-Wing
122	123	69

The most striking developments over the last decade have been the steady and massive erosion of the old Gaitskellite Social Democratic right wing of the Party, and the rapid growth of the left-wing (including a number of hard-line Marxists). For the purpose of simplified calculation let us assume that the April 1979 Parliament contained 300 Labour MPs (instead of about 315) and that they were divided equally between the 3 sections of the Party (this will over-state the strength of the right-wing so it therefore represents a conservative estimate of the extent of left-wing advance).

Left-Wing	Centre	Right-Wing
100	100	100

Let us count left-wingers at 1 point each, centrists at 2 points each, and right-wingers at 3 points each. It follows that the maximum score is 900 and the minimum score is 300, and the present score is 600. The corresponding political complexion is shown below:

300 —MINIMUM SCORE: MARXIST REGIME: HEFFER/MIKARDO/MAYNARD

550 —LEFT-WING REGIME: FOOT/BENN/SHORE

600 —PRESENT SCORE: WILSON/CALLAGHAN/ HEALEY

650 —MODERATE REGIME: WILLIAMS/OWEN/ HATTERSLEY

900 —MAXIMUM SCORE: SOCIAL DEMOCRATIC REGIME: JENKINS/RODGERS

The April 1979 score of 600 (which itself is an over-estimate) is the lowest ever for any Labour Government and is an indication of the extent of left-wing advance over the last decade. It can easily be seen that replacing just 25 right-

wingers by 25 left-wingers will make a substantial difference
to the political complexion of the Parliamentary Labour
Party and jerk it violently to the left.

What might be termed 'natural vacancies' offer a bigger
target for Marxist infiltrators than seats where they have to
remove an incumbent Moderate first. About 84 of the
present Labour MP's are sixty or over. Assuming that about
60% of these retire at or before the next election there will
be about 50 natural vacancies. Assuming that natural wastage
(death, illness, bankruptcy, criminal conviction, lucrative
offers outside Parliament, family problems, business commit-
ments etc.) depletes the ranks of those under sixty by about
10%, there will be a further 23 vacancies. In both cases some,
but not necessarily all of these, would be seats where automatic reselection could remove people who would otherwise
naturally fall by the wayside.

Taken overall there could be about 75 natural vacancies
and perhaps even a further 25 artificial vacancies (caused by
re-selection). This presents plenty of opportunity for the
Marxist infiltrators. Of course they are not yet able to
penetrate all areas. Trotskyist strength is concentrated in the
London constituencies, in Bristol, Leeds, Bradford, York and
Sheffield. In these areas Marxists from Polytechnics and
Technical Colleges have taken over their local Labour Parties.
The Social Educational Association, ASTMS, and the Young
Socialists have usually been the spearhead for the attack. The
Trotskyists are becoming stronger in Wales.

The defeat of the Labour Party on 3 May 1979 has not
altered the general trend. Some well-known left-wingers
(like Arthur Latham) in marginal seats were defeated, but
many centrists and right-wingers were defeated too. The
relative strengths of Labour's left, centre and right in Parliament have not changed markedly. The defeat has weakened
the power of Labour Party Moderates like Jim Callaghan who
no longer has the Prime Ministerial patronage to help tame
left-wing Labour MP's. Above all, the constituency activists
who usually go quiet in the run-up to an election to avoid
frightening the electorate, are now beginning to renew their
offensive. The crucial election will be the next one due in
1984 (if the present parliament) runs its full term). The
Labour party when it goes into that election is likely to be
more left-wing than ever before.

What has happened in Newham North-East is the model of how a Marxist takeover is accomplished. There is nothing unusual, special or peculiar about how the Marxists took over between 1972 and 1976 — it is a copybook example of how it is being done everywhere that these takeovers are occurring. That is why it has been important to examine it in detail. Not only are the methods and techniques of the Marxists much the same nationwide but the Newham North-East constituency Labour Party is a pretty average Party and in many ways typical of the majority of parties. Mr Underhill in his affidavit stated: 'a CLP (Constituency Labour Party) usually consists of about 1,000 paid-up members divided into six to eight branches; normally about 150—200 of the 1,000 are active within the CLP; 70—80 could control a CLP; a branch may contain only 15—20 members (he means 'active members') so that only eight or nine people could control it.' I accept all this as broadly accurate, although obviously there are many local variations. But this has been the general pattern ever since individual Labour Party membership began in 1918. These facts do mean that a determined group, acting in concert, can win control of branches or even of a CLP (Constituency Labour Party). Newham North-East was typical in these respects — it had about 1,000 members, nine Party branches (wards) whose membership varied from about 60 to about 140, and only a small portion of these — ten to twenty per cent were active members. Newham North-East was typical in the constitutional sense because it shared the same basic constitutional structure laid down in the Rules for constituency organisations. So in writing about Newham North-East I have been writing about a constituency whose main features are shared by a fairly large, and growing number of constituency Parties.

Newham North-East between 1972 and 1976 has provided a glimpse of the rather horrific future that awaits constituencies that are taken over. In that sense it may foretell the shape of things to come. Newham North-East could become the *norm* for most Labour constituencies in the 1980s. Islington North is in just this position at present. Newham North-East has two models for us — the model of a Marxist takeover and the model of a vigorous Moderate resistance.

Of all our institutions the political parties are in the worst state. They are positively primitive. You cannot be a Cabinet

Minister, Prime Minister or (with rare exceptions) and MP without belonging to a political party. It is the parties who select councillors, MPs and our political leaders. Yet their legal basis is that of a golf-club and they are subject to fewer regulations than a street corner off-licence. They are in many respects inefficient and they have comparatively few resources. I do not know so much about the Tory Party or the Liberals. But the Labour Party is in a rotten state. Bureaucrats at Transport House and Regional Office exercise enormous power — and they should not be exercising any. Membership figures are completely false. Minutes and records of meetings are patchy and often inaccurate. The Rules are regularly flouted. Labour Party membership is steadily declining.

There are now only about 400,000 Labour Party members (official figure for 1976 was 659,058 but this was false). Of these only about forty thousand are active, so twenty-one thousand people form a majority. This is a very small number. Looked at another way — there are some 620 odd constituencies. Forty people in each constituency Labour Party should be enough to dominate it. Of the constituencies we are only interested in the ones Labour needs to win in order to form a government, say about 320. In order to control *all* these the Marxists need to find only some 12,800 constituency activists. In order to control the majority of these they only need to find about 6,500 activists and get them to the right places.

Now, 6,500 is a very, very small number of people out of about 56 million people in Britain. There are more than 6,500 Marxists in Britain today. A system which is vulnerable to a takeover by such a small handful of people is a rotten system. It is just like the rotten boroughs of the early nineteenth century. But it would not be of very great significance how rotten the system was — were it not for the fact that organised groups of totalitarian Marxists have set out to exploit its weaknesses. The system has always been pretty rotten — though in the past at least more people took part. But the decline of membership is *not* the crucial factor. Small organised groups could have taken over the constituency Labour Parties in the past.

The *new* factors are the strategic decision taken by Marxist groups to organise large-scale infiltration and the fact that the

Labour Party's defences have been dismantled. The pro-scribed list (banning Communists from Labour Party membership) has been abolished and the right-wingers have lost their majority on the NEC. The NEC no longer, as in the past, intervenes to stop Marxist takeovers — it now intervenes to help them. Marxist infiltration on a large organised scale is a new phenomenon. Consequently many people have not realised its significance. The large-scale infiltration of the 1970s is completely new to British politics. Weaknesses and faults in the system that could once be ignored are now a serious danger. For the last couple of decades, under Wilson and Callaghan, Labour leaders have let the situation slide and now it has started to get out of hand.

I have dubbed Marxist infiltrators 'Enemies of Democracy' and they have emerged by their political views, their modes of organisation, their personalities and behaviour and their methods as virulent opponents of all the civilised values that are summed up by the word 'democracy' used to denote the liberal democratic system that they are dedicated to destroy. Ultimately their politics leads, whether they know it or not, to a Party elite dictatorship enforced by a secret police and a bevy of bureaucrats and state officials. But they hold out in the short-term something which they have the gall to call 'democracy'. It is not.

It is the false ideal of *activocracy* i.e. the rule of the active. It holds that only those who show a high level of commit-ment and expend a great deal of time and energy are entitled to exercise political power, and that those who do not should be effectively excluded from having any influence. Their ideal system is one in which the Marxists, as political *samurai*, are each equivalent, in political terms, to ten ordinary people. This is not the 'one man, one vote' principle of political equality which underlies democratic theory. So they support a system which permits multiple voting (the wearing of many hats) and all the latterday variants on the pocket boroughs and rotten boroughs of the past which historians tell us went out in 1832. They did not. They were simply transferred from the constituency seat to the constituency party. Where the real power is, the rottenness is usually to be found — and the spring-cleaning job is done on those rooms which no longer house real power and are just for show.

In addition to an activocracy they uphold the ideal of the

hack. The person whose human values are so distorted that he neglects his wife and family, neglects the pursuit of knowledge, neglects his work, neglects his service to the community, and instead wishes to spend his time on intriguing, petty organisational manoeuvres, filing clerk's work and other bureaucratic specialities, and on the manipulation of institutions, is the political hack *par excellence*. Indeed he is the Stalinist hack as we have seen. This dismal ideal of *hackery* is the second component. And the last is fanaticism — a false religion, a dreary scholasticism, a blind faith, a vision peopled with mechanical images, a dismal sub-utopia, an obsessive and cock-eyed perspective on the world — these are the hallmarks of the Seventh Day Marxists. And they wish to put us all through that baptism of fire. They preach the politics of hate and they practise what they preach.

And so to describe this witches' brew in the barbarous neologism that somehow seems to fit it — the Marxists hold out for us the ideal of a *'fanbacktivocracy'* and they call it 'democracy' though all the two have in common is the 'ocracy'. It may be that *they* cannot distinguish between the Rule of the People and the Rule of fanatical, activist hacks — but we need not suffer the same incapacity.

Just because these 'ideology addicts' try to press their goods on us — does not mean that we need to accept them. It is time to take the kid-gloves off when dealing with such specimens. For too long now they have been resisted by pussy footers who give them credit where none is due, recognise their sincere and benevolent intentions where none exist, and engage in fruitless debates with them, aiming to persuade them — the unpersuadable. Enough of this! The Marxists have had more than 50 years to impress us with their examples and 100 years to impress us with their arguments. Their doctrine has been tried and found — not merely wanting, but absolutely deadly. The debate is over. We now no longer, *pace* Shirley Williams, should try to persuade them, but simply try to beat them. For too long we have shadow-boxed with these people and given them too many benefits of too many doubts.

The Marxists have the impertinence to talk of raising the level of political consciousness of the workers. But the political consciousness of the Marxists is actually lower than that of the untutored workers. The Marxists think of themselves as superior, as the leaders of the workers — but they are way behind them. The workers have nothing to learn from the likes of Andy Bevan or Norman Atkinson.

The Marxist infiltration in the constituencies goes one better than Lenin — he acted in the name of a largely non-existent working class — they kick the real workers out of Party positions and pursue policies that are diametrically opposed to those that the real workers support — and they do all this in the name of the very same working class that they are trampling on! The Marxists kicked the authentic working people out of the Newham Party positions and took the name of the working class in vain while doing so. Who is the worker — Transport House bureaucrat Bevan, Polytechnic lecturer Bradbury — or Mr Milsom, the bus-driver?

Like political *poseurs* they mouth revolutionary slogans, though like Napoleon in *Animal Farm* they are not carried away to the extent that they put themselves in the firing-line. It was interesting to watch the Newham Marxists on trial for contempt of court. They longed to be revolutionary heroes but they did not want to pay the price. They wanted martyrdom on the cheap. They wanted to be martyrs without having to die. Andy Bevan was torn between the desire to show contempt for the courts that he was always attacking and yet not be sent to prison even if only for a few days — so he posed outside the court with the Rentacrowd making revolutionary noises but inside he wore a three-piece suit, brushed his hair, and employed (at the Labour Party's expense, of course) a clever Tory QC to get him off the hook on technicalities — he need not have bothered as Mr Justice Pain looked after his interests very satisfactorily.

The Newham Marxists were not even authentic revolutionaries, just Stalinist hacks. They were very brave when they had 40 of them in a meeting and 4 of us; some of them were very brave over the other end of an anonymous telephone call — but not so brave outside these contexts. In almost every respect they are bogus and false. They call their take-overs of constituency parties 'the advance of socialism' but looking at the way the forty Marxists on the GMC took over Newham North-East and stole it from its rightful trustees, the Newham workers, it seems to me that these class war warriors are merely the 'Forty Thieves'.

I am frankly tired of their absurd pretensions. To some it

may appear ironic or paradoxical or even dialectical that
middle class political inverts should engage in workers'
faddism while abusing the workers, call themselves Marxists
while distorting Marx, pretend to be seeking the common
good while striving after power for its own sake, damnify
Stalin while practising Stalinism, and cheat and intimidate
their way to power. I am tired of their half-baked panaceas
and regimented utopias and of their socialism that always
seems to have an 'accident' somewhere along the line where
everyone gets burned. Who wants an accident-prone system?
If socialism exalts the humble, fosters individuality,
creativity, diversity, and the general happiness and emancip-
ates the human race, then there is a lot to be said for it. But
their doctrinaire socialism will make everything a great deal
worse. There is really very little more to be said about the
Marxists. They are 'Enemies of Democracy' and our job is to
fight them until they are well and truly beaten.

They are the primary enemies of democracy in Britain
today. What about the Fascists you ask? Yes, they are just as
bad. But they feed off the Marxists. They are the Marxists'
best friends. In fighting the Marxists we are automatically
weakening the Fascists at the same time. The Marxists played
a very big part in Hitler's rise to power. They attacked the
Social Democrats as 'Social Fascists' and as worse than the
Nazis and undermined the resistance to Nazism from the
Social Democrats. They won Hitler business support by
frightening bankers and industrialists with the spectre of
nationalisation. They won Hitler electoral support by
creating a backlash against their street violence and their
attacks on property.

In Britain today the Marxists are increasing support for the
National Front among workers especially, who grow exasper-
ated with them and yearn for the National Front's short,
sharp treatment for them. They increase racial tensions,
aggravate racial disputes, and exploit grievances thereby
increasing support for the National Front. They organise
street attacks on the National Front and try to ban racists
from exercising free speech — thereby increasing people's
sympathy for the National Front. In Newham time and time
again our canvassers came across people who said — 'The
Reds are getting into the Labour Party. I'm going to back the
Front — they'll sort them out'. People like Tom Jenkins in

the schools naturally provide the National Front with power-ful ammunition for their schoolkids' 'spot the Red teacher' campaign. In Germany in the 1920s and 1930s it was official Marxist policy to encourage Fascism which was seen as the last stage of capitalism thereby hurrying the Revolution for-ward. Perhaps the Marxists of today really *want* to encourage the growth of the National Front for much the same reason — whether they want it or not that is what they are doing. Like two grizly animated skeletons the Fascists and Communists are locked in a grim embrace each propping up and at the same time trying to tear to pieces the other as they try to dance their dance macabre on the grave of democracy.

Fascism is a dying creed. It is much the lesser threat in Britain today — though it must still be taken seriously. But there are not gigantic Fascist empires in the world nor are the Fascists trying to organise extensive infiltration of one of the two major parties. But it should not be thought that the Fascists are not a threat to Democracy — they are, just as the Marxists are. There is little to choose between them — would you rather burn to death or freeze to death? Is there much to choose between the Big Flame of class war fanned by the desire to seize absolute power or that icy racial hatred that comes with 'the chill North wind flaunting the swastika banner in the sky'?

Some say the world will end in fire
Some say in ice
From what I've tasted of desire
I hold with those who favour fire
But if it had to perish twice
I think I know enough of hate
To say that for destruction ice
Is also great
And would suffice.					[Robert Frost]

Ironically, the best chance the Marxists have to destroy our democracy is not by seizing power for themselves but by causing sufficient disruption and disorder or by threatening the social and political fabric to such an extent that they pro-voke a military coup. Once again, wherever we find the military dictatorship, we find the Marxists. They have usually been instrumental in bringing about the military coup. I blame the Marxists for their major contribution in bringing General Pinochet to power in Chile. Without them his regime would have had no *raison d'etre* and Chile would still be a democracy. The Marxists who scream about repression in Chile should be reminded that it is their fault that this has come to pass.

There is no instant cure for the political disease described in this book. But it is treatable. It may be that the disease will turn out to be self-limiting or that there will be a spontaneous remission or that natural defence mechanisms within the body politic will cure it without the need for any treatment at all.

That is possible — but it would be a quack doctor who took a chance on it when there was a feasible and reliable scientific course of treatment available that was almost certain to cure it.

I have little doubt that the treatment would work but much doubt whether it will ever be tried. Most people will agree that Marxists are enemies of democracy. But this is mere talk. The standard response is 'Yes, I agree with you but I am not going to do anything about it' — they usually say 'can't' rather than 'won't', and if they are politicians they say it is 'politically impossible' which means that they lack the political courage to do it.

The treatment consists of a combination of private action and official action. Private action includes action by private individuals, private associations, companies, and private foundations. Official action includes legislation and action by the government, public bodies and public officials.

The first move must be to knock out the very effective and despicable methods from which the Marxists derive so much unfair advantage. Intimidation is illegal. But usually the police do not prosecute. They are wary of becoming involved in political battles even if one side is using criminal methods.

As we have seen the *threshold of endurance* of the Moderate tends to be low. Consequently it only takes a little pressure to put him out for the count. There is no need for grievous bodily harm when intimidating the Moderate — common assault is sufficient. But in cases of common assault — where someone is punched or kicked but no blood is spilt — the police have a policy not to prosecute. Normally one would not want to put people in court for the odd punch in the heat of the moment. But is is a very different matter when it is done as a calculated systematic tactic to gain unfair political advantage. The police should be instructed to prosecute for common assault in such cases. If they fail to act private prosecutions should be brought. In all appropriate cases actions for the tort of intimidation should be brought. After a short while the Marxists would get the message and this particular technique would be eliminated.

Similarly, after a number of firmly-prosecuted slander and libel actions and actions for injurious falsehoods the bottom would be knocked out of the defamation campaign. The anonymous phone calls are more difficult to deal with, as are verbal threats. Here one would possibly need expensive equipment to nail the culprits.

The cheating can be stopped by legal action. Civil actions can be brought to stop insufficient notice, surprise business, failure to notify people and so forth. Falsification is more difficult to tackle. The best defence is to set up papers, magazines and to issue pamphlets which counter the lies and provide full and accurate information.

The aim in all this must be to bring to a halt the use by Marxists of Marxist methods and confine them to the ordinary democratic methods that the rest of us use.

The second move must be to galvanise ordinary people into action on a larger scale and inspire them with the necessary fighting spirit to pursue a hardline strategy. This is very difficult but we did it in Newham. It can be done with the right kind of organisation. Most important of all, the tough-minded and energetic people in society who could become active democrats must be persuaded to involve themselves in the political battle *within* the Labour movement instead of engaging in destructive attacks on it or dissipating their energies elsewhere. This book will be worthwhile if it persuades some people to join this fight.

All this will cost a great deal of money. We must not be squeamish about this. The Marxists have vast resources and all good democrats must realise that they too will have to raise vast resources. The Marxists have turned control over the Labour Party into a money game — and democracy will not be able to play, let alone win, without putting a great deal of money on the table.

This means that private individuals must make regular

financial contributions and that moderate trade unions, companies and private foundations must make substantial contributions. Democracy yields no dividends and there may be no obvious financial return on any financial contribution. However, political stability is vital to economic life and the Marxists threaten it.

Legislation is required to facilitate private efforts. For example, the laws concerning business donations should be relaxed, legal aid should be made readily available to those seeking to bring public-spirited actions for the public good such as representative and relator actions. Actions to stop the Marxists cheating and intimidating could then be brought on legal aid by ordinary Labour Party members or members of trade unions or other Labour organisations.

Above all, legislation is required to *restructure the whole system*. The truth of the matter is that the Labour Party as at present constituted has a built-in bias in favour of political extremists. The Moderates have to run in order to stand still because the system works against them. The same applies to the trade unions.

In theory the necessary changes to the Labour Party Constitution could be made by a two-thirds majority at the Annual Conference. But this is unlikely until the trade unions which control it are themselves made more democratic.

There is one other way and that is to use legislation to restructure the Labour Party. It is a wholly novel approach.

The point about legislation is that, although the disease mainly affects the Labour Party and has left the Liberals and Tories largely untouched, legislation would have to be even-handed.

How can legislation help? Legislation can restructure the system in such a way that the Marxist bias is eliminated. Instead of favouring the activist — the highly-committed, fanatical ideologue — the system can be made more truly democratic. Our campaign was called, you may remember, the Campaign for Representative Democracy (CRD) because we wanted a system whereby the people in power were representative of the majority of people. Most Labour supporters (at least 90%) and most Labour Party members (at least 80%) are firmly opposed to Marxism, whatever they think about other matters. If the system were altered to encourage Labour supporters to be Labour Party members and then to put the power to choose in the hands of the Labour Party members, instead of the activists on the GMC (as at present), there would be a fundamental change.

Political Parties are in many respects feudal in character. They control the access to positions of power yet their internal organisation is slipshod, their internal management is casual, they have little in the way of financial resources or of high-calibre personnel to run them, the protections for the minorities and for the ordinary member in them are scanty. They select people who will control the largest slice of finance in the country − the vast public sector with its gigantic nationalised industries and all the government agencies financed by the taxpayer. The Parties choose the people who will pull the strings to control billions of pounds. A Minister will often make decisions involving £500 million expenditures. Yet the Party that chooses him has a tiny budget. In Law it is treated as a private club − no different from a golf club. While companies are regulated down to every tiny detail by law, as are public bodies, the political parties are treated as private associations and not regulated by Statute at all. There is not even the equivalent to the Statutes against commercial fraud.

Political Parties need to be recognised as a special class of public associations − different from private clubs and different again from companies. They need to be thought of in terms of constitutional law and special principles should apply to them. It is farcical that every single vote should be counted with scrupulous care by thoroughly impartial Returning Officers at a General Election in a safe Labour seat where the Labour candidate will win by a landslide − when the all-important decision, where every vote counts, when that candidate is selected by the Party, is made by a tiny minority of unrepresentative people in a slapdash way with ample opportunity for corruption, where cheating and intimidation are rife, and with no legislation to regulate the process.

It is scandalous that while industry, the Press, education, the civil service, the army and the police, and even the courts, have become modernised to meet the changes in society of the twentieth Century, the political parties which ultimately control them all are still living in the Dark Ages. This is not the case to anything like the same extent in the U.S.A. or

many other western European countries. The primitive stage
of development of the political parties, most of all the
Labour Party, makes them vulnerable to infiltration. There is
even a potential danger of the National Front infiltrating the
Conservative Party.

However, the following pieces of legislation would largely
solve the problem. It would be ironical if it fell to an incoming Tory government to democratise the Labour Party. It
may be that the degeneration of the Labour Party has gone
so far that it is no longer capable of putting its own house in
order. The measures I advocate would have their best chance
of success with all-party support. They are not partisan
measures. They are measures for the good of democracy and
should be enacted without delay:

(1) The National Executive Committee and the National
Officers of all political parties should be directly elected by a
secret ballot of the entire membership of the party. Left-
wingers like Ron Hayward (General Secretary of the Labour
Party) and Marxists like Andy Bevan (National Youth
Officer) would find it very difficult to be elected under this
system. Men like Reg Underhill who would like to be Moderates but are shackled by left-wing committees would be freed
of these and at the same time given a mandate to act as they
would prefer to.

The only other satisfactory alternative for keeping out
extremists is to have the Parliamentary Leader appoint the
officers and committee members. The Tory Leader at present
nominates the Party Chairman. Each system has its attrac-
tions. The first has more democratic respectability; the
second greatly reduces the danger of the national officers
getting above themselves and trying to dictate to the Parliamentary Party. I would advocate the first as a more
permanent and acceptable system with added safeguards to
protect the autonomy of the Parliamentary Party. (The
Parliamentary Party would continue to elect the Parliamentary Leader).

(2) Constituency Party Officers and Executive Committees
must be directly elected by a postal ballot of the constituency party members with each member having one vote and
no-one having more than one vote. They should be elected

annually as at present. The legislation should provide that the Constituency Party should have a Chairman, a First Deputy Chairman, a Second Deputy Chairman, a Secretary, an Assistant Secretary, a Treasurer, and an Assistant Treasurer and not more than four other officers and between six and ten ordinary committee members and that these people should form the Executive Committee. There would then be a representative committee of between seventeen and twenty-one and either the radical option of 'primaries' on the American model which can be 'closed' (restricted to party members), 'half-open' (restricted to registered party suppor-ters) or 'open' (in which any member of the electorate can vote) or the conservative option of entrusting the selection of Parliamentary and Local Government candidates to the local Party's Executive Committee. I think that the best bet would be a 'combined option' leaving the selection in normal circumstances in the hands of the Executive Committee with the provision that if 15% of the members of the party sign a petition objecting to the short-list within 3 weeks of its being announced, then all the candidates shall be presented to the ordinary members and the selection shall be made by a postal ballot. This would be a long-stop against an Executive Committee that had gone off the rails and would indicate grave dissatisfaction among the membership. It would only be rarely invoked — if, for instance, all the names on the short-list were unrepresentative or some important and widely-supported figure had been omitted.

There is a third alternative — to let the EC choose the short-list and throw open the final selection between them to a mass meeting at which all party members could vote or, preferably, to a postal vote of the members. I think there would be a great deal to be said for the EC conducting a rigorous screening and interviewing process to ensure the short-list candidates were up to the mark, leaving the final choice to the ordinary members. But however the compon-ents are arranged the important thing is to ensure an element of control (as direct as possible) over the process, for the mass membership of the local Party. It is true that Labour Party membership has been declining over the last twenty years — but this is partly because the ordinary member has so little power. If he is given an important role it would be a tremendous incentive to recruitment of members. The effect of this would be to turn Labour supporters into Labour members so that extremists would constitute less than 10% of the total — then they would hardly get a look in in the major parties. Even the extremist parties would tend to field more moderate candidates as the extreme fanatical element would be diluted by an influx of, and greater influence for, the more casual and apathetic members. In order to protect the interests of sitting councillors and sitting MP's, who get a rough deal if suddenly sacked from their job, they should receive compensation. More importantly, they should only be sacked by a 2/3 vote (of the Executive Committee or ordinary members as the case may be) instead of a simple majority. If the MP has become bone idle or betrayed the party it would be easy enough to obtain a 2/3 majority — but if he retains substantial support he should not be sacked.

(3) There must be built-in provision for a referendum of constituency party members if requested by a petition of 15% of the constituency members; and of the national membership if requested by a petition of 15% of the members. No-one is going to go to the trouble of collecting a large number of signatures for a petition unless something is seriously amiss or there is a serious controversy and split within the constituency Party or the national Party. If there is, it is right that the final verdict should rest with the membership. The referendum will act as a long-stop against infiltration of the Executive Committee by extremists by stopping them implementing extreme policies. Moreover there should be power for a censure motion on any officer or officers to be put to a referendum and the officer to be dismissed. But a referendum should be the *only* way of dismissing officers or ordinary committee members. If an officer resigns in the middle of his term of office his place should be automatically taken by his elected deputy. This would remove one little avenue by which extremists creep in through the back-door.

(4) The autonomy of the Constituency Party must be guaranteed by law so that decisions taken by the Constituency Party's Executive Committee or mass membership cannot be overruled by bureaucrats, 'higher' organs within the Party

and the rights of ordinary members should be guaranteed by law against any other committees or bodies within the Constituency.

(5) Two very important areas for manipulation are conduct of elections and referenda, and interpretation of the rules. It should hardly be necessary to say this but centuries of political experience, to say nothing of common sense, should have taught us that you do not leave the cat to look after the cream-jug. You cannot have a fair election or a fair interpretation if the person who decides has a vested interest in the outcome. It is absurd to expect politicians, of all people, to be people of such boundless integrity that they can be left to be judges in their own cause and to supervise their own, or their friends', elections. For Transport House officials to pose as neutral, fair judges on disputes over constitutional interpretations is laughable. To have them, regional office officials, or members of the local party running an election for officers, for the council or parliamentary candidates — and expecting the result to be wholly above-board is living in cloud cuckoo land. How many people would not cheat in an exam if they were given exam papers with the answers printed on the back? How many people would not break the speed limits or shoplift if there were no traffic wardens, store detectives or police? In examinations we use the time-honoured principles of invigil-ation (careful direct scrutiny by independent persons to ensure no cheating) and *outside* examiners (examiners who do not have a vested interest in the outcome) and *unseen* examinations with a rigid time-limit equal for all candidates, careful checking of the identities of candidates, and even the examiners themselves are monitored. When I marked 'A' level history papers not so long ago I was struck by the checks, double-checks, and the scrupulous care taken to ensure that candidates did not cheat, that they got a fair and careful hearing, and that none had special advantages. The same prin-ciples must be applied to Party elections as to General Elections — independent, outside Returning Officers. The same goes for rule-interpretation. The *independent-external* principle not only makes the system fair in fact it also makes it look fair so that people can have confidence in it.

(6) All the secret postal ballots should be made as simple as possible. They should be accompanied by a note in red urging people to exercise their democratic rights and pointing out that it is their duty to their party and as a citizen to take the trouble to vote. To make it really easy for them a stamped addressed or freepost envelope should be enclosed. The number of places for election should be as few as possible so that filling in the form does not become too much of a chore. The key offices should be printed in heavy type to draw attention to them.

(7) There should be an unequivocal legal right of access by all members to the records of the party – especially the membership details, the constitution and rules, the accounts, and minutes of meetings. It should not be necessary to have confrontations with hostile Party officials belonging to some other faction in order to obtain such information. A simple expedient would be to require the Parties to lodge up-to-date records in the public library. This would also do a lot to stop jiggery-pokery over members – new members being added who are not members, people being left off the list who are members and so on.

(8) There should be a statute incorporating some of the standard provisions (eg those to be found in Company Law) to protect the rights of members by stipulating minimum periods of notice, irrespective of what the rules say.

(9) There should be statutory regulation of the process of joining the party and being expelled or suspended from it. To join a party there should be one standard form of application and it should simply be a question of filling this in and paying the prescribed fee. To be expelled or suspended from a party is a serious step. It should have stringent safeguards built in. The only grounds for expulsion or suspension should be a serious criminal conviction, violent or intimidating behaviour towards other party members, membership of another party, or action or views which demonstrate hostility towards democracy. Expulsion or suspension should also be taken out of the hands of the party completely because it becomes a judge in its own cause. It should be handled as a semi-judicial matter by outside agencies with the party organ

which wants to expel acting as prosecutor.

(10) There should be a statutory quorum of 30 per cent of eligible members at all party meetings open to ordinary members and 50 per cent for committees. This would put a stop to a handful of members making decisions in the name of their absent colleagues and would discourage the holding of too frequent meetings which enable extremists to conduct a war of attrition against Moderates.

I have sketched the broad outlines of a simple legislative programme. The basic principle in all this is to shift the power and the initiative from a tiny unrepresentative elite to the mass membership, to make it easy for people to particip-ate instead of making it difficult (at present they have to run something of an obstacle-course), and to abolish the indirect element. If I said 'indirect, multi-stepped elections in a multiple-tiered organisational system foster extremism' you would probably start gaping! That sounds like the political scientist's gobbledygook. But it does make sense. In simple language, if A elects B who elects C who elects D we get further and further away from A. Eventually we reach Z who claims he was 'elected' by A in the same way that someone like Norman Atkinson can claim to be elected by ordinary Labour Party members because they elect their GMC delegates, the GMC delegates elect delegates to Annual Conference, and these then vote for or against Norman Atkinson. We have gone down a chain and each link takes us further away from the person who is supposed to be repres-ented. Z may have been indirectly elected by A in the same way I am related to my most distant cousin, but Z is a long way from A. In the same way, Norman Atkinson would be most unlikely to be elected as the Labour Party's Treasurer if there were a direct vote of all Labour Party members. They would not want a person with very left-wing views in that important position.

The device by which these indirect elections occur is the Annual Conference. There is no need to abolish these Annual Conferences. They are good fun and make for good TV. But there is a need to take away their powers. They should be talking-shops and discussion-forums where activists can sound off on policy questions. It would be up to the Parliamentary

Parties to decide whether they wanted to take any notice of them, which would depend on whether or not they were talking sense. Of course, there would still be a small element of indirect representation in my proposed scheme — but it would be confined to a local level and would have a procedure for reverting to direct control if it were abused.

The legislative programme I have outlined may sound rather complex. Actually it is very simple. To prove it I will show how it could work cheaply, efficiently, and fairly, in practice. In each constituency a Constituency Parties' Officer would be appointed with an office and a small staff. He would be a person of high integrity who had never belonged to any Party. The obvious candidate would be a civil servant or lawyer. He would need to have a small amount of legal knowledge and administrative competence. In fact he would be just the sort of person, perhaps the very same person, as the Returning Officer for General Elections. He could continue this job with private practice as a solicitor or State work of some kind or he could be a retired person. He would have the crucial qualities of independence and externality — he would not take sides between factions within one party but would act strictly according to the rules of each party.

He would keep a Register of each party's members and this would be the official register of membership. He would be empowered to admit people to the Party. Indeed, instead of being signed up at home by Party canvassers, members would often join at the Constituency Parties' Office. Any member of a party would be able to inspect the list of members of his own party on request. On joining a Party a person would pay the required fee and sign an application form: 'I wish to become a member of the ... Party with immediate effect. I declare that I am over 18 years old and not a member of any other Party. I enclose the annual fee of ...'.

The Constituency Parties' Officer and his assistants would be responsible for conducting all elections and all referenda. The assistance of the Electoral Reform Society could be invoked. The Parties' elections would be held in different months, staggered through the year eg Tories in January, Labour in February, Liberal in March. All Parties which fielded more than 10 Parliamentary candidates would be required by Law to register. This would be enforced by fines, the provision to make court orders directing registration (backed up by committal for contempt and sequestration of assets) and the disqualification of candidates whose election literature or entry on the ballot-form indicated that they were standing as Party candidates for an unregistered party.

Elections would be held annually by postal ballot. At the annual election party members would vote for their local officers and Executive Committee and for the national officers and National Executive Committee. The Constituency Parties' Officer would have an addressograph so elections and referenda would be simply a question of putting some duplicated forms in the post.

Who would bear the cost of this? The cost would not be enormous − the salary and office expenses of 600+ CPOs and the cost of 2nd class post. I hate to advocate any increase in bureaucracy but this would in fact be replacing incompetent, partisan, amateur bureaucrats by professional ones. The cost would be insignificant in comparison with the benefits. The State should pay for it as it will be the State which benefits from it. This would help the parties which would no longer have to pay for their own elections and would have more money for other things. It would also encourage bigger memberships which would generate extra revenue for them. Copies of minutes of meetings, accounts (to be subjected to a compulsory external audit) and other Party records should be deposited with the Constituency Parties' Officer. This would also ensure that more reliable records were kept, and kept safely, which will be of benefit to historians and other scholars.

This only leaves the question of interpretation of the Rules. This should be taken out of the hands of partisans within each Party and entrusted in the first instance to a Constituency Parties' Tribunal. This body should be similar to an Employment Tribunal, Rent Tribunal or Supplementary Benefits Tribunal. It should be for the Tribunal to decide whether a case has been proved for expulsion or suspension of a Party member and whether the rules are being correctly interpreted by the Party officers and Executive Committee and the Constituency Parties' Officer. There should be a 3-man Tribunal. None of the members should ever have been members of any political party. The Chairman should be a qualified lawyer.

A similar structure should operate nationally with a National Parties' Officer and staff. He would supervise the overall conduct of the national part of the elections and national referenda. He could also do the trade unions' secret ballots. In all cases at both constituency and national level there would be the right to take the matter to the High Court. What I have advocated, however, would greatly restrict the necessity of costly and time-consuming litigation. By making the system fair in the first instance it would only rarely be necessary to go to court because there would be fewer abuses and irregularities which needed to be rectified. There is only one major point I have left out — what happens if, despite the democratic safeguards, extremists congregate in one area and capture a constituency party by joining up en masse. I have stressed the need for constituency Party autonomy because the greater danger comes from undemocratic central control. Nevertheless, to prevent this there should be a device whereby at a referendum (or the annual election) a 2/3 majority of the national membership can disaffiliate from the Party a constituency organisation that has gone off the rails. This would be a rare event.

If you have followed the arguments so far you can now see that the Marxists would not get anywhere in such a system. They could achieve very little by intimidation — how do you intimidate hundreds of people in a secret postal ballot? They would lose the opportunity to cheat and manipulate to a large extent. Even falsification would be made more difficult for them. They would lose their multiple votes: instead of having ten votes while everyone else has one they would be brought down to the level of the ordinary working man they are always talking about. They call for 'Redistribution' — but redistribution begins at home and what better way to start than by redistributing their votes! Here is a case for expropriation without compensation if ever there was one! However many meetings they went to they would no longer be able to out-run the ordinary member. They would be completely outnumbered by Moderates. There would be three pressures leading to larger numbers joining — the work of candidates for election as councillors and MP's, the attraction of being able to participate in important decisions, the work of Moderate organisations fighting against Marxists. I think it would be possible under these circumstances to produce a

Labour Party where over ninety per cent of its members were anti-Marxist. This would put a virtual stop to Marxist infiltration of the Labour Party. The Marxists would largely abandon it. It would no longer be an attractive home for them.

There are two other measures which would bring about a great change in British politics, both of which would make politicians more representative. One is full-scale American primaries. The other is proportional representation. The first is greatly to be preferred.

My scheme goes along the primaries road. It can be considered as a final settlement of the parties question in itself or as a major step towards full primaries.

Its virtue is that as it stands it solves the problem of infiltration without disturbing the Conservative and Liberal parties which are not at present being infiltrated, and without introducing fundamental constitutional changes. It solves the problem without resorting to bans, mass expulsions, or victimisation.

With appropriate modifications the scheme could also apply to the trade unions and other parts of the Labour Movement such as the Co-op. The British Labour Movement could be made the most truly democratic in the world. This would be the biggest advance in democracy for over a century — in fact, since 1867, when the Tory Prime Minister, Disraeli, first gave the vote to the urban working class.

The Newham North-East saga has been an extraordinary one and I doubt if anyone could have predicted some of the strange turns it has taken. At Newham we found out what happened when an irresistible force met an immovable object. The story certainly captured the imagination of the Press. Nestling opposite the page 3 girl in the *Sun* on 24 February 1977, was a long report on the serving of the February Injunction headed 'Fury as Writs Wreck Prentice Meeting', and the story made the front page in a number of papers.

The Guardian (14th July 1977) did a long feature article (by David Leigh) about us: 'A couple of students, with strong ideological convictions, move in on a working-class Labour constituency. One takes a bed-sitter in the area ... the other stays at his university, master-minding the plot.

The latest twist in the story stars a pair of right-wing Labour crusaders fighting fire with fire they say, against Marxist "weevils" and "cheats". Tony Kelly and his left-wing supporters, who made Newham famous by voting out Mr Prentice when he was a Cabinet Minister, gained a reputation as enemies of democracy. Mr Paul McCormick, and Mr Julian Lewis, by contrast see themselves as the Batman and Robin of the political struggle. Sweeping down into Newham in their Votemobile, armed with only righteousness, a knowledge of legal procedure, and their theoretical studies of Marxist tactics, they have already wreaked some mayhem.... The lily-pond outside Paul McCormick's rooms in Nuffield College, Oxford is a far cry from the grime of Barking High Street in East London. But this is the nerve-centre of the "Campaign for Representative Democracy". McCormick, an intense, rather suspicious-minded 26 year-old with a moustache and a research fellowship, is talking on two telephones at once, dictating affidavits and telling Julian Lewis down in Newham to get out 124 telegrams to delegates making sure they turn up.'

The *Financial Times* (15th December 1977) saw it a little differently in an article headed 'Two Men's Holy War Against the Left — Labour's Nightmare at Newham' which begins: 'There is a very good moment in the film Butch Cassidy and the Sundance Kid when Robert Redford and Paul Newman, having fled halfway across America, look back and spot the tiny figures of their implacable pursuers far below in the sierra. They turn to each other in bewilderment: "Just who are these guys?" And however improbable the comparison may appear, that feeling of bafflement and despair sums up perfectly the word of top Labour Party officials at Transport House at the goings-on in Newham North-East. Their tormentors, of course, are not a Sheriff's posse, but two Oxford graduates. Once upon a time the campaign to save Mr Reg Prentice, MP for Newham, from an undignified ejection by left-wingers was little more than a joke. Today, the names of Paul McCormick and Julian Lewis, the Oxford men in question, elicit dismay at Transport House — coupled with the prayer that a kindly High Court judge will put an end to the misery. To the uncommitted, the sight of the two men using the rule book ruthlessly to beat the left at its own game was hugely amusing ... but for Transport House, which felt that the MP's troubles were largely self-inflicted, any humorous side the affair might have had has been transformed into a nightmare.'

In all the reports attention has been paid to the leading figures — perhaps understandably — and according to the writer's prejudices he has portrayed either the Marxists or Prentice or Hart or myself and Julian as the heroes. But the real heroes, whom no-one has noticed, are the Newham workers — who fought, not for themselves, nor for a faction, nor a Party, but for democracy. They are indeed unsung and unknown heroes. They do not have titles and honours. They are not MBE's like Hart or CBE's like Underhill and Hayward or JP's like Prentice and Hart. They do not have exalted titles like 'National Agent' or 'National Youth Officer' nor are they able, like Prentice, to preface their names with 'The Right Honourable' or, even 'Honourable' as in 'The Honourable Mr Justice Peter Pain'. They do not think of themselves grandly, like Andy Bevan, as the leaders of the working class. They are merely workers. So to the workers' Faddists and those who worship at the shrine of power they are of no account. But I tell you this — if these Honourable Leaders could raise themselves to the moral level of the people they claim to represent, the Labour Party — and the country — would be in a much healthier state.

The Newham workers have shown by their fine example what can be done when ordinary people are prepared to make the effort and are assisted by effective organisation. It is now vital that our political leaders rise to the occasion and show themselves worthy of their high positions by putting democracy before party or personal interests.

The Newham North-East affair has already had a major impact on British politics. Without it, Mr Prentice would not have voted for a 'No Confidence' motion against the Labour Government in April 1979. If he had voted the other way (or even abstained) the motion would have been lost and there would have been no General Election on 3 May 1979. When it did come the General Election result might have been different. As a result of Newham North-East major changes have been made in the Labour Party Constitution. Perhaps the most important result of all has been to turn the searchlight on the violent lurch to the left in the Labour Party and the activities of Marxists inside it.

This book has been about enemies of democracy — not the collapse of democracy — because there is no reason why the fight should be lost. Unfortunately the present Labour leaders do not have the 'fight, fight, and fight again' spirit of Hugh Gaitskell. But Newham North-East has shown that a hard fighting approach can beat the Marxists even with the present rotten system. If the system is changed they can be put off the political map altogether. I have proved they are not invincible. Nor is their rise to power inexorable. If they ever win it is because we let them.

It would be a tragedy if the valiant fight of the Newham workers turned out to have been in vain. They won the local battle against the Marxists. But then the National Executive Committee and Transport House were called in to crush them. They were crushed and burnt to ashes.

It may be that a Phoenix will rise out of those ashes — and turn defeat into a glorious victory. The Marxists will curse themselves if they find that they have won the battle of Newham (thanks to the intervention of their friends in Transport House and the National Executive Committee) but lost the whole war of infiltration as a result.

Whether this happens depends upon what *you* as a democratic citizen are prepared to do for democracy.